Skip Brown &
John Graham
# Target 26
A Practical,
Step-by-Step,
Preparatory Guide to
Running the
Marathon

With a Foreword by Tom Fleming

**Collier Books**
A Division of Macmillan Publishing Co., Inc.
New York
**Collier Macmillan Publishers**
London

Macmillan Publishing Co., Inc.
866 Third Avenue
New York, N.Y. 10022
Collier Macmillan Canada, Ltd.

Library of Congress Cataloging in Publication Data
Brown, Skip, 1949–
   Target 26.
   Bibliography:  p.
   Includes index.
   1.  Marathon running.  I.  Graham, John, 1933–
joint author.  II.  Title.
GV1065.B76      796.4'26     78–32031
ISBN 0–02–028820–4

10  9  8  7  6  5  4  3
Designed by Jack Meserole
Printed in the United States of America

To my long-suffering aid and support team, Claire and Jenny, and to another multi-marathoner, Paul.
—John Graham

To my wife, Cindy, for eleven years of love, understanding, and encouragement.
—Skip Brown

# Contents

# Acknowledgments

We are extremely grateful for the advice and assistance given to us by Nick Marshall, Phil Stewart, and many of our marathoning friends in the Pittsburgh area. We also add special thanks to Dave Burkhart for the illustrations, Bonnie Kosor for help in typing the manuscript, George Shaw for photographic assistance, and Connie Rollins and Glenda Bergman for a variety of assistance.

# Foreword

The marathon—26 miles 385 yards!

*"I have trained the many miles. I have prepared my mind to go the distance. I am now ready to undertake the most difficult challenge in distance running."*

You may have said the same thing to yourself. The marathon is the most rewarding, satisfying event that a distance runner can undertake. I am always thrilled when I finish one, not just because I may have run my fastest time, but also because I have once again fulfilled my expectations of finishing the marathon distance.

My first marathon, at age 18 in Boston in 1970, is still the most memorable of them all. The main challenge of going the distance, of making it to the Prudential Center, was my goal. As I toed the starting line, I felt that I had trained properly and was confident that I could make the distance. Yet, although I was confident, ambivalent feelings of apprehension and curiosity were with me.

The beginning was, as expected, very easy, and time passed quickly. With Heartbreak Hill ahead, an urge to run faster grew within me, because, as we know, the last 5 miles are all downhill from there! But of course, there was "the wall," the notorious enemy of all marathon runners. This is where the marathon really starts. This is where the mystique of reaching the finish line becomes everyone's favorite post-race story. To this day, I can't remember those last 5 miles. I was weary with physical fatigue, and mentally tired of telling myself to push on. I knew somehow I'd fulfill my expectations of finishing this first marathon, and I did.

Running 2 hours, 37 minutes, 36 seconds was worth all the training and preparation. I was at once extremely tired and yet ecstatic about the accomplishment of finishing 63rd. From this experience, I progressed to a different level of understanding both about myself and about the marathon for the next time out.

No marathon will ever be like that first one. Memorable impressions of traveling 26 miles will never be quite the same in any future race, and yet every marathon you run will leave you with some new and unique impression. If you run a dozen marathons, you have had a dozen different experiences. I've had twenty-nine of these individual trials. They were similar in that in each I crossed the finish line, but different because of the conditions and time taken, and the thoughts that went through my mind.

Why do you want to run the marathon? This question is often put to marathon aspirants—competitive runners and recreational joggers alike. It is a difficult question to answer, yet it can be easily passed off with the reply, "It's just fun and enjoyable to run." In most cases, this is a truthful answer. The beginner is generally a person who has taken up jogging as a form of physical fitness. He or she may not have thought then of ever running, much less competing, in the marathon. But sooner or later the challenge and thrill of running 26 miles may be too tempting to pass up.

Such was the case with me. I started running at 17 years of age, but soon discovered that "fun runs" were not enough motivation to keep me going. I needed more. I needed the challenge of running long distances, and improving my times along the way. Marathon running soon became the principal type of running I wanted to do.

I'm not quite sure how people view the marathoner. Are we special people blessed with a gift of endurance? Are we dedicated workhorses who thrive on the pain and agony of the marathon? Are we egotistical marathon maniacs who seek glory by running 26 miles 385 yards? Or are we normal people wanting to achieve the highest level of fitness and to succeed personally in an ultimate test?

If you relate most closely with the last of the possible definitions, then *Target 26* is valuable to you. This book is for the runner who feels ready to enter the marathon competition. Your physical and psychological preparation for running the marathon are of utmost importance. This book discusses the methods of preparation and enables you to decide whether or not you have properly trained for the marathon experience.

Seven out of ten marathon entrants run for the sole purpose of completing the full distance. *Target 26* emphasizes that with organized, consistent training, and with proper goals in mind, the first-time marathoner will successfully fulfill his or her running expectations. It outlines the many different methods, enabling the individual runner to choose the method best suited for his or her ability.

Chapter 4 discusses the racing and training effects that the marathon has upon the running body, and the gradual adaptation the body makes to these stresses. The principal ways of encouraging this adaptation are the methods involved in developing an efficient cardiovascular system through training. Recognition of the psychological stresses, which are primarily initiated by the physical intensity of the marathon, is of equal importance. This physical and psychological survival struggle in running the marathon is best fought, as Chapter 4 indicates, by the runner's perception of his or her success.

Chapter 7 deals with the race itself, and the many rituals marathon runners settle into on that day. From the moment you wake up, to the pre-race warm-up, to the clothes you wear on your back, all aspects of final marathon preparation are covered. These necessities must be coordinated, as they are as important to you now as they were in the many months of training. In the actual running of the race, the anticipated racing pace is now the most important consideration in the runner's mind. The initial pace is the crucial first stage of the long, long distance ahead.

*Target 26* can aid the runner by helping in selection of the training method most compatible to his or her individual needs. There is certainly no one way of training for the marathon. Many marathoners complete a race only to reexamine previous training procedures. By doing so, they establish more firmly in mind their "target 26" next time out in the marathon world.

—**Tom Fleming**
(2:12:05, best marathon)

*New Jersey*
*August 1978*

# Preface

Not another book on running!

Can there possibly be a new word to say about the sport? Since running became the thing to do and the general populace flooded onto the roads by the thousands, the publication of journals and books has almost kept pace with the torrent. Running magazines once had tiny circulations; they have now become chic, and are aimed at the mass market and displayed everywhere on magazine racks. Books on running were once dry tomes for those concerned with physical education; now they speak of psychic powers, total health, total fitness, the total experience.

It is no wonder then that the thousands of newly arrived joggers try to reap these wondrous benefits by quickly aiming at that "ultimate experience," the marathon. This is unfortunate. Under pressure from the media, following the now fashionable sport, thousands of ill-prepared runners are attempting to run 26 miles 385 yards with very little conception of what that entails. Two very large marathons in 1977, the Mayor Daley in Chicago and the New York run, set records for nonfinishers. Whereas a dropout rate of some 15 to 20 percent might be expected, at the Mayor Daley event the dropout rate was an unenviable 60 percent.

And despite all the books and magazines, there is yet no good book devoted specifically to preparing for the marathon. There is one which claims to be complete but is simply a collection of articles. Another, from Germany, has yet to be made available in this country. Therefore there is a distinct need for a book aimed at the runner who can run upwards of 5 miles and has just begun to aspire to longer distances leading to the marathon (and beyond). This book is designed to enable this runner to achieve his first successful completion with a minimum of pain and with a great deal of joy.

We decided to collaborate on this book because we feel that our opinions and experiences are complementary, and that together we can help more runners than either of us could alone. Skip Brown is 31 and has run twenty-four marathons in times down to 2:19:17 at the time of writing. He runs competitively at the front of the pack and emphasizes speed in his preparation. Being in the open section of any marathon, his principal objective is a good time and a high finishing place. John Graham, on the other hand, is 47 and has run forty-one marathons in times down to 2:43:34 at the time of writing. He started five years ago after a layoff from college running of some nineteen years, and at present is still improv-

ing. He also runs competitively, but his targets are somewhat different. Clearly a high open finishing position is very important, but his targets also include running any master in the race into the ground (if possible!). His training emphasizes endurance and freedom from injury.

We do overlap in our objectives a great deal and to a lesser extent in our capabilities. In terms of knowledge that can be of value to the embryonic marathoner, we can speak from wide experience. To date, we have no DNFs (*Did Not Finish*), although a couple of times we have come close! The lessons we learned in those experiences are herein distilled.

In this book we have given some advice of a medical nature which, based on our own experiences, we believe to be useful. However, you should always contact a qualified medical practitioner, preferably one who understands runners and running, if you're in any doubt. He should be able to diagnose your problem at first hand. Don't take our word for it—check your own special needs.

We are both firmly convinced that a "lonely long-distance runner" loses much in running alone, and that he or she will get much more out of running with company. Therefore the aspiring marathoner should first make contact with local long-distance runners, preferably through contacting the local Road Runners Club (address from RRCA, Jeff Darman, RRCA President, 2737 Devonshire Place, N.W., Washington, D.C. 20008, 202-462-3245.) We are firmly committed to the value of the Road Runners Clubs of America in their promotion of good running company and in their lowering of barriers between the closed clubs and ordinary runners. The Road Runners Clubs are managed by runners, seemingly in most cases now by marathoners, and they understand the needs of runners and 26-milers.

With the information in the present volume, together with training and racing company, preparation for a marathon need not be an endless grind of hours of loneliness. It can be great fun and enjoyment (coupled of course with some satisfyingly hard work!). The marathon should be a climax of your efforts in which all this knowledge is brought to a successful completion at the finish line.

The joy and satisfaction of finishing a successful first marathon cannot be better expressed than in the poem on page xvi by a young finisher.

Photo 1 (OPPOSITE)
Bill Rodgers wins Boston 1978 in 2:10:13, just 2 seconds ahead of Jeff Wells. It was the closest finish in the history of Boston, a finishing duel which Rodgers won by a mere 12 yards.
(Photo by Sue Swigart)

*Marathon Legs*

My legs are Marathon Legs now!
So ask my time and ask me how
(And help me walk a little now).

The title is a modest prize
For legs whose strong endurance lies
In miles of training on the roads
Through blisters, strains, and other woes,
Through snow, through heat, high wind and rain,
(And fun!), and being called Insane.

So ask me where and ask me how
'Cause I have Marathon Legs now!

—Cheryl Dorko

We hope that this book will enable you to finish your next marathon with as much pride as Cheryl shows.

And we must give tribute to those long-suffering partners of ours. Even though they are runners both, tolerance of running authors is not something achieved easily. They have listened to long passages and given useful critical advice which has contributed to the value of the book. They have put off meals and waited around while we ran our miles *and* wrote our words. We are grateful, too, for their encouragement when things were not going as well as they might have!

—John Graham
—Skip Brown

"The marathon people are meant to run and they do it."
—Sir Laurence Olivier

# Target 26

# Chapter 1
# The Target
## Aiming at the Marathon

In 1897, fifteen runners lined up to run 24 miles into Boston in the second marathon on American soil. In 1964 the entry reached 301. Yet only fourteen years later in 1978, despite new qualification standards, no less than 4,212 official entrants left the starting line at Hopkinton. In 1976, 17,300 runners completed at least one of the 166 marathons staged, while in 1977 the number of entrants had again jumped, to some 25,000! Such has been the explosion in marathon running in recent years.

Yet the marathon itself is not old. It was first instituted as a long-distance footrace at the revival of the Olympic Games at Athens, Greece, in 1896, even though no marathon had ever been run in the original games. It commemorates the performance of a Greek soldier, Phidippides, who according to tradition ran 23 miles in 490 B.C. from the plains of Marathon to Athens to announce victory over the Persians. The most romantic accounts have it that he had been engaged in running some hundreds of miles only a few days previously, and that shortly after proclaiming, "Rejoice, we conquer," he died.

The revival as an Olympic event in 1896 was run over 24 miles 1,500 yards, but at Paris (1900) the distance was set logically at 40 kilometers. It stayed the same length at St. Louis (1904), but in London (1908) it grew to 26 miles 385 yards. In Stockholm (1912) it was 24 miles 1,725 yards; in Antwerp (1920) it was 26 miles 990 yards; but from Paris (1924) onward it was standardized at the same distance as that in London: 26 miles 385 yards. The original reason for the London distance was to accommodate the Royal family, one of whose members was sick but still wished to view the start. It so happens that Windsor Castle is 26 miles 385 yards from the finishing stadium, and ever since, countless runners have run those 2 extra miles in honor of British royalty!

Even 24 miles would be enough, for the physical and mental stresses of the marathon are severe. They can be too much for the competitor who has not prepared adequately for the task. This has never stopped marathon participants either in the past or now. Nevertheless, far too much has been written about the rigors of the race and the legendary breed of athlete who can complete such a distance. Because of this the public has come to look upon the marathon as the ultimate test. We can remember in our youth when the marathon was so unattainable that it was not even a goal. Supermen ran marathons, and suffered for their ambition. Mortals ran single miles, or cross-country trails, and even then only while in school. Thereafter we settled down to normal pursuits of home and family, leaving running for those apparently born with some special capability.

Even today, the media glory in themes of agony; pictures of runners lying down, feet being peeled out of hot shoes, and the inevitable blisters take precedence over pictures of runners' enjoyment. Any history of the marathon will include at least two classic moments. The first was in 1908 in the London Olympics when an Italian baker, Dorando Pietri, ran into the stadium first in a kind of delirium. After being helped to continue in the right direction and to get up after falling down, he was disqualified in favor of the American who entered the stadium in second place. The second classic, caught on movie film, was that moment when the immortal Emil Zatopek, running in his first marathon in the Olympics in Helsinki in 1952, ran past the British champion, Jim Peters, who had led the whole way and who finally dropped out exhausted a couple of miles from the finish. Both of these events decorated the fabric woven around the supermen who ran marathons.

The fact is that these men were unprepared for the marathon—they knew very little about how the body reacts to stress placed upon it, and they knew nothing about how to train for it. In fact, they ran very little by modern standards. British professionals in the nineteenth century used training dominated by running at even speed, but not daily nor all the year round. Then at the beginning of this century the Americans added repetitions over shorter-than-competitive distances around the track. This type of training was used for all running events, including the marathon. It wasn't until about 1920 that a combination of fast and slow repetitions began to be used. This format became standard for the next thirty years. Even Zatopek trained on horrendous repetition work combined with long distances.

In the late '40s, long slow distance work began being introduced into training regimes, first by van Aaken in Germany and then by Percy Cerutty in Australia. Lydiard in New Zealand, working in the late '50s, refined a combination of high mileage and hard and easy days, a training regime that is followed by most in one form or another even today. (More of this in Chapter 2.)

Due in part to these new training methods, improved equipment such as shoes, and increased knowledge of diet and running physiology, times have improved remarkably. The open qualifying time for Boston Marathon starters currently is faster than the times of all but two medal winners in the first three Olympics, and Olympic winning times even as late as 1956 would be considered mediocre in minor local Road Runners' events of today. Thomas Hicks won the 1904 marathon, over a mere 40 kilometers in St. Louis, in 3:28:53, while Waldemar Cierpinski in Montreal in 1976, running 2.195 kilometers longer, had to finish 1 hour and 19 minutes earlier to win!

## Marathon races

Of all the marathons, the Olympic event is the most glamorous and the most competitive, even if it doesn't necessarily produce the best times. There the runners are competing for only three places—those bearing the medals. A fourth place is unremembered even if it was a superlative time. Nevertheless the Olympics have produced glorious performances. Zatopek in 1952 took first place to get his third gold medal for the games in his first marathon. He had earlier won the 5,000 and 10,000 meters. He was the iron man, a colonel in the Czech army who trained alone through his native woods, running intolerable workouts in boots. He seemed to personify the idea that the necessary training had to be the sort that only supermen could endure.

Then there was Abebe Bikila, a tiny slim man from Ethiopia, who ran barefoot through the streets of Rome to break the Olympic record set by Zatopek only two olympiads before by an enormous 8 minutes! It was the first real breakthrough in Olympic times to the modern era: 2:15:17 against Zatopek's 2:23:04. Then four years later Bikila came back again to break that record in Tokyo with 2:12:12, running to start with in

**Figure 1**
Olympic Marathon winning times over the years.

shoes but then abandoning them during the race in favor of bare feet. At the height of his fame he was struck by a car and paralyzed for life. It was left to his countryman Mamo Wolde to win the next Olympic Marathon in Mexico City and to come in third in Munich; Wolde ended an Ethiopian era.

Then it was that Frank Shorter won easily in Munich for the U.S., the first American winner since 1908, and in near record time, only 8 seconds slower than Bikila's Tokyo time. He beat that time in Montreal by nearly 2 minutes but was still a full 50 seconds behind the winner, Waldemar Cierpinski of East Germany, finishing in 2:09:55. Figure 1 shows how Olympic winning times have improved over eighty-one years.

### Boston fever

After the Olympics, Boston is *the* marathon. Certainly it is the event which marks the zenith of marathon aspirations for many excellent runners. For nonrunners, Boston is often synonymous with the marathon race.

A few months after marathoning was born in the 1896 Olympics in Athens, an American race was held in New York. Boston staged its race on April 19, 1897, and thus was the second on American soil. However, since the New York event had a short life, Boston is now the oldest marathon, having missed only a single year. By 1978 there had been eighty-two Bostons compared to only eighteen Olympic races.

On that first occasion, fifteen runners gathered at Ashland in Massachusetts to race 24 miles 1,232 yards of unpaved and dusty roads. John McDermott won in 2:55:10, even though he walked three times in the last 10 miles, and was caught up in a funeral procession at one point along the way. The Boston marathon race was on, and the times came down over the years (Figure 2).

Since then the race has spawned individual legends. Clarence De Mar, who won seven times and finished in the top ten altogether fifteen times and yet was robbed of competing in his nine most competitive years by the ignorance of the race doctors. The Kelleys—John A., the older, who won twice, was second six times, and third once; and John J., the younger, who won once and was second four times. They were not related to each other, but for twenty-nine years between 1934 and 1963 there was always, it seemed, a John Kelley in the very early finishers! Then there was Tarzan Brown, the Narragansett Indian who won twice. And Gerard Cote, the French Canadian who chalked up three first-place finishes. Finally, Bostonian Bill Rodgers has won twice since 1975 in times more than a minute faster than any other winner.

Yet with all this talent, and the fact that Boston was of such preeminence in the marathoning world that it had always attracted the very best of international runners, not once has Boston ever been won by an

4

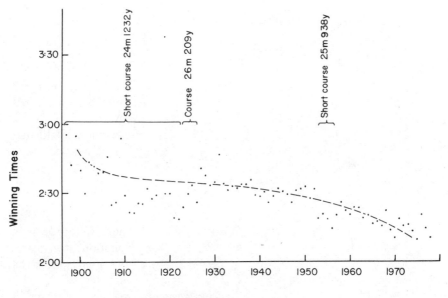

**Figure 2**
Boston Marathon winning times over the years.

Olympic champion. Three have managed second places: Hicks in 1904, Hayes in 1908, and Stenroos in 1926. Bikila managed only a fifth place in 1963, while Mamo Wolde was 12th in the same race. Shorter finished in 20th position in the 1978 race, six years after his Munich gold-medal triumph.

There are other marathons, of course—in 1978 there were over 240 races planned in the United States alone, and Appendix II lists 290 events worldwide. Some of these have already made a name for themselves, and some have in the last few years attracted a greater number of entrants than Boston. New York has had two marathons for a long time, one held on a hilly course in Yonkers and the other until very recently in Central Park. The latter was always fairly small, run on monotonous laps within the park and hidden from the eyes of the public. However, in 1976 New York went public with a race encompassing all five New York boroughs, starting from Staten Island and ending in Central Park. It is flat, with broken city streets and plenty of sharp turns. Yet because of the enormous media coverage, and the attraction of the best runners at some cost, the race has grown to be the largest in the States. In 1977 it was officially the largest, at 3,701 finishers. Another new race in Chicago, called the Mayor Daley Marathon, also had major sponsoring and great publicity and came in fourth-largest in 1977, with 2,131 finishers. The Honolulu Marathon—which is a much lower-key event with, as they

5

**Photo 2**
Frank Shorter, two-time Olympic Marathon medalist, fails to beat
the Boston jinx, as he becomes the sixth Olympic winner to fail at
Boston. His 1978 time was 2:18:15, good for 20th position.
(*Photo by Sue Swigart*)

## Table 1
### Largest 1977 marathons in terms of finishers

| | |
|---|---|
| New York City Marathon | 3,701 |
| Honolulu Marathon | 2,366 |
| Boston Marathon | 2,321* |
| Mayor Daley Marathon | 2,131 |
| Palos Verdes Marathon | 1,707 |
| Skylon International Marathon | 1,624 |
| Maryland Marathon | 1,547 |
| New Jersey Shore Marathon | 1,400† |
| Mission Bay Marathon | 1,106 |

\* Under 4:00:00
† Approximately

say, two record times that they encourage you to beat, the shortest and the longest—was second-largest with 2,366. Boston was third with 2,321 finishers under the 4-hour cutoff time. Other big ones are shown in Table 1 in terms of numbers of finishers.

These numbers are deceptive, of course. One of the disturbing developments of 1977 was that because of the high media coverage and commercial sponsorship, a large number of very badly prepared runners entered some of these races. The New York and Chicago events had very high dropout rates. One expects about 15 to 20 percent not to finish; the Mayor Daley event set a world record for people who didn't finish at something approaching 60 percent of the starters—not a statistic of which to be greatly proud. Boston, on the other hand, with a qualifying time for all entrants, probably had less than 5 percent dropouts if the times for finishers after 4 hours had been recorded. It is certainly the event with the most "electricity."

Thus for an aspiring marathon runner, another listing is appropriate, one which lists the races in order of preference based on course, organization, atmosphere, usual weather to be expected, and so on. Such a list has to be very subjective, and so we offer two lists, one for each of the authors of this book (see Table 2). We have made no attempt at relative numerical rankings but the lists are in order of preference. Any other experienced marathoner would probably have a somewhat different list.

In our minds, to be qualified for such a list the race must have an attractive course, well measured and timed. Efficient preregistration, changing rooms and toilets at the start, and changing rooms and showers at the finish help. Aid stations and transient help are necessary, as well as post-race results issued on a reasonable schedule. Even with all these things, however, the race will not be worth returning to if the atmosphere

**Table 2**
Preferred marathons

| Brown's list | Graham's list |
| --- | --- |
| Boston Marathon | Boston Marathon |
| Honolulu Marathon | Skylon International Marathon |
| Nike Oregon Marathon | Marine Reserves Marathon |
| Pikes Peak Marathon | Fiesta Bowl Marathon |
| Paavo Nurmi Marathon | Paul Masson Marathon |
| Rice Festival Marathon | Paavo Nurmi Marathon |
| New York City Marathon | Mission Bay Marathon |
| Fiesta Bowl Marathon | New York City Marathon |
| Maryland Marathon | Presque Isle Marathon |

is not right. This could be just the friendliness of the organizers or the competitors who return year after year, but it appears to be the single vital ingredient that marks a good marathon.

It is apparent from the sizes of races shown in Table 1 that fields have grown large. Once upon a time you could run alone most of the way, but now there are other runners with you the whole way. The day of the "lonely long-distance runner" has long since gone. Nevertheless, there still are smaller races with under 200 runners that are worthwhile. Your choice of a marathon for a first run or just your next run is worth spending some time over. Don't be misled by some advertising flair or even by a convenient date or location. Finishing happy, *with* a good time and *having had* a good time, is much more important. Chapter 7 will have some pointers to help you make the choice.

### Why?

During the past few years the number of marathons being staged around the country grew as more and more people found the urge to run them. Now there are over 200 marathons annually and we have simply run out of weekends! On a recent weekend it was noted that there were ten marathons available in the eastern half of the country. Yet as we are slowing down in the increase of new marathons, the number in each has exploded, as the numbers in Table 1 show. In 1977, 25,000 runners had entered the sport. The biggest question still remains: *WHY?*

It is not just the race, but the dedication to training that is amazing. The morning light barely penetrates the bedroom when the runner rises at the strident bidding of the alarm. He stiffly dresses in shorts, T-shirt, and favorite worn running shoes before opening the door to confront the morning, and he remembers the adage that the most difficult step is the first one. The scene is repeated across the country. More and more ordinary people of all ages are running at dawn, or at midday, or in the evening, joining the growing number of marathon runners.

The current boom in running started back in 1967 and 1968 with writings by Bill Bowerman and by Kenneth Cooper. Running became respectable, and Cooper promised measurable fitness by the invention of aerobic points for the amount of heart and lung exercise in which the participant indulged. He was also able to distinguish between the benefits of running, swimming, and cycling, and the relatively small benefits obtainable from tennis or golf. We might all, following this introduction to a balanced exercise program and the resultant fitness, have remained with a maintenance diet of regular exercise amounting to no more than a couple of miles run four or five times a week. Yet we didn't. A large and growing number went beyond this, far beyond, to upwards of 60 to 100 miles a week, in order to run marathons. What motivates the runner who climbs out of bed at dawn to strive for a grueling 26-mile-385-yard goal?

During the last year we have heard of studies such as one performed at Harvard to determine what had become of Harvard alumni in the past fifty years and to determine whether their incidence of heart disease could be correlated to the exercise in which they had indulged. The results showed the surprising fact that there seemed to be a *threshold* of activity level. Below this threshold there was very little protection against the normal population levels of heart disease, but above the threshold the measure of protection increased remarkably. This level corresponded to activity hard enough to make the participant sweat and expend 2,000 calories. This level was equivalent to running 20 miles, so it was a little more than Cooper recommended for general bodily fitness.

Dr. Thomas Bassler, a California pathologist, has affirmed that no one who has finished a marathon in under 4 hours has contracted heart disease. Such a flat statement can be attacked by other less positive medical authorities. It well could be true, however, not because running the marathon provides immunity but simply because the marathoner's way of life is a healthy one. Generally a marathoner takes fairly regular and strenuous exercise, does not smoke, sleeps well, and is aware of his or her body to the extent of caring for it, and moreover usually has a diet which includes fresh fruit and vegetables and is low in fats, especially those in muscle meat. There have been many studies which showed that smoking, eating too much (especially of fats), and lack of exercise are bad for you, so it may be that simply combining all of the positive factors in a single life-style improves one's longevity.

Be that as it may, we have yet to meet a marathoner who runs in order to avoid a heart attack, even those who were originally put onto an

Photo 3 (OVERLEAF)
Start of the 1978 Boston Marathon. (*Photo by Phil Yunger*)

exercise program as a result of suffering a heart infarction in the first place. There is another motivation for running the marathon, but it is not entirely clear what it is.

It is probably a combination of a number of things. At least at the start of the race it has all the aspects of a fun run in which runners joke and laugh among themselves. Outsiders have always been amazed at the jollity of the crowd that is about to put in three hours of very hard activity.

Since it is an endurance race, older runners can perform very well, and it becomes an event in which age is not the great divider. Chapter 4 shows that 10-year-old and 60-year-old males have equivalent performances, as do 17-year-old and 40-year-old males. For women, it's 10-year-olds and 45-year-olds, and 17-year-olds and 35-year-olds.

The personal challenges arise in the later stages of the race, and it becomes a matter of self-fulfillment whether the runner is there to complete the event or the racer is there to win it. Both are being essentially competitive, the runner being driven to improve his own last best time and the racer to improve his position.

### Motivation?

I'm not into running to be fit.
That's, most emphatically, not it!
I'm not here for cardiovascular gain
Running through the snow and in the rain.

Five further inches off my waist
Are surely no reason for my haste,
Nor is a pulse of only thirty-eight
If I'd rather dawdle and be late.

I'm not trying to show I'm nifty
Just because I'm reaching fifty.
I'm out here on the road, and lap by lap
Simply trying to beat the other chap!

So when anyone has to ask
Why I take on this running task,
It's not to be as fit as twenty
But it sure as hell helps plenty!

Marathoners are, in the main, competitive, but it is not necessarily for material awards. There are very few except the odd medal or trophy which is soon relegated to a bottom drawer. There is, however, an immense fund of satisfaction and self-discovery. We put ourselves into a position where no other person can help and we have to rely on our own strength of purpose, our own resourcefulness, and our own ability. It is very often a matter of searching for the limits of our own capabilities, something in this modern world that we are very rarely in a position to do. We are all competitors in the marathon, and the main competition is ourselves. That's why the personal record has so much meaning to the marathon runner.

Whatever *your* motivation is, even if you have no well-expressed or well-understood reason for running, in order to run well and to complete a marathon without pain, it is necessary to train to persuade the body and the mind of their ability. Chapter 2 tells you how to go about this.

# Chapter 2
# Put Your Best Foot Forward
## Training Methods

Despite the reputation of the marathon as the ultimate challenge in athletic competition, almost any healthy individual with a high level of persistence and a modest training program can complete a marathon. Startling as this may seem, it is true. Nowhere is this more evident than in such highly publicized races as the New York City Marathon, where a sizable fraction of the entrants, attracted by the glamour of the event, are poorly prepared to attempt the distance. In the 1977 race, nearly one-fourth of the finishers came in after 4 hours. Even more telling was the Mayor Daley race where nearly 60 percent failed to finish. The very late finishers might more appropriately be called *survivors*. True, they may have covered the required distance, but they have likely missed the greatest reward of marathoning. In fact, their memories of the event may even be painful rather than pleasurable. It is doubtful that their experience was much more satisfying and enriching than that of the nonfinisher. Thus, for the novice or aspiring marathoner, the purpose of this chapter is not to explain the secrets for surviving a marathon. Rather, it provides the guidelines for training which can lead to the *successful* completion of a marathon.

For the experienced competitor, the goals are different. For the majority of these runners, the goal is usually the achievement of a personal best time. It may seem strange in an event that requires more than two hours to complete, but every second of improvement is a cherished treasure. An additional target of many runners is the Boston Marathon qualifying standard (3 hours for men under 40 years of age; 3½ hours for women and for men over 40). Boston is the Mecca of the marathoning populace; and running in the event is a recognized symbol of competence in the sport. With the rapid increase in the popularity of road racing, the organizers of the traditional event established qualifying standards in 1970, hoping to limit the number of entrants to what they believed to be a manageable size. However, because of the dramatic increase in the quality as well as the quantity of marathoners, the race has actually grown—from 1,011 starters in 1970 to 4,212 in 1978.

Finally, for a very small fraction of marathoners, the quest for victory supplants time as the primary objective. The U.S. Olympic Trials are the

14

most extreme example of this type of competition. The goal of the entire field is a finish position in the top three, which earns a place on the Olympic team. Such competition is not restricted to the front-runners. It can be just as intense within various age-group classifications or among female entrants. Because of the different goals of the more experienced marathoner, his training may be oriented differently from that of the novice. The approaches and techniques commonly employed by these types of runners are also presented in this chapter.

> I always enjoy my training. It's never been a chore to me.
> **—Ian Thompson, Great Britain**
> (Third best performance in history—2:09:12)

Too often words like "pain," "discipline," and "sacrifice" are used to characterize training. This is unfortunate, as those who view their running in these terms are certainly not obtaining the maximum benefits of the sport. Their performances may even be falling short of their potential as a result of this attitude. In order for one to achieve the maximum physical and psychological benefits from running, the training must be enjoyable. The daily runs should not be thought of as some chore which must be dispatched.

This is not to say that training does not involve work. Successful marathoning does require a significant effort. However, a fallacy common in America is that work must by definition involve sacrifice, discomfort, and inconvenience. Somehow work and pleasure have become antithetical. In fact, the sense of accomplishment achieved from working toward a desired objective can be more satisfying than actually attaining the goal or any associated material benefits which might result. A large fraction of the satisfaction from completing a marathon results from achieving a goal to which you have devoted a long period of preparation. Quoting Thompson again:

> Races are over in a flash, relatively speaking. . . . So it's the enjoyment of training that keeps me going too.

Thus, a true love for running is the essential ingredient in molding an effective training program.

## Which way do we go?

Running and training are not the same thing—although training certainly involves running. Training is orienting your daily, weekly, and monthly running, and even, in a sense, your life-style, to help achieve a goal. It is more focused and defined than a random day-to-day accumulation of miles on the roads. In addition to physical conditioning, training the mind is also essential. Mental confidence as well as physical competence is required for successful completion of an extended ordeal like the marathon.

Just because a training program has a sense of direction does not mean that there must be a rigid schedule of workouts which are programmed to produce the desired result. Successful approaches can vary from a very structured format with each workout planned to the nearest tenth of a mile, to a general approach where the runner determines his needs on a day-to-day basis within an overall set of guidelines. The important factor is that the training must be individualized. There is no single approach that is best for all runners. Training programs should be developed to achieve the runner's personal goals, which, as we noted earlier, are varied. Different goals are likely to require different emphases in training. The person attempting to crack the three-hour barrier for the first time is probably in more need of endurance than the experienced competitor who is trying to qualify for the Olympic Trials. Thus, the former may have a plan primarily based on long slow runs, whereas the national-class competitor may be emphasizing speed work to cope with the near 5-minute-mile pace he must maintain.

In addition to the runner's needs, a successful program must consider the runner's likes and dislikes. If a person abhors running on a track, a rigidly defined program of intervals may not be the optimum method for improving speed. Other alternatives should be explored that do not impose a negative mental factor, which is potentially hindering.

Even more important than an individual's goals and needs, his likes and dislikes, and his ability is his response to training. The running must be stressing, otherwise there will be little improvement. However, the workload must be balanced to avoid excessive strain, which could lead to chronic fatigue and possibly injury. The intensity level which maximizes conditioning and avoids breakdown is very individualized, as each athlete responds differently to the stresses of training. Striking the proper balance is an art and not a science (although the East Germans are removing some of the guesswork by their tremendous advances in sports medicine). They key is listening to your body. More about that in Chapters 4 and 6.

Since no one can be certain how he or she will respond to an increased workload, it is impossible to program this balance into a training plan. Hence every program should be flexible. You must determine each day's running based on your physical and mental condition. If you still feel washed out and achy from Sunday's 20-miler, it might be best to delay Tuesday's intervals another day. In addition to day-to-day flexibility, the entire program should be open to periodic adjustment. If you find 70-mile weeks exhausting, don't push on to the 100-mile weeks you had planned.

Numerous training theories can be found in the running literature. Everything from charging up sand dunes to frolicking through the forest has been proposed by coaches and practiced by world-class athletes. Each method has its drawbacks as well as its advantages. No single program has yet been developed that is the "best"; and probably none ever will be. This is because each runner is an individual with his own personal needs, limitations, and goals. Hence a single method will not suffice for all marathoners. However, there have been some trends in training methods which have resulted in improved times over the past century. Thus each individualized program has some of these improvements as common components with most other programs.

The purpose of this chapter is to present the most common training techniques and the rationale that support these theories. The benefits as well as the pitfalls of the various methods will be presented. This should provide the information necessary to establish the personal training plan which will best help you achieve your goals.

## Coping with stress

Although individual theories and programs vary dramatically, nearly all successful marathon training is based on a single underlying principle—that of *stress adaptation*. Because this concept is the foundation of all marathon training, a general description of the theory is presented as an introduction to the various training methods. The physiological changes which occur are considered in detail in Chapter 4.

Stress can be defined as almost anything a person encounters in his environment which is subjectively associated with unpleasant feelings. Each day every one of us is exposed to many types of stress. Some examples are emotional stresses, such as anxiety or boredom; environmental stresses, such as temperature changes or pollution; and physical stresses as a result of one's work or recreation. These stresses come in a wide variety of intensities. Hans Selye, a Canadian medical researcher, has spent years studying the reactions of animals and man to various types and degrees of stress. This research led him to formulate the General Adaptation Syndrome—a theory which describes the manner in which an organism reacts to a stressful situation. A key element in this theory, and the one which is of most interest in athletic conditioning, is stress adaptation.

Stress adaptation is the increased resistance to stress as a consequence

of prior exposure to stress. Selye's theory states that the body has the capacity to rebuild following the application of stress. In addition to this recovery process the individual develops defenses to accommodate similar stresses in the future. It is this principle which controls and determines physical conditioning. In training, the runner applies a stress which is within his current capability for adaptation. A recovery period is then provided to allow the body to adapt and generate its defenses. The body is then restressed in the next training session and the cycle repeats. Gradually the adaptive capabilities of the runner are increased and greater workloads can be tolerated. In other words, he is "getting in shape."

Selye has demonstrated that only continuous exposure to stress will result in an increased resistance to that stress. Thus the aspiring marathoner cannot be a weekend athlete. He must train regularly. Most marathoners train daily, and many run twice each day.

Of course, there are limits as to the number of workouts per day. In addition to the everyday personal and business conflicts, multiple workouts can have their drawbacks. The danger in this level and frequency of stressing is that the recovery period is quite short, and the runner may not be allowing enough time for effective recovery and rebuilding of defenses. Quite often the athlete exceeds his current adaptive capability and an injury results. Thus, more training is not necessarily better training. Selye also notes that chronic exposure to a certain type of stress can reduce the overall resistance of the body to other stresses. This is frequently observed in distance runners who after several weeks of intensive training often contract a cold or infection because the body resistance to disease has been reduced. This is just as much an injury as a muscle strain would be. The key to optimum training is to find the stress level that is just within the athlete's current adaptive capability and then allow the proper recovery to obtain maximum benefit. Because each of us is different, no coach or book can dictate what these factors are. Thus, training is a never-ending experiment, with each runner continually searching for the method that works best for him. With this in mind, let's proceed on to examine some of the methods employed in this trial-and-error process.

## Long slow distance

In order to determine the kind of preparation that will result in a successful marathon, the runner must first understand that the marathon is an endurance event. Therefore, although the goal of most marathoners may be to achieve a faster time, the primary emphasis in marathon training is not to develop speed. In fact, studies have shown that a person's speed is greatly influenced by genetics and can be improved only so much by training. Muscle biopsies have shown that fibers composing the muscle structure come in two types. In layman's terms, these are known as fast-twitch and slow-twitch fibers. Fast-twitch fibers contract rapidly and quickly exhaust their available glycogen. The metabolism of the slow-twitch fibers utilizes glycogen more efficiently over longer periods and at lower intensities. As the name implies, those endowed with a higher than normal fraction of fast-twitch fibers make the better sprinters. Individuals with a high percentage of slow-twitch fibers are more suited for endurance events. Tests on world-class distance runners indicated that performers of this caliber have in excess of 90 percent slow-twitch fibers. For example, Garry Tuttle, two-time AAU Marathon champion with a personal best of 2:15:15, was found to have 98 percent slow-twitch fibers.

Even the "perfect" training program cannot transform an inherently slow runner into a champion sprinter. However, training seems to have a dramatic effect in improving endurance. Although individuals naturally endowed with a large fraction of slow-twitch fibers are likely to progress further, everyone responds dramatically to endurance-type training. This is particularly noticeable in beginning runners who are far more deficient in endurance than speed. A primary reason for the larger effect of training in developing stamina is that running long distances involves cardiovascular as well as muscular conditioning, whereas speed is determined mostly by muscle strength alone. Probably the best example of a runner who is not hampered by his genetics is Don Kardong. Testing performed at the Dallas Institute for Aerobics Research showed Kardong to have only 59 percent slow-twitch fibers. Yet he surprised Americans by making the 1976 U.S. Olympic marathon team, and shocked the world with a fourth-place 2:11:15 at Montreal.

Endurance is developed gradually through aerobic conditioning. For our immediate purpose, running *aerobically* is simply moving at a pace such that the body's requirements for oxygen over the duration of the run can be satisfied through respiration (we'll postpone the complexities of the physiology and biochemistry to Chapter 4). Running at a pace faster than your aerobic limit will produce an oxygen debt. In other

19

words, the muscles are not receiving enough oxygen to meet the demands of the workload. Running *anaerobically* for extended periods will eventually temporarily impair the muscles' ability to contract by a buildup of lactic acid, thus forcing you to slow down dramatically. The body demands that the oxygen debt be repaid quickly. Most of us who have attempted to run an all-out 440 on a track know this sensation all too well. As you came out of the final turn, ready to sprint for the tape, the muscles begin to tie up. The whole race seems to become slow motion as a rigor mortis sensation envelops the body.

Of course, the marathon is entirely different from the quarter-mile. Studies have shown that during the marathon, 99 percent of the oxygen requirements are supplied aerobically. Hence, the primary goal of marathon training should be to improve endurance. Numerous tests with both athletes and untrained individuals have demonstrated that endurance is developed through extended periods of aerobic exercise—in other words, running long distances at a comfortable pace so as to avoid oxygen debt. This kind of running develops one's aerobic capacity by keeping the stresses near the point of optimum respiratory efficiency (again, that principle of stress adaptation crops up!). The circulatory system is conditioned as well. The heart becomes a stronger, more efficient pump. In addition, there is an increase in the number of capillaries feeding the muscle tissue and an improvement in oxygen utilization. Chapter 4 has the details on these phenomena as well.

Dr. Ernst van Aaken was the first to champion running long distances as a training philosophy. He boasted that the successes of Harald Norpoth (5,000-meter silver medalist in the 1964 Olympics and former world record holder) and, more recently, the phenomenal performances of Germany's women marathoners were the result of a training program based on high mileage at a relaxed pace.

The surge in the popularity of this approach is probably due in large part to the enjoyment of this training method. The running is relaxed and the pace comfortable. Workouts are essentially pain-free and can be run conversationally with friends. Furthermore, the probability of injury is much less than with other methods. This is in sharp contrast to the rigid interval training which was in vogue in the '50s and '60s, in which each workout involved a near-maximum effort. Because of the high concentration of anaerobic running, interval workouts can very often be exhausting and even painful. In contrast, the long slow distance runner usually feels pleasantly tired after his run. In fact, not infrequently he feels energetic and inspired, as long slow training runs often have a pick-me-up effect.

Because of the fundamental importance of endurance in the successful completion of a marathon, numerous runners have adopted this philosophy as their total training program. For the beginner, the high-mileage runs at slow pace will usually produce a rapid improvement in condition over the first several months. But even for well-conditioned, experienced runners this method will yield improvement (although much more gradually). Cardiovascular-system performance will continue to improve over several years, as long as the program does not exhaust one's adaptation energy reserves. In addition to aerobic conditioning, over-distance training usually develops a smoother running style. Gradually one's carriage and motion evolve into a more efficient form. Wasteful arm and head movements are often eliminated.

The key to developing an effective long slow distance training schedule is to understand the definition of the adjectives "long" and "slow." Each has a different meaning for every runner, but the principles are still the same. The following sections will help you determine how long is long and how slow is slow.

## Those long training miles

Several investigators have attempted to discover the magic formula for marathon success. Exercise physiologists have considered the factors that would assist the runner and then statistically correlated those factors to finishing times for a number of participants.

Paul Slovic back in 1973 considered the following factors to be important:

· the fastest mile time within the past year
· whether or not a marathon had been completed previously
· miles run during the past eight weeks
· the length of the longest single run during those eight weeks
· the maximum mileage in a week in the past eight weeks
· the number of runs over 20 miles during the previous eight weeks

and from these factors equations were produced to show the final expected time.

Then came Carl Foster and Jack Daniels in 1975, who chose instead the following:

· estimated maximal oxygen uptake
· the length of the longest single run during the past eight weeks
· miles run during the past eight weeks
· the habitual training pace for steady runs.

In addition, they tried to differentiate between novices and experienced marathoners. They also found that they could integrate many of these factors into mileage, so they also published an equation for runners who had covered more than 490 miles in training during the past eight weeks. This equation then only depended on the estimated maximal oxygen uptake.

21

Finally, John Graham in 1976 derived an even simpler correlation based only upon

· the pace of the most recent 10-mile race

which integrated the effects of maximal oxygen uptake and training in a single race result just long enough to have elements of speed and endurance.

However, to be honest, none of these correlations was accurate. While they worked well for the data on which they were based, they had no general application because they didn't take into account the motivation of the runner, the severity of the course, or the weather at race time.

One piece of analysis, however, has stood the test of time. Ken Young in 1973 came up with the Theory of Collapse, which also showed that the training mileage volume was important. Moreover, there was a threshold which it was well to exceed. Young's theory was that one could run three times one's normal average training distance in a race without reaching a point of collapse. The average training distance was the number of miles covered in the past eight weeks divided by 56 days. Thus in order to complete the 26.2 miles of the marathon without collapse the average training distance ought to be a minimum of 8¾ miles, which means that 56 × 8¾ miles would have to be run in the previous eight weeks. This works out to be 490 miles, and that is why Foster and Daniels used that number in their simplified equation.

This theory of Young's has held up well under trial; 8¾ miles per day on average, or more than 61 miles per week, is the statistical minimum training required to reach the end of the marathon without collapse, or "hitting the wall." It effectively measures the point of energy exhaustion. We have tried this theory out many times to predict when a runner who has trained less than this minimum might be expected to hit the wall, and it works pretty well.

· A 49-year-old runner entered his first marathon with only an average of 38 miles in his last four weeks. Starting out at a 3½-hour pace, he maintained the 8-minute-mile speed for the first half of the race. At 15 miles he began to slow and finished the marathon in 3:54 (slower than a 9-minute-mile average).
· A young boy training at 52 miles per week before his first marathon effort with a daily average of 7½ miles could be expected to reach a point of collapse at 22½ miles. In the race at this point his pace slowed by some 4 minutes a mile! He did manage to complete the race; however, other runners may well have quit at his collapse point.

Young's theory, of course, assumes that the runner isn't subjected to other, more dominant stresses. For example, a runner is likely to collapse for other reasons if the day is very hot and humid, or if he or she starts out

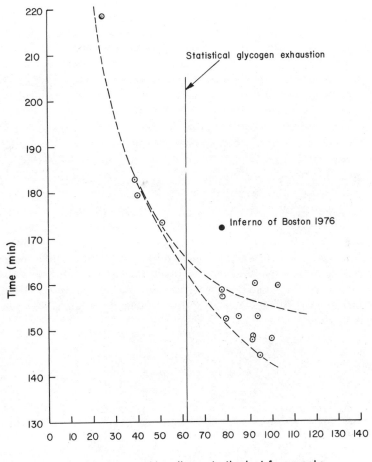

**Figure 3**
The effect of running mileage on performance. The runner, Brown, is age 17–28 through this improvement period.

at far too fast a pace. However, for a reasonably prudent runner, the effect appears predictably tied to training mileage.

Each runner is an experiment of one: Sometimes we fit the average statistical mold and sometimes as individuals we do not. So any statistical theory like this must be sampled and tried and, if necessary, modified to fit with our own results.

Figure 3 shows an experiment for the younger of the two authors of this book. This graph illustrates the marathon time as a function of training distance. As we would expect, the finishing times of his marathons improve as the average mileage increases. For mileages less than 61 per week the finishing times are much higher, and in each of those races he suffered a survival finish. For mileages greater than that threshold there is a scatter which appears to be dependent principally on variations in the course itself and in the weather on race day. One such obvious point is the result of the 1976 Boston Marathon, run in excessive heat. If this time is corrected for heat (as shown in Figure 7), it falls right along with the points within the trend curves.

This figure uses the average weekly mileage over the last four weeks rather than the eight-week preparation period which we discussed above. Other unreported studies showed that if you test the effects of the last thirteen weeks, eight weeks, four weeks, and two weeks, the four-week period appears to give the best results. It does assume that there has been a reasonable level of training before that, of course.

Figure 4 shows the equivalent experiment for the older of the two authors. Again the effect of the threshold is evident, as well as the scatter beyond it due to weather and course variations. Also there is another 1976 Boston inferno result which can be corrected for heat to lie among the companion points between the dotted curves. Two points showing bad times noted as being in the low hemoglobin period are due to iron-

**Figure 4**
The effect of running mileage on performance. The runner, Graham, is age 41–45 through this improvement period.

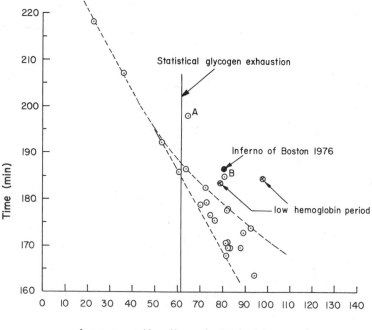

Average weekly mileage in the last four weeks

deficient anemia, a condition which is discussed in Chapter 6. Finally, two points marked A and B are poor times for another reason. In both cases the runner started out at much too fast a pace, thus exhausting the body's stores of glycogen far too rapidly. In both cases a wall was encountered, and the rest of the marathon became a survival shuffle. To be fair in the case of point B, the race was run only eight days after a previous marathon, and so the initial pace should have been about 30 seconds a mile more prudent.

These curves tell us that there is a minimum mileage to be run during training and that a sensible pace must be selected. (More about pacing later in Chapter 7.) The curves also seem to imply that the more mileage, the lower the time possible. Both of the runners ought to run at least 110 or 120 miles a week. Right? Well, not exactly, since not all runners are capable of very high mileages without something happening to them. For example, with high mileage the runner is not always able to recover from the previous training run and thus becomes susceptible to injury. In the case of Graham, trial and error seems to indicate that an average of 95 miles a week is about the limit before the body starts experiencing excessive pain and colds appear from nowhere! Brown is still exploring his limits, but certainly experience to date seems to indicate that 110 to 120 miles a week average is excessive.

Ernst van Aaken, the originator of slow over-distance training, believes that the key to successful marathoning lies in increasing one's upper limit. Consequently, he believes the marathon aspirant should run the 42-kilometer distance often in practice. Further, the runner should steadily progress to even longer runs, up to 60 to 80 kilometers each week! It should be noted that his program is a cautious one in which the runner increases his distance very gradually. He recommends a three-to-five-year period to reach the 80-kilometer distance. Van Aaken is also an advocate of gentle-paced running with frequent walking breaks.

Impressive mileage totals are also recorded by many international marathon champions. The training programs for many of these elite average in excess of 20 miles per day. For example, Jerome Drayton (1977 Boston champion and several times winner of the prestigious Fukuoka Marathon) regularly churns out 150 miles per week. Once during the final week of preparation for the 1970 Fukuoka race he upped his training to 175 miles, convinced that his legs could use the extra strengthening. He noted that "150 miles per week had begun to seem easy." However, a beginner should be warned not to jump in and try to emulate a runner who not only has rare ability but has been conditioning himself for years.

Clearly mileage has a big effect. Thus after having exceeded the minimum you will have to explore the upper reaches of training distance to determine your own capabilities for high mileage without injury. However, you should recognize that factors other than training also affect marathon performance, as evidenced by the scatter in the preceding graphs. These include choosing the right course, favorable weather, avoiding injury, and selecting the optimum pace for the time you intend to achieve. Other chapters have advice on all of these ideas.

### Distribution of mileage

Knowing that overall mileage total seems to make a difference, there are still some questions to be answered:

- How often should I run longer than 20 miles at one go?
- Are two 5-mile runs as good as one 10-miler?
- How should the mileage be distributed in the week?

For every one of us the answers have a bearing on how much time we have to allot to training and when we can get off during the day. An important point to keep in mind when establishing your training goals is to make your program compatible with your other daily activities. Don't make things hard for yourself or the sport will be all too easy to relinquish if there is a disturbance in your daily routine, such as change of job or an injury.

You do not need to run over 20 miles a day to run a successful marathon. Even some world-class marathoners don't reach this level. For example, Steve Hoag, who captured second place in the 1975 Boston Marathon (2:11:54), averaged only 90 miles per week in preparation. However, long training runs are an essential part of marathon preparation, as they serve several important purposes. Long runs teach the body to live off its reserves. Unless you are severely depleted from extensive training or are on some special diet, the glycogen storage capacity in the body is certainly enough to carry you beyond 15 miles. However, as the distance approaches 20 miles this fuel supply becomes exhausted, and the body must switch over to living off its reserves. This means a higher percentage of the energy is supplied by fats. As discussed in Chapter 4, utilization of this energy source requires more oxygen intake and is slower. Thus the running may become more labored. However, the more frequently a runner ventures into this zone, the more conditioned the body becomes in performing this transition in energy source. It becomes accustomed to working off its reserves, and the shock to the system is not as dramatic in the race as it would have been without this training. It has also been claimed that long runs increase capillary formation in the muscles (more so than shorter runs). Hence, the oxygen supply to the leg muscles may be increased.

In addition, the long training runs are excellent mental training. The self-discipline required to complete a run lasting longer than 2 hours is much greater than that required for two shorter runs. Long runs get the runner accustomed to the mental stresses of extended periods on the road. They also provide a boost in confidence for the less experienced marathoner who may still have doubts about his ability to complete the distance.

In conclusion, long training runs are beneficial. Once some basic level of conditioning has been achieved, a long run of at least 15 miles is a good idea at least once each week. An occasional 20-miler (or longer) can be thrown in to obtain the benefits noted above. The frequency of long runs depends on your current condition and adaptive capability. Once a month would be perfectly adequate, especially if you have run several marathons in the last year as well.

Hardly ever is a run longer than 26 miles necessary, even though some very rare people do believe in testing the system occasionally. If you feel like a good long run, then do it. It is largely a matter of listening to the body and doing what feels good. But it is not *necessary* that you exceed the race distance during training runs. As an example, practice has shown that Graham is very comfortable with training runs in the 12-to-16-mile range. He has found that the transition to 26-plus miles on race day is not difficult.

How about breaking up the day's distance into two runs? This is a common practice many marathoners use to increase their total mileage. It is also helpful to those whose time available for training is limited (like a lunch hour). A question frequently asked is: Are two short runs as beneficial as one long one of the same total distance? There have been no conclusive studies to prove that one way or the other is best. It probably doesn't make much difference as long as the training is not composed *entirely* of 5-mile runs. As noted previously, long runs are necessary. However, a successful program can be built around running shorter distances twice a day during the week and leaving the long runs for the weekend. What really matters is *total mileage*, and any difference in conditioning that might result from combining smaller runs is probably marginal. In terms of race performance, this effect is much less significant than, say, a 10° temperature change on the race day.

Running twice a day also cuts into the recovery period following each run. As we noted earlier in this chapter, the risk of injury is higher when multiple workouts are performed. However, if approached cautiously and gradually, running twice a day can be effective in conditioning the body to recover more quickly. Van Aaken's program for the college-student runner involved five workouts per day!

Having said this, it is nevertheless worthwhile trying to maintain all runs above a certain minimum of approximately 5 to 6 miles. This is because after you are conditioned to a base level of about 70 miles per week your body doesn't reach an equilibrium until a few miles into the run. The first 2 miles are spent, even after pre-run stretching, in working out the newly created lactic acids in the exercising muscles, and in settling into a rhythm of activity. Thus it is worthwhile to run a few miles past this threshold of breaking into the run.

Finally, there is the question of how to distribute the desired mileage throughout the week. Some runners mistakenly believe that if they want to achieve, say, 70 miles per week, the best way is to run 10 miles each day. However, experience has shown this not to be the case. Under a program developed by Bill Bowerman (former track coach at the University of Oregon), runners alternate hard days (or long days on over-distance training) with easier, shorter days. Brian Maxwell, one of Canada's best marathoners (his personal record, or PR, is 2:14:43), is a practitioner of this philosophy to an extreme. His hard days are often in the 30-to-35-mile range, while the recovery days are relaxed runs of 6 to 10 miles. This hard/easy approach is simply an extension of Selye's stress-adaptation theory over a longer period than just the interval between workouts. Under Bowerman's program the easy days are an important part of the recovery phase, but it is a dynamic recovery as opposed to rest.

Just how do all these puzzle pieces fit together to form an effective training program? Table 3 is an example of a schedule which a runner might follow if he or she adheres to the long slow distance training philosophy. We should emphasize that this schedule is provided only to illustrate how the various points discussed earlier can be incorporated into a sound program. Your own program should be based on your own limitations, preferences, and personal constraints. In developing Table 3, we used a runner whose personal limitations on weekly mileage are in the

## Table 3
Sample long slow distance training schedules

Daily mileages

| DAY OF THE WEEK | REMOTE FROM MARATHON | | FOUR WEEKS BEFORE MARATHON | |
|---|---|---|---|---|
| | Non-race week | Race week | Non-race week | Race week |
| Monday | 6 | 6 | 8 | 8 |
| Tuesday | 8 | 8 | 13 | 13 |
| Wednesday | 12 | 10 | 16 | 16 |
| Thursday | 8 | 8 | 12 | 12 |
| Friday | 10 | 10 | 15 | 15 |
| Saturday | 8 | 5 | 10 | 5 |
| Sunday | 15 | 15* | 20 | 15* |
| **Total** | 67 | 62 | 94 | 84 |

* Race day. The schedule assumes this mileage comprises a 10-mile race plus some warm-up and post-race jogging.

range of 90 to 95. He trains primarily on long slow distance and uses shorter races to develop his speed (see the section later in this chapter on racing as training). The training is divided into two types of periods. One is the four weeks immediately before the week of the marathon, and the other is the remainder of the year when there is no marathon in the near future. Within these two categories, typical mileage distributions are shown for both racing and non-racing weeks.

The sample schedules reflect the importance of peaking in the month before the marathon. Comparing the last-four-weeks preparation to the remainder of the year's training, you can see that the total distance covered is significantly greater during the pre-marathon period. However, the relative distribution of mileage throughout the week is similar. Notice how the hard/easy concept is woven into the week's running. During a non-race week, both schedules have the longest day on Sunday. Monday is then a short recovery day just to get loose and work out the kinks. Tuesday acts as a day of intermediate effort, the distance being determined by the individual's recovery needs, and Wednesday is the other long day of the week. Each week has one long run (Sunday) to accustom the body to extended periods of stress. While you may find it easier to divide the weekday mileage into two runs, it is important that at least one long run be retained per week. As we explained before, the mental and physical conditioning of long training runs is essential marathon preparation.

For the weeks in which there are races, the same hard/easy approach is followed. Notice that the early part of the week is identical in both the race-week and non-race-week schedules. This is because the race is being utilized as a part of marathon preparation and thus minimum impact on the training routine is desired. If the race is an important one, you may wish to begin cutting back earlier in the week. Because of the strenuous demands of racing, the Monday recovery run might be shorter and/or slower than during a normal training week. If the race is a particularly exhausting effort, more than one day of recovery may be necessary.

The total distance covered on race day depends a great deal on the distance of the event. In the sample schedule, we have assumed that the race was a 10-miler. Normally one jogs a mile or two for a warm up. Following the race it is wise to jog a couple of miles very slowly to help flush the waste products out of the muscles. This generally alleviates some of the stiffness that could result the next day if one did no post-race running. Thus the runner in our example gets a good 15-mile day, with 10 miles being at a hard effort. However, it is important that the runner not be overly concerned with mileage on race day. If, for example, a hard 10-kilometer has left you exhausted and cramped, don't go out for a 6-mile run "just to get the miles in." Jog what you can and be satisfied with an 8-mile day. Remember the purpose of the race was to obtain speed work and not to accumulate miles.

## What pace?

Having discussed distance thoroughly, we now turn to the question of speed. What pace is considered slow? As you might expect, the answer is again an individual one. A 6:30-per-mile clip may be a relaxed run for the 2:20 marathoner, but it is an all-out effort for the novice who hopes to crack 3:30. There are guidelines to apply in determining what pace is best. In general, the pace should be easily achievable. The run should be entirely within your aerobic capacity (except for perhaps a brief period when a steep hill is encountered or possibly a run in at the end). If you can chat to a companion, so much the better, but hardly ever should it be so fast that the necessary heavy breathing is too much for conversation. Of course, as you train, aerobic capacity will improve, and this measure of pace will probably mean that later on you will be able to run faster. As long as you remain within the "conversational limit," your pace will be safe. Keep in mind the advice of Arthur Lydiard, the renowned coach from New Zealand: "You can never run too slow to improve oxygen uptake; but you can run too fast!"

Another measure often used to determine correct pacing is pulse rate. You may know your maximal pulse rate from a stress test. If not, one easy way to estimate this value is to *subtract your age in years from 220.* Thus, on the average, a 40-year-old has a maximum pulse of about 180 beats per minute, while that of a 28-year-old is a higher 192. Whatever your particular figure is, you can determine an upper limit for your long training runs by taking 75 percent of that maximum value. You can estimate your pulse during the run by stopping and taking your pulse (say at your neck) for 10 seconds. Multiplying this value by six will give your heart rate. If it is greater than 75 percent of your maximum, you are probably going too fast and should reduce speed. As an example, the 40-year-old with a maximum pulse of 180 should train at a level of about 135. This corresponds to 22 or 23 beats in a 10-second counting period. However, most runners don't want to be bothered with taking their pulse and may feel a bit foolish clutching their throats intermittently during the run. If you don't want to be bothered by the numbers or taking your pulse, the rule is simple: Just keep within the conversational limit.

Some mileage, of course, ought to be run at a faster rate, if for no other reason than to let your legs know what it feels like. However, surprisingly enough, even if you didn't do any speed work you would find that the long-distance training would enable you to do better in races. Many runners are worried that if they don't run better than a 7-minutes-per-mile pace in training then they will never be able to run at 6:15 per mile in their next race. However, they will be pleasantly surprised to find that they can. Jerome Drayton, for example, has stated that 90 percent of his running is at a 7-minute-mile pace, which is some 2 minutes per mile slower than his marathon race speed.

Having alluded to the benefits of some speed work, we should note that there are some disadvantages to a training program composed entirely of long slow distance. Even its staunchest supporters recognize that some additional work is required to develop speed. The basic drawback of a program entirely based on slow-paced running is that it is nonspecific. The workouts do not develop the muscle strength and high-speed coordination required for racing. The fast-twitch muscle fibers receive little conditioning. Speed work can be accomplished in a number of ways. The remainder of this chapter explores these methods. We will attempt to put the relative merits of fartleks, intervals, hills, and racing into perspective as they relate to marathon preparation. However, suffice it to say here that a sound endurance base is of fundamental importance to the marathoner. This conditioning is best and most safely acquired by long runs well within one's aerobic capacity.

## Hill training

Hill training is one method of developing speed which is used by some, but by no means many, runners. Its unpopularity can probably be attributed to the difficult and exhausting workouts, which are nearly as strenuous as racing. Hill training is strongly advocated by Lydiard, who used it to produce Olympic medalists in the middle-distance events. Although the importance of speed is not as great in the marathon, it can provide the competitive edge that separates the champion from the runner-up. More important, the strength and efficiency which can be obtained from hill-running training is beneficial to marathoners of all abilities.

Although, as discussed in earlier sections, long-distance training is the foundation of successful marathon conditioning, hill running does provide some benefits which cannot be attained by over-distance work. Hill training resembles weight training in principle, as it is resistance work. Running hills develops strength in certain muscle groups to a much greater extent than coasting over flat terrain. In particular, the hip flexors, calves, and quadriceps will become more powerful. The quads, for example, are often one of the most painful muscle groups in the few days following a marathon. This is because most runners' normal training creates an imbalance in overall muscular strength, with the muscles on the front of the thigh doing relatively less work. Toward the latter stages of a marathon these muscles (which serve to extend the leg forward) begin to tire and the runner's stride slowly decreases. Thus while the effort and cadence may remain constant the runner is gradually losing speed. The strain resulting from forcing these muscles well beyond their training stress levels often manifests itself as a severe throbbing pain which accompanies any movement in the next few days. They are even sore to the touch!

In addition to muscle strength, hill running develops specific efficient

31

uphill and downhill running techniques. This can be quite important in marathon racing as well as shorter, hillier road races. In an event like the Boston or Maryland marathon where you are confronted with a tough hill near the 20-mile mark, you don't need to waste your dwindling supply of energy. Hill training can help you conserve the energy by minimizing wasted motion.

First, before plunging into the fundamentals of hill training, a word of caution is in order. Serious hill training should be undertaken only by the well-conditioned runner. It is a mistake to tackle the slopes without a strong endurance background. Even with many weeks of aerobic conditioning behind him, a runner usually finds transition to hill running quite taxing. Anyone desiring to train on hills should work into a routine slowly. Maximum effort should not be employed during the first several workouts. Moreover, before beginning the hill workout sequence, a good warm up is essential. The strenuous effort of hill workouts can lead to muscle strains or even pulls if the runner starts into them cold. Generally, 2 miles of slow jogging and some stretching is adequate.

Hill training can be as unstructured as a fartlek or as rigidly scheduled as an interval session on the track. Some runners hill-train by selecting an especially rolling terrain for their normal run and assault each rise at a much higher effort than their normal workout pace. Many (such as Graham) find this approach the best, as it avoids the mental strain that can accompany more disciplined workouts. However, while such runs are beneficial, they are not specific, primarily because the route of the run dictates the nature of the workout. Also the irregular frequency of hills and different nature of each hill force the runner to concentrate to obtain maximum benefits.

Arthur Lydiard, one of the modern-day champions of hill training, recommends a more disciplined approach. His "classical hill workouts" have been modified extensively to fit the different needs of individual runners. However, the guiding principles remain basically unchanged. One variation which works well is to select a hill of approximately ½ mile with flat stretches at the base and the top. After the warm-up, try the following sequence:

- stride the first 200 yards leading to the hill
- drive up the hill at a hard effort
- stride another 100–200 yards at the top
- jog 200 yards for recovery
- run downhill hard
- stride hard for 200 yards immediately after descending the hill.

Between each sequence, slowly jog a 440 or 880 for recovery. Four (or more if you can manage it) repetitions of this sequence will produce a most beneficial (and taxing!) workout.

The striding segments immediately before and after the ascent and following the downhill are nearly as important as the hill itself. These phases are vital in developing a smooth running form and style for racing. A smooth transition both when starting up a hill and when coming off it are important. Too often runners slow down when approaching a hill to save themselves for the strain ahead. This does not really save a significant amount of energy. The runner who employs such a tactic probably loses ground to runners who maintain a sensible pace and flow smoothly up the incline. After reaching the top of the hill, another common fault is easing off. Runners slow down to catch their breath instead of running "over the hill." Very often this is a result of poor uphill running technique. The runner is tied in knots and has incurred an excessive oxygen debt from an inefficient or too-strenuous attack up the hill. From proper hill training the runner will learn what his capabilities are and will not make such mistakes. He will learn what effort he can maintain and reach the top in good form. The striding after completing the uphill helps to condition the runner in regaining his normal stride rapidly as the slope levels off. Likewise, after flying down a steep slope, regaining proper posture and efficient stride and cadence is difficult after the long but rapid and jarring strides of the downhill. This training sequence conditions the runner to these situations. After a few sessions of this type of workout the transition in style in coming on and off the slopes is smoother and more efficient.

Although this hill workout is primarily designed to develop speed and strength, it is also an excellent distance workout. Counting the warm-up and jogging recovery, the runner who completes four or five of these sequences has logged more than 10 miles without stopping. Thus a good hill workout does not have to have the effect of decreasing mileage.

Lydiard throws an additional twist into his hill workouts. He recommends springing up the incline instead of simply running. In springing the runner ascends the hill on his toes. Each stride is typified by a hard, driving thrust upward. The runner lands on the fore foot, and as his weight comes down, the heel drops below the level of the toes. The net forward progress is quite limited—perhaps only a foot—as the runner is intent on springing upward rather than striding out. Lydiard believes this bouncing, kangaroolike action produces maximum flexion of the ankles and is beneficial in stretching the calf muscles. It also trains the knees to maintain proper lift when running uphill.

Despite Lydiard's promotion of this technique, we are not yet convinced of these benefits. If you are prone to Achilles-tendon ailments, springing up hills can cause injury. Even if you are extremely careful, the new running style can leave you with some aching ankles the next morning. For the runner who is just beginning a hill-training phase, it is best to introduce springing gently. Don't attempt to use the technique completely on every hill the first couple of times. Try to spring on only one hill or perhaps a 50-to-100-yard segment of each uphill during the first hill session. See how your body responds. If you can tolerate the severe stresses on the

Achilles, gradually increase the amount of springing on the uphill portions until you achieve what you feel to be an optimum level of intensity. Remember that any benefits derived from springing can in no way offset the very severe detriment of any injury to the Achilles. This kind of damage can take months to correct.

The alternative to springing is just to run the uphill sections hard, while concentrating on maintaining good form. This technique places a somewhat greater emphasis on strengthening the quadriceps, whereas springing puts more emphasis on the calf muscles. Even if you can cope with the stresses of hill springs, it is still advisable to forgo the bouncing motion occasionally and just run the uphills hard. This will allow you to work on efficient uphill running technique, which is not developed as well by the bouncing motion of hill springs.

Although there is no "perfect" form for uphill running, there are several guidelines one can follow which apply to most runners. When ascending a hill, the stride length should be shortened and the cadence quickened slightly. The back should be kept relatively straight and the hips forward with the hands held a little lower than normal (see Photo 4). The head should be kept up, eyes looking straight ahead. Many runners will positively avoid looking up, as they don't like to see how much farther it is to the top. However, if the head drops, there is a tendency

**Photo 4**
Uphill running form. (*Photo by John Graham*)

for the hips to fall back, thus destroying the erect posture. This bent-over running style is very inefficient.

The key to efficient uphill running style is to avoid wasting energy. Probably the most common and noticeable fault is exaggerated arm movement which is out of synch with the runner's progression up the hill. While the arc of the arm swing is larger for uphill running than on the level, uncontrolled flailing or jerking movements can actually slow you down. The arms should move in a pendulum fashion, bending at the elbows with a smooth rhythm that matches the cadence of the stride—just as in level running. Side-to-side arm motion which brings the forearms across the front of the chest should be avoided.

Keeping the upper body relaxed is another way to avoid wasting energy. Let the legs do the work. Many runners in assaulting a hill unconsciously tighten their neck and shoulder muscles. This muscular tension diverts energy to nonessential muscles and can interfere with a fluid running motion. Runners are often unaware of this habit until cramping sets in, and then it is too late. Hence the runner must get in the habit of relaxing the upper body. He must constantly monitor his condition when working up a hill and be aware of any tendencies toward tightening of the neck and shoulders. Again these habits and a relaxed running style will become second nature to the runner during a marathon, if he has developed these capabilities in training.

Downhill running style is an area that is ignored by many runners. More emphasis is placed on efficient uphill style. Perhaps the reason for this is that most runners consider downhill running to be easy. A popular misconception is that gravity is doing all the work, so running downhill just comes naturally. This really isn't true. There is a knack to efficient downhill running, one which can be difficult to perfect. However, after a few sessions on the slopes almost everyone will show a definite improvement. This effort will pay off too. In fact, compared to uphill technique, there may be a greater benefit in time from developing a proficient downhill style. The yardage you may lose going up the slope can easily be regained by fast downhill sections. In addition, hard downhill sessions in training condition the quadriceps to the pounding of intense downhill running. This can pay off in a race like the Boston Marathon, where the last 5 miles are mostly downhill. Many runners when reaching this stage find their thighs hurting so much that they can't cope with the jarring of fast downhill racing. Hence, they lose valuable time over those last downhill miles. Thus, if you decide to try hill training, don't neglect the downhill.

In traveling downhill the idea is to let gravity do the work. Many runners mistakenly lean back and relax on the downgrades. This actually slows them down, as the impact of the heel with each step has a braking action in the runner's speed. The runner should concentrate on keeping his body perpendicular to the slope of the road, as in Photo 5, and just let himself go. The primary concern is just to keep the legs up with the upper body. Conscious braking upon heel impact should be avoided. Ron Daws recommends complete relaxation of the heel upon contact with the road. The arms are used mainly for balance and when running downhill may move in fast, rather jerky motions which are unlike the smooth rhythm needed for all other types of running.

A word of warning is in order at this point. Hard downhill running is very stressful. The pounding absorbed by the skeletal structure (ankles, knees, back, etc.) is tremendous. The quadriceps also take quite a beating. Hence it is best to exercise some caution on the first few downhill sessions—more so than on the uphills. If possible try to find a gentle slope for early training in descending hills. Give yourself a few workouts before bashing full tilt down the hills.

Hill workouts should always be run in protective training shoes. The shoe should have excellent cushioning beneath both the ball and the heel to absorb the shock of the downgrades. In addition, a good solid heel cup is advisable to help stabilize the heel on impact and prevent, to some degree, the twisting and rotation which often lead to knee and ankle injuries. Shoes with flared heels are also believed to be beneficial in this respect.

As we noted earlier, you should not consider serious hill training until you have developed a strong endurance base. Once you have decided to incorporate hill running into your overall training program, how should you introduce the workouts into your weekly schedule? First of all, begin slowly. Your first several sessions should not be an all-out effort. Allow several days for recovery between workouts. Monitor your body carefully for signs of overtraining and injury. As you gain in strength and confidence, slowly increase the intensity and reduce the number of recovery days. However, even when you hit peak training still allow at least one recovery day between hill workouts. Hill training on successive days invites an injury.

Another point to keep in mind is that your weekly mileage should decrease slightly when hill training. This is to be expected, as you can't maintain both speed work and long distance without courting disaster. Don't use your rest days to try to build up the mileage. A weekly routine during a hill-training phase for the runner in our earlier example might be as follows:

| Sunday | Monday | Tuesday | Wednesday | Thursday | Friday | Saturday |
|---|---|---|---|---|---|---|
| 18 miles | Hill workout | 8 miles | Hill workout | 8 miles | Hill workout | 8 miles |

All of the non-hill-training days are run at an easy relaxed pace. Notice that a long run is maintained to help keep up the endurance. Assuming

**Photo 5**
Downhill running form. (*Photo by John Graham*)

each hill session is about 11 miles (including warm-up, recovery jogs, and cooldown), the total weekly mileage is 75 miles—down about 20 percent from the 94 per week our marathoner was covering in his endurance training (Table 3).

In conclusion, hill training is an excellent way to build muscular strength and speed. While these factors are certainly not as important as endurance to marathoners, they can provide that little bit extra that gets you under three hours or gets you by your archrival in the home stretch. Just as important as the physical benefits is the confidence hill training can produce. The hill-trained marathoner knows he can cope with hills and is not intimidated by them. He acquires a great deal of mental toughness that is essential to successful racing.

### Interval training

As we noted earlier, it is possible to attain considerable success in the marathon using a training program consisting only of aerobic long-distance runs. However, it is probable that the runner who utilizes this approach may not be performing up to maximum potential in the marathon. He may lack some of the adaptability of his competitor who does some anaerobic conditioning. Those who train exclusively on long slow distance may encounter difficulty in hilly marathons, or may experience considerable difficulty in recovering from faster sections in the race.

While the marathon is an endurance event, exercise physiologists and medical researchers have determined that some small fraction of the race—1 or 2 percent—is run anaerobically. Thus some anaerobic training could be beneficial. Let's examine exactly what speed training does provide. First of all, it improves mechanical functioning and coordination. The legs become accustomed to the different stride length and cadence which faster running requires. In addition, speed training may increase the fraction of the runner's maximum oxygen uptake at which he can perform aerobically. Thus, while anaerobic work does develop basic speed, its *most* important function for the marathoner is to develop a more efficient running style at speeds which he formerly was struggling to maintain.

As we noted with hill training, any type of anaerobic training should be avoided unless the runner has a sound background of endurance training. Aerobic conditioning is the foundation and structure of marathoning, and speed workouts are only the shingles on the roof. Thus it is useless to do speed work if the endurance base is not present. Furthermore, once you have developed stamina, intervals are much easier to cope with. Oxygen debt is not created as quickly, and you have the ability to recover rapidly. Secondly, daily speed workouts are not necessary and in fact could be dangerous. The marathoner should never require more than two or three anaerobic sessions per week—even when peaking for a big race. Many accomplished marathoners find that one speed workout per week suits them well.

Interval workouts are very often unpopular with marathoners. In fact, the reason why many younger runners abandon track and turn to road racing after leaving school is that they want to get away from the monotonous, painful, and exhausting interval workouts which formed the bulk of their training. However, interval training does not have to be this way. In fact, to be effective, interval workouts should generally not be painful and exhausting. (More about this later.) It is not even necessary to run on a track. Percy Cerutty (Australian coach of thirty world-record setters, including Herb Elliott) recommends that speed workouts be performed on soft surfaces to avoid leg injuries. His sessions on the beaches and sand dunes near Portsea have become legends in the history of athletic training. However, since many of us don't have beaches nearby, golf courses, wooded trails, or open fields (provided the surface is not rough) can be used. Of course, if your legs are made of iron, you can run your intervals on the road. In fact, when peaking for a race, it is probably wise to do some of your anaerobic training on the road. The rhythm and stride length developed on a soft surface will be different than those on hard pavement. Since marathons are run almost exclusively on roads, you should have some feel for how your stride and tempo adjust when changing to a hard surface.

There are some benefits to running intervals on a track. Obviously, you know exactly the distance of each repetition. On the roads or beaches, this is often left to judgment. That eighth quarter may unconsciously shrink to 300 yards. More important, it is easiest to gauge your progress when the speed workouts are done on the track. By recording the statistics of each session in a training diary, you can readily visualize the development of your basic speed.

A seemingly infinite number of interval workouts can be found in the running literature. However, these can all be classified into three categories:

· sprint intervals—short distances run at top speed
· pace intervals—short to medium distances (440 to mile) at approximately 90 percent effort
· endurance intervals—longer distances (880 to 2 miles) at less than 90 percent effort.

Sprint intervals, as the name, implies, are most beneficial to dash men. With the exception of a head-to-head confrontation at the finish, marathoners never sprint, and even in this instance, should have paced their early effort so as not to have to approach their maximum speed at the end. Thus, sprint intervals are of no significant benefit to the long-distance runner. However, pace and endurance intervals can be of benefit to the marathoner. The distinction between these two classes is not a sharp one, but can be described qualitatively. *Endurance intervals* are run at a pace which is very near or perhaps just above the aerobic/anaerobic border. This speed, while faster than your marathon pace, is one you can maintain for a significant period without incurring a large oxygen debt. This varies for each runner. However, for example, a runner who averages a 6:00 mile in his best marathon might average 5:30 for a sequence of mile intervals. He has to push a bit to achieve this pace, but it is just a matter of maintaining tempo, and he is not exhausted at the end of each mile.

*Pace intervals* are somewhat faster and develop greater muscular strength—similar to hill training. Because each repetition is run closer to maximum effort, significantly longer recovery periods are necessary. Using our 6:00-mile-average marathoner again as an illustration, he might run his miles at 5:15 pace if he desires more anaerobic work. Of course, rather than a 2-minute recovery period which he used for the 5:30 miles, he increases his jogging interval to 4 minutes. He may also reduce the number of repetitions as well. Eventually, as his confidence and condition improve, he can begin to cut back on the recovery periods and perhaps increase the number of repetitions.

If your concern is solely with marathon preparation, then endurance intervals should compose most of your speed work. A couple of the faster, pace-type intervals can be thrown in when peaking for a major event.

However, if you are like most of us and run road races of shorter distances periodically, an equal mix of pace and endurance intervals is preferable.

The biggest mistake a runner makes when beginning anaerobic training is running too fast, too soon. The body requires time to adapt to the sudden transition from relatively slow roadwork to short bursts of speed. Your goal is to build from your endurance base, not break it down. One way to avoid pushing too hard too early is to leave the watch at home for the first few workouts. This helps diminish the urge to go all out. In order to minimize the shock of this sudden change, the initial ventures into anaerobic training should be relatively long distances at a pace well below your maximum effort. The rest period should be short. Then, as your body adjusts to this new intermittent style of running, you can venture into the more intense endurance intervals. It is not uncommon for a runner who begins speed work to feel awkward and uncomfortable running faster than his race pace. However, if you follow this break-in procedure, this feeling will be minimized. Before long you will adapt to the faster pace and will become more comfortable with it.

As we said earlier, there are an infinite variety of interval workouts that have been used. It would be foolish to recommend any specific workout or schedule. You must experiment to find what's best for you, using the guidelines presented in this chapter. Don't make the mistake of trying to emulate the workouts of a specific international-class marathoner. Such practice can lead to injury.

Whether you choose quarters or 2-milers as your repetition distance, one thing to keep in mind during the runs is to maintain a smooth, economical running style during the interval. Concentrate on keeping the upper body relaxed and the stride even. If you tie up over the last 100 yards, you may be defeating one of the primary purposes of speed work, which is to develop an efficient running style at faster speeds.

There is a tendency for interval trainers to be overly concerned with the time for each repetition and ignore a very important aspect of the workout—the recovery interval. A good rule of thumb is to allow enough time between repetitions to maintain a consistent speed for each fast segment. Here again, don't try to emulate the Herculean feats of a Frank Shorter. Find what recovery period is best for you. You'll find that as you become more accustomed to intervals, this recovery period can be (and should be) shortened. Most coaches agree that one should jog between each fast repetition. As previously stated, jogging helps eliminate the waste products and lactic acid from the muscles more quickly. Walking, or worse yet, stopping, often results in tightening up, and thus the runner experiences difficulty in getting started on the next repetition. This loss of momentum can be psychological as well as physical. If you stop, it's often easy to lose the motivation necessary to complete the workout.

40

## Frolicking with fartleks

If you despise repetitive hill workouts and find circling the track monotonous, there is yet another way to acquire anaerobic work in your training. Fartleking was developed in the 1930s by a Swede, Gosta Holmer, who was seeking an alternative to these traditional types of workouts. It can best be described as an unstructured interval session in which the faster segments are of different distances and are run at varying paces with varying recovery periods. When used properly, a fartlek combines the endurance-building qualities of long-distance training with the sharpening of intervals. The English translation of the word is "speed-play," and in its true form that is what a fartlek is. The runner inserts the anaerobic bursts whenever and for as long as he wishes. It is more of a creative, imaginative type of workout. It has been claimed that fartleking is most successful when the runner loses himself in the run and just does what he feels like.

Holmer advocated that fartlek sessions should be 1 to 2 hours long and should be run without a watch. He also preferred that the runs be on cross-country terrain such as golf courses or trails. An example of a fartlek workout might be: easy running or jogging for 5 to 10 minutes for a warm-up; a hard steady run of ½ to 1½ miles; easy striding with occasional short sprints of 60 to 100 yards; full speed uphill; freewheeling down the other side; jogging or walking for a rest; etc.

There are drawbacks to the fartlek approach which explains why it is seldom practiced properly. First, the unstructured nature; fartleks lack specific goals which are essential to many of us. Because nothing is timed or measured, and no two workouts are alike, the runner has no tangible means to measure his progress. Unless the runner is experienced and can monitor his body for its current condition, he may have no idea if the fartleks are doing him any good.

In addition, many runners feel that speed-play and hard anaerobic work are incongruous. They believe that if they lose themselves in the run, they will really be loafing and not getting the benefits they desire. Hence, it does require a creative breed of runner to run fartleks as Holmer devised them. Very often, modern-day athletes subconsciously turn their fartlek sessions into interval workouts on the roads or trails. For purposes of physical conditioning, this is certainly beneficial. However, these runners are not really getting the mental relaxation for which fartleks were developed.

## Racing as training

Having discussed the traditional types of anaerobic training, we should note that to many of us, especially the older runner, hills and formal track intervals are a form of cruel and unusual punishment prohibited by Article VIII of the Constitution. For one thing it seems that for those of us who were not bred to run in circles (or ovals), interval training merely brings one close to injury, especially of the Achilles tendon. Moreover, speed intervals are not necessarily any more prototypic of racing speed in long-distance running than running at less than racing pace.

Nevertheless, it is a good thing to get some faster running in, as we've just mentioned, to give the legs and body an idea of what the faster pace feels like and to be able to measure the increase in cardiovascular performance that the higher rate demands. It is possible, for example, to rate one's pace simply by how hard one is breathing at any time. How do we get this training if not by some form of regular anaerobic workouts? The answer is in racing.

Experienced runners have discovered this for themselves. Garry Tuttle (age 30, 2:15 marathoner) observes a trend away from interval training. "My legs get sore, and at my age, I'm afraid of getting hurt. My races are my intervals." Bob Bourbeau, age 40 and capable of 1:55:21 for 20 miles, says, "The best way for me to get in shape for racing is to race regularly." Finally, Alex Ratelle, with a 2:33 marathon at 53, rarely does speed work and competes instead in a large number of races both at marathon distance and below.

Probably the best example of the benefits of frequent racing is American marathon record holder Bill Rodgers. Rodgers, who trains at some 140 miles a week with peaks of 170 miles, is on record for one day of interval training a week. But he also runs a lot of races. In 1977 he ran six marathons, one half-marathon, and eight other high-quality races at 8 miles or greater. This doesn't even count the shorter races or fun runs in which he participates. These races probably have more influence on his speed than the weekly interval workouts.

Recent tips published by Brian Maxwell, the Canadian marathon champion, specifically recommend running shorter races every one to three weeks. In discussing speed work, he makes three suggestions: (1) regular shorter-than-marathon races; (2) take a day or two at faster-than-marathon training; and (3) add 5 percent fast running to each day's longer, slower run—that is, run fast for ¼ mile for each 5 miles you run. He never mentions intervals at all!

Another advantage is that racing not only provides physical speed training but mental conditioning against real competitors, something a successful road runner must have. The message again is to try what suits you best. Mileage within reason is required to maintain adequate endurance. You can get the needed speed training by racing those 10-kilometer and 10-mile races between your marathons. If track intervals turn you on, then that is probably best for you, but for many of us the combination of miles and racing is enough. Keep in mind that if you are racing, your mileage may be reduced slightly during the week of the event (see Table 3). This is especially true if you hope to do well in a race, in which case you should ease up in the few days prior to the race.

### Putting the puzzle together

Having discussed the various training methods, the question now becomes one of developing a program that fits your individual needs. We began this chapter by stating that marathoners of different abilities and levels of experience have different training needs. In selecting an approach for your training, you must first assess your present condition and your immediate goals. Then establish a training program that accommodates your personal likes and dislikes.

As we have stated repeatedly, the foundation of successful marathon preparation for the novice and Olympic champion alike is a strong endurance base. Without this it will be difficult to complete a marathon, much less run a good one. Remember—we are not trying to tell you how just to finish a marathon, but how to run one successfully.

For the first-time marathon aspirant, we believe the best approach is to base a training program almost entirely on long slow distance workouts. This develops the maximum cardiovascular efficiency that is necessary for the event and minimizes the probability of injury. An occasional short road race can be used to provide a little speed work, although the first-time marathoner should probably not attempt to race his first marathon. This method has been used successfully by many marathoners, especially older runners who seem to recover more slowly from injury, and those who are returning to running after a layoff of several years. If you have been running shorter distances for several years and are used to anaerobic training sessions, then a few speed workouts probably won't hurt. However, keep in mind that intervals coupled with high mileage can be demanding, and are not important at this stage.

After having completed a marathon or two, and thus being "bitten by the bug," you will obviously want to improve your performance and try to discover your personal limits. At this point, many runners turn to a more structured program involving a bit more anaerobic training. Many experienced marathoners simply replace one or two of their normal training runs with some type of speed workout each week.

Other marathoners structure their workouts into phases of several weeks' duration with the idea of peaking for a certain race (like Boston) or racing season. This approach is becoming more popular in the late '70s, due in part to the wide publicity of Arthur Lydiard's training philosophy in the running literature. The Lydiard program divides training into four distinct phases:

43

- base conditioning
- stamina development
- competitive sharpening
- rest.

Each of these phases has a distinct purpose. The base-conditioning phase is for the development of your aerobic capacity. This is accomplished by running long distances at reasonably relaxed efforts. Follow the principles discussed earlier for long slow distance training. Slowly work up to your target mileage and then increase the pace. Avoid the urge to do anaerobic workouts and watch for symptoms of overuse (Chapter 6). How well you perform in races depends on how well you develop your aerobic capacity. Hence, this phase is the longest of the four noted above. If you really desire to get the most out of a Lydiard approach, allow at least eight weeks for general distance training, or more if you can fit it in.

Once your aerobic base is developed, then progress to developing the strength and stamina needed for racing. This is best accomplished by hill running—particularly the type of workouts we discussed earlier. Work into hill training slowly and allow about four to five weeks for this phase.

Finally, spend the final few weeks before the major event developing your basic speed with some short races, and interval or fartlek training. Again, to avoid the shock of a transition to a new type of running, take it easy the first few times out. Once the important racing season arrives, cut back on the training load and allow for plenty of rest before the events. For the marathon, the week before the event should be at an easy relaxed pace with no goals in mileage—especially if you are using the carbohydrate-loading diet that is explained in Chapter 3. For shorter road races, where the demands of racing are less severe, some normal training during the week is possible. Try to include one long run and one speed workout in the week's running.

Runners who follow this system can expect a one- to two-month period of optimum performance. You can generally tell when you are past your peak as motivation and race performance decline. At this point, it is not worth pushing harder, as it may lead to injury. The best thing is to take a week or two of rest. A regularly scheduled rest is beneficial. It gives the body a chance to recover physically from the previous hard season, and it allows you to recharge mentally for the events in the months ahead. During this break, all running should be very slow and mileage drastically reduced. A day or two off is fine too, although your nerves may get to you for periods much longer than this.

Photo 6 (OPPOSITE)
Two world-class performances in four weeks! Tom Fleming triumphs in Cleveland (2:15:02) less than a month after a 2:14:44 in the 1978 Boston Marathon. (*Photo courtesy of New Balance Athletic Shoe, Inc.*)

Among the more notable runners who follow a Lydiard-type approach are Jerome Drayton (1977 Boston champ and 2:10:08 best) and Lasse Viren (fifth in '76 Olympic Marathon and 2:13:11 best). To illustrate an example of such a training program (but not one you should attempt to duplicate), we quote Viren's regime from *Track and Field News:*

> Lasse kicks off his training in November after a month of active rest. This basic conditioning period lasts until April, when he begins a month of hill work and strength training. Then from June until September he does competitive-season training.
>
> During the basic conditioning phase, Viren will run three times a day, covering 22-30 miles, with the longest run about 13½ miles. Should he run only once or twice a day, his longest effort could be over 22 miles. Training venues are changed regularly to head off boredom.
>
> As summer approaches, the percentage of long work is decreased and hill running instituted. As he does no weight training, Viren's strength results from these repetitions up an 800-meter hill.
>
> During the racing season, races are sometimes used as supplemental speed work to sessions of fartlek. Long/easy running is retained, however, and his long runs will reach 25-30 miles.

The Lydiard approach is designed for the runner who wants to reach his maximum potential. If used as outlined here, it forces you to select a period of a month or two in which you aim to peak. This can be a very difficult choice, as there are now important marathons in nearly every month of the year. However, if you feel that two or three good marathons per year and a reduction in your personal best are more important than five average performances, then this approach may be for you. We should add that just because you are peaking for a few months a year (say once in the spring and again in the fall), you don't have to forgo racing entirely during the buildup phases. You can still compete in road races, and even marathons if you don't run all out. The point is to make these races contribute to your training rather than disrupt it. For example, if you are in your long slow distance phase, don't back off in mileage three days before a 10-kilometer run in hopes of getting a PR. First of all, at this stage in the program you're not in condition to run your best time. Furthermore, if you include a recovery day, you've lost nearly a week of your base conditioning.

## Warming to the task

Most runners give only lip service to warming up before their daily training runs, the authors included. When your time is limited, you would rather spend it on the road than in some motionless stretching position. Generally it takes a serious injury to convince runners of the importance of supplementary exercises. The authors' own experiences

46

are helpful here: Brown has had three lengthy injury layoffs in the last three years and is now a firm believer in stretching; while Graham (blessed with a perfect foot plant) has never had a serious injury and considers 30 seconds of leaning against a wall to be adequate stretching (to be fair, he does a little more before important races).

As you are well aware by now, distance running can easily result in stiffness and inflexibility of the posterior muscle groups (lower back, hamstrings, and calves). Try touching your toes the morning after a marathon! Exercise physiologists have linked injuries (muscle pulls and connective-tissue problems) to inflexibility and imbalances in strength of opposing muscle groups. Thus the primary purpose of supplementary exercises is to prevent injury.

If you are susceptible to injury, as most of us are, you would be wise to devote a few minutes before and after each run to some very simple stretching exercises. Photos 7 through 10 illustrate a routine that we have found to be a good one. It is not too lengthy (requires only a few minutes) and stretches all of the critical muscles and tendons which runners are prone to injure. If you desire a more rigorous regime of stretching exercises or wish to get into yoga, consult the reading list at the end of this book for some references to get you started.

In performing all types of stretching, avoid jerky, sudden movements. All movement should be slow and controlled. Hold each position for a minimum of 15 seconds. The bouncing motion associated with the traditional calisthenics actually tightens up the muscles by initiating a reflex contractive action. Never strain to reach a given position. Overstretching can also injure muscle fibers. You can tell if you are overstretching if the tension in the muscles is not somewhat relieved in the first 10 seconds. If you experience quivering of the stretched muscle, back off. Finally, breathe normally when stretching. Don't hold your breath.

About the only other exercise worth your time is bent-leg sit-ups. As we noted earlier, muscular imbalance is the cause of many a runner's injuries. Sit-ups will reduce this imbalance by strengthening the abdominal muscles and reducing the likelihood of a painful attack of sciatica.

As for the act of running itself, begin each run easily, slowly working into the rhythm that suits your fancy. If you plan a hill or interval workout, do at least a mile of jogging plus a bit of striding before attempting any anaerobic work.

### Stepping out in style

As a general rule, reasonably smooth and efficient running form evolves after many months and miles on the roads. Because each of us is structurally different, you would expect that individual styles would vary. As long as you are progressing well in your training, you are probably better off not changing your style. We must recognize that the best

Photo 7 (ABOVE)
Warm-up stretching: wall push-up. (*Photo by John Graham*)

Photo 8 (OPPOSITE, TOP)
Warm-up stretching: toe toucher. (*Photo by John Graham*)

Photo 9 (OPPOSITE, CENTER)
Warm-up stretching: backover. (*Photo by John Graham*)

Photo 10 (OPPOSITE, BOTTOM)
Warm-up stretching: quadriceps stretch. (*Photo by John Graham*)

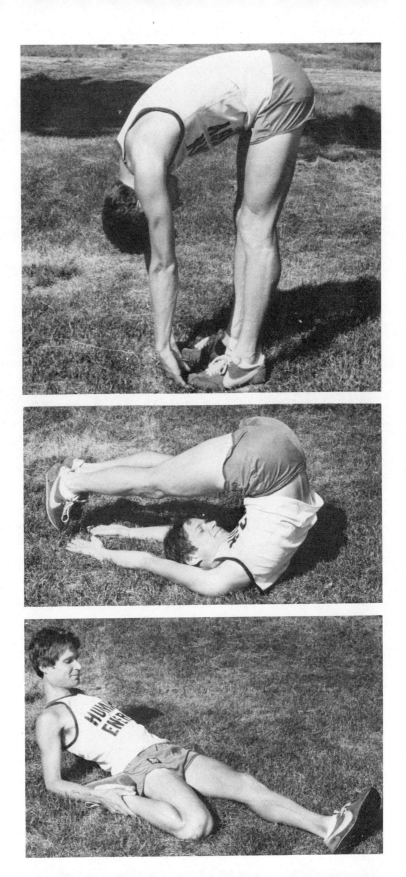

coaching in the world won't give us the fluid grace of a Frank Shorter. Emil Zatopek, when asked about his ragged, arm-flailing form, replied, "Track and field is not ice skating. It is not necessary to smile and make a wonderful impression on the judges."

Having heard that, there are a couple of points to keep in mind—especially for inexperienced runners. As you are well aware, marathoning requires a tremendous amount of energy. Hence, it would be beneficial if one could eliminate all wasted motion and conserve energy stores for the task at hand. Bill Bowerman (former coach at the University of Oregon) has made an exhaustive study of running style. He believes the most important element is to be in an upright posture, and therefore in balance above the stride. Many runners try to lean forward to gain maximum thrust with each stride. Bowerman states, "A forward lean may be useful for someone trying to bash down a wall with his head, but in running it merely gives the leg muscles unnecessary work." If you lean forward, you are wasting energy, as work must be performed to keep the body from falling over as well as to propel you forward. A good way to assure an upright posture is to keep the buttocks tucked in.

The other common faults are associated with wasteful movement in the arms and upper body.

- Avoid flapping your wrists (leave your hands loosely cupped).
- Don't swing your arms across the centerline of your chest (this twists the upper body, which disrupts fluid forward movement).
- Avoid excessive head movement (a rolling motion is a common waste of energy).

To repeat, nearly all marathoners develop a reasonably efficient and relaxed running style with experience. However, a self-evaluation of your form occasionally is beneficial to be sure you haven't picked up any bad habits.

### Keeping track

There is an additional activity to which all serious marathoners should devote a few minutes each day. That is recording the day's running in a training diary. A personal training log should be maintained as an aid to better training. Since the preparation involved in successful marathoning spans many months, many details can be forgotten if a written record is not kept. Knowing what you have done in the past can serve as a helpful guide to what you should do in the future.

Depending on your personal preference, this diary can be as brief or as comprehensive as you wish. As a general rule, record-keeping should be brief enough not to become a chore, but still contain enough information to make the diary useful. In this regard, each day's entry should be more than just a listing of the distance (or time) of the run. A brief

description of the workout should be provided. If the workout was an interval or hill session, the pertinent details (repetitions, splits, etc.) should be recorded. Some indication as to the effort or intensity of the run should be included (e.g., hard, moderate, easy). Recording this information can be beneficial in avoiding overtraining, as the runner can recognize if he or she is stringing together an excessive number of consecutive hard days. Moreover, the runner will be able to see the results of having done this before.

A brief summary of one's physical condition and energy level are also useful. Any unusual aches and pains or injury should be noted. This is especially important for those coming off an injury. They can better monitor their recovery and may identify techniques which enable more efficient training during this period. If used properly the diary can also help avoid injuries by identifying trends that might be leading to a breakdown.

Other data, which are not as essential but are often recorded, are the time of day, the weather, the runner's weight, basal pulse rate, and the shoes worn during the run. Also worth noting are events in one's personal life which could affect training, such as: "Worked late previous night—only five hours' sleep." An example of a typical daily entry is illustrated on the next page.

In recording the results of races, you should include more information than just distance and time. Your finishing position (open and age group) is important, as it allows you to chart your improvement relative to others in your age group. Recording split times is also valuable in assessing the effectiveness of your pacing and race tactics (Chapter 7 shows how this can be done). Also your physical and mental experiences are important. Such post-race evaluation may identify factors which you can change to improve performance.

In addition, many runners also include a brief summary of each week's training. In addition to the total distance completed, you may want to provide a brief synopsis of the week's running, which may involve such

51

---

Tuesday
May 16

Morning (45°, breezy)

- 7.0 miles at slow relaxed pace

Evening (60°, sunny)

- Interval workout on track
  Warm-up of 2 miles slow jogging and some stretching
  4 × 880, 440 recovery
  Times: 2:36, 2:33, 2:35, 2:30

- Left Achilles tendon still a bit sore from Sunday's race; hence, only
  ran 880's at ¾ effort. Used ice on tendon after run as a precaution.

**Total Distance:** 12 miles

---

things as the number of long runs or the number of interval or hill workouts. Such a review allows you to determine if your immediate training
goals have been accomplished. By reviewing the distribution of daily mileage totals for the week, you can determine if your training has a proper
balance, and whether or not you are implementing the hard day/easy day
routine essential to effective training.

Also, to provide a handy reference and a goal for future training, you
may include a complete listing of your competitive performances. This
can be in the form of a table listing the distance of the race, time, place
(open or age group), date, and location of the event (see Appendix I).
Accompanying this summary, you may wish to include a complete listing
of your personal best times for all distances and the date and location of
the particular event where your personal record was achieved.

Concurrent with the explosion in jogging is the appearance of various
types of log books on the market. These range from small notepad-sized
logs that will fit in your shirt pocket to massive 400-page volumes with
graphs to plot every possible statistic. The price range for these diaries
also varies tremendously. Some of the fancier versions are approaching the
cost of a good pair of running shoes! Since personal preferences vary so
widely, these standardized logs do not always fit the exact needs of many
runners. Hence, frequently marathoners record their training in a spiral-
bound notebook or a lined record. This allows the runner to put in what
he feels is important to him, and not waste money on a book which was
designed to fit the needs of the three-day-a-week jogger. No matter what
you select for your diary, remember that it's not what you keep it in,
it's what you keep in it that counts.

## Motivation

If your aspiration is to run a marathon eventually, then your total mileage and the time you spend on the roads will have to increase. Some runners have difficulty making themselves do this, and are liable to quit simply because of the boredom—they don't like being alone so long! However, if you truly enjoy running, then boredom is only rarely a problem. In fact, boredom or a lack of enthusiasm is often a symptom of overtraining and may indicate the need for a rest. However, we do have some hints for enhancing the enjoyment of your training and overcoming any temporary lack of motivation.

The most effective one is to run with someone else. Choose a running partner of your own caliber and interest so that aerobic training can offer the opportunity to exchange ideas and views. Running partners assist each other, especially in the difficult parts of training—emerging from the warmth of home on a cold, wet morning, or perhaps toiling up some excruciating hill in the heat. They bolster each other to raise mileage and enhance each other's ambitions to speed. Fartleks can become an order of the day without prior programming!

Another solution is to vary your training routes: hills one day, valleys the next. It's difficult to be bored when the scenery is changing and you have to pay attention to the exigencies of the course. Even running a course in the opposite direction is as good as a "rest"—for one thing, hills can be appreciably different.

Many runners disassociate from the difficulties they may find in running by daydreaming. Graham has run many an important international event in a long training run—difficult hills become quite easy when in the mind the legs are driving toward the Olympic Trials finishing tape! Articles have been written (principally by nonrunning psychologists) on the aspect of disassociating as if it were, firstly, surprising, and, secondly, detrimental. It is neither. It serves a very valuable function for a runner in training; it motivates him. However, as you become more trained and more competitive you will find that thoughts will veer toward monitoring your body in response to the training (or the competition in a race). This can be valuable, since you can identify stresses ahead of time and modify your pace to avoid excesses. Thinking about the pains or discomforts or success that your body may be experiencing in an objective way is still disassociating yourself from the pains and discomforts, since you tend to "step outside yourself" to do it. Competitive runners find this disassociation more beneficial to their results.

In any case, whether you run with someone, vary your runs, or disassociate from the run itself, you should have no difficulty with boredom on the road.

53

## The little extras

Two other important aspects of your daily activities which should not be left to chance are diet and rest. Because of the extreme physical demands of serious marathon training, proper rest is essential to allow repair and rebuilding (remember stress adaptation!) of the muscles. Like almost everything else in this chapter, sleep requirements are an individual need and vary from runner to runner. Whatever your needs, you'll find that if you're not meeting them, your workouts will suffer within a day or two. Your energy level sinks, your legs turn to stone, and a 5-mile jog can be exhausting. You may even catch a cold or a more serious infection.

We don't believe in scheduling days off, except just before marathons. This doesn't mean that we don't miss days. Occasionally extreme fatigue, illness, injury, or personal or business conflicts force us to miss a day. However, these days aren't predictable. It is just a matter of listening to your body and learning how to respond to its warnings.

The food we eat plays a more subtle role. Its effects are generally only apparent over a much longer time interval (like the iron-deficient anemia noted in Chapter 6). Although nutrition is still as much an art as it is a science, it makes good sense to eat a well-balanced diet, and thus leave one less variable in the training dilemma to chance. Chapter 3 has the details on the dietary requirements of marathoning.

# Chapter 3
# You Are What You Eat
## Diet

Running a marathon, and indeed training for one through the several months before the actual race, involves a large expenditure of energy. The running of a single mile at about 7½-to-8-minutes per-mile pace consumes approximately 100 calories. So an average day's training of 10 to 12 miles uses 1,000 to 1,200 calories, quite a considerable percentage of the average full day's requirements of an inactive person, which is about 2,000 to 2,500 calories (assuming the person doesn't overeat).

Moreover, as the following chapter will show, this energy required for running is taken from storage of glycogen and fats within the muscles. Thus not only is the total energy a consideration, but also the type and balance of food consumed to store that energy is important. Every aspiring marathoner eventually realizes that he has to pay attention to what and how much he eats. It is as important in preparation for the marathon as is the actual physical training we have discussed in the previous chapter.

Therefore we are interested in what basic foods do for the body, and how much is needed for normal requirements. Then we need to examine the additional and specialized requirements of marathon running and what foods can best supply these needs. We need to know how much of these foods are advisable. Finally we offer some judgment on special diets that have been recommended for racing preparation.

### Basic food constituents

CARBOHYDRATES are energy foods, so called because they can be stored as glycogen within active muscles and then used during exercise by a chemical conversion process. They are composed basically of carbon, hydrogen, and oxygen, hence their name. They come either as complex molecules like starches or as simple sugars like glucose, fructose, and sucrose. These are readily converted into glycogen, which in turn is very quickly broken down by enzyme activity into useful energy. Hence they are very valuable athletic foods.

Moreover, they are far easier to digest than proteins or fats and have a very quick transit time through the body. They also provide significant water for the body during this digestion process. All of these are advantages for the runner.

Curiously they are not absolutely necessary for the sedentary person, because they perform no vital function like binding vitamins or providing some essential compound. The normal metabolism of the brain does require some carbohydrates, but the body would provide this from fat conversion if necessary. Thus there are no minimum requirements for carbohydrates in our diets. However, since carbohydrates are so advantageous to the runner in providing an inexpensive and rapidly usable form of energy, they are the mainstay of his diet. More on this later.

FATS are also made of carbon, hydrogen, and oxygen like carbohydrates, but in different proportions. Whereas the ratio of hydrogen to oxygen in the carbohydrate is 2 to 1, as in water, in fats the hydrogen content is relatively higher. The more hydrogen there is, the more the fat is said to be "saturated." Excesses of saturated fats have been linked with vascular disorders. Saturated fats are most commonly found in meat and dairy products; unsaturated fats come from corn oil and nuts.

Fats are higher in calories than carbohydrates (about $2\frac{1}{2}$ to 1), but they are unfortunately not quite so easily digested and used by the body. However, they do have a more vital role than their quick-energy cousins, since the fatty acids are essential to maintain health and growth. Without a certain minimum the tissue would lose viability in the skin and in organs like the kidneys. Furthermore, fat serves as protection for vital organs.

Moreover, fats are carriers of soluble vitamins (A, D, E, and K), they make food more palatable, and when eaten satisfy the consumer better than carbohydrates, which often leave you feeling relatively empty. They perform some other vital functions in hormone synthesis and in structural synthesis of the cells themselves. Thus they are required by the body. However, fats are available in both plants and animals. For example, while a typical American diet composed of well-marbled steak can be as high in fats as 45 percent of the diet, even a "fat-free" diet would rarely drop below 5 percent of the diet. This is quite sufficient for minimum daily requirements.

Thus there is no reason to go out of your way to consume fats; the unsaturated varieties found in plants will be quite enough for the body.

PROTEINS are compounds in which nitrogen has been added to the carbon, hydrogen, and oxygen, possibly with some trace minerals. They are essential to growth and in building and rebuilding the body, and they are absolutely vital to the body in terms of regulating supplies of hormones, vitamins, enzymes, and antibodies. In addition, they supply some energy.

Proteins are composed of varying amounts of *amino acids*. These amino acids have exotic names, and many can be synthesized by the body itself—in fact, fourteen out of the twenty-two necessary for growth. Four others are very common in foods, so one need be concerned only with providing for the other four: trytophan, lysine, isoleucine, and the sulfur-containing amino acids.

Although many runners, as we will see later, turn to vegetarianism, one of the dangers of vegetarian diets is that by neglecting certain meat proteins an imbalance of these amino acids can easily occur. Amino acids are necessary to maintain growth and to keep the nervous system and brain in working order. However, they must be balanced. Thus not only is protein required by the body, but a proper mix of protein is needed to give the right mix of amino acids. Curiously it also appears that the correct mix must be eaten in the same meal rather than just during the same day for the benefit to be obtained. Eggs contain the best balance, while fish and meat are rated as 70 percent of the balance value of eggs. Milk is 60 percent of the value of eggs. Table 4 shows these and other foods in order of preference for amino-acid content.

## Table 4
Amino acid content of foods

| Food | Percent balance | Food | Percent balance |
|------|-----------------|------|-----------------|
| Eggs | 100 | Rice | 56 |
| Meat | 70 | Corn | 41 |
| Fish | 70 | Peanuts | 34 |
| Soybeans | 69 | Potato | 34 |
| Milk | 60 | Flour | 32 |

Combinations of foods which are individually deficient in one or another of the amino acids can also give balances that are close to that of eggs.

VITAMINS are chemicals which must be present in the correct quantities for the correct functioning of the body. Tests have shown that extreme deficiencies can cause death; this happened with white mice back in 1880 tested with an artificial vitamin-free diet. On the other hand, excessive amounts of vitamins are also associated with damage to vital functions.

*Vitamin A* is very common and carried in fats of all kinds, both plant and animal, and there is very rarely a deficiency. It is concerned with the healthy growth of teeth, skin, and mucous membranes. However an excess of Vitamin A can produce damage to the eye, liver, or brain, so it is not necessary to artificially add it to the diet.

*Vitamin B* is not one but a complex of vitamins such as thiamine ($B_1$), riboflavin ($B_2$), niacine ($B_5$), pyridoxine ($B_6$), and $B_{12}$. They are all necessary to the healthy body and with the exception of $B_{12}$ are well distributed in common foods. Thiamine ($B_1$) is important to runners, since it is linked to carbohydrate metabolism into energy and in the oxidation of lactic acids, which, if they are not oxidized, cause cramps (see Chapter 4). A high-carbohydrate diet then requires a little more of this vitamin than usual. It can be obtained in meats, nuts, and seeds.

The other B vitamins are less needed by runners. $B_2$ is needed for cellular growth while $B_5$ prevents pellagra. $B_2$ can easily be obtained in milk and rice, and $B_5$ in corn or flour. $B_{12}$ is vital, since without it anemia or even damage to the brain and spinal cord can occur. It occurs in milk and meats and is rarely deficient unless you edge toward vegetarianism and forgo meats. More on this point later in this chapter.

*Vitamin C* is essential to the diet to maintain proper growth of connective tissue and the normal growth of teeth, bones, and blood vessels, and to prevent infection and to aid in the healing of injuries. Fortunately it is abundant in fresh fruits and vegetables, especially in citrus fruits, tomatoes, strawberries, turnip greens, onions, potatoes, peppers, and string beans. There has been a suggestion that megadoses help prevent and cure the common cold, but this so far is unsupported. Moreover, reports show that large doses of Vitamin C can do harm, in blocking the necessary $B_{12}$ vitamin and in possibly causing kidney stones.

*Vitamin D* is also very common and need not be supplemented. It is contained in fats, milk (where it is added generally), and egg yolk. Vitamin D promotes bone calcification and regulates the absorption of calcium and phosphorus from the gastrointestinal tract. Nevertheless in excess it can cause kidney damage.

*Vitamin E* will be discussed later in this chapter.

MINERALS are at last being recognized as important constituents of diets. They are many and varied, each having different functions. Table 5 shows the minerals that are necessary to us, and why.

The trace elements assist in maintaining active nerves, providing the proper alkalinity of the blood and other fluids, activating enzymes, and so on. Some of them, as we will discover shortly, are particularly important to the runner. Table 6 shows the best sources for the most important of these minerals.

From a glance at Table 6 one can see that Popeye's adherence to spinach as a source of energy is not so far wrong. Not that it gives him strength or energy, but it does provide him with the vital elements to use his energy properly in disposing of the villain!


### Our running needs

Knowing the uses of food building blocks, we can already see that some things are going to help us more than others. Table 5 has already mentioned such things as cramps that we could do without during a marathon. Moreover, some foods are required for the development of

## Table 5
Minerals necessary for the human body

| Mineral | Quantity required | Function |
|---|---|---|
| Potassium | Large | Balance in fluids and salts |
| Calcium | Large | Bones, blood coagulation and muscles |
| Magnesium | Large | Preventing cramps in muscles |
| Sodium | Large | Balance in fluids and salts |
| Cobalt | Trace | |
| Manganese | Trace | |
| Aluminum | Trace | |
| Iron | Trace* | Essential ingredient in hemoglobin |
| Molybdenum | Trace | |
| Copper | Trace | |
| Zinc | Trace | Good bone metabolism |
| Boron | Trace | |
| Vanadium | Trace | |
| Phosphorus | Large | Bone growth, nerve and brain tissue |

\* More in women.

the very necessary muscles. Our first and most basic need is energy to keep us going for 2 or 3 hours. This clearly comes from the carbohydrates in our foods, and the next chapter explains in detail how they are used. First, however, it is important to know *how much* we can eat before we speak specifically about *what* we can eat.

Since in normal training we burn a lot of calories, you will find that using your weight as a guide, you can eat a surprising amount. In fact, you can eat as much as satisfies you! It eventually occurs to most marathoners that perhaps they run so much so that they can eat all they want.

Of course, it is not that simple. One of the factors that will assist you in running well is to be relatively light. Most marathoners manage to look gaunt and undernourished despite eating ravenously, but this is by design, because you feel better and race better with less surface fat on you. A recommendation that you should weigh 10 to 20 percent less than the actuarial tables for "normal" persons is difficult to follow at first, but after some months of training and racing you will find a new pride in the capabilities of your body, enabling you to take care of the weight. A daily check on the scales is probably a sufficient weight-control mechanism. Then you will fit in with those other skinny racers at the starting line without feeling bloated and unsightly!

Thus to start with you should set your weight goals based on your

**Table 6**
Sources of minerals in foods*

| Calcium | Iron | Magnesium | Phosphorus | Sodium | Potassium |
|---|---|---|---|---|---|
| Milk | Meat | Nuts | Dried peas | Vegetables | Citrus fruits |
| Hard cheese | Turnip greens | Soybeans | Dried beans | Fruits | Vegetables |
| Turnip greens | Kale | Wheat germ | Brussels sprouts | Grains | |
| Broccoli | Chard | Spinach | Sweet corn | | |
| Cauliflower | Lettuce | | Peas | | |
| Spinach | Cabbage | | | | |
| Celery | Spinach | | | | |
| Carrots | Mustard greens | | | | |
| String beans | Dried peas | | | | |
| Raw cabbage | Eggs | | | | |
| Peas | | | | | |

*Vegetables, fruits, milk, eggs, and whole-grain cereals are excellent sources of the other trace elements.

height and build, and then eat sufficient to reach those goals slowly over a month or so. Too rapid a weight loss, for example, would not be very healthy and you would be unable to continue training at the same level. It is rarely necessary to add weight!

Having set the goals and attained your weight, then you can eat as much as you like and whatever you like as long as you keep a regular eye on the scales. Marathoners are notorious for eating hideous combinations of foods. But generally, there will be a distinct emphasis on carbohydrates, for two reasons. First, that is the energy food base that we know we need, and second, we find after a little while almost without conscious thought that since carbohydrates are easier to digest they don't leave you feeling as full as fats do. Thus your next training run isn't encumbered by your last meal. Meats are particularly bad in this context, since good red muscle meat takes nearly 12 hours to digest, whereas carbohydrates can typically be digested in about 3 hours.

Bill Rodgers was perhaps the most successful marathoner in the world in 1977, and recently Kenny Moore spent time with him. He reported: "Rodgers spends much of his time in the kitchen, eating. He will sleep 10 hours a night, if permitted, but even so will rise at three a.m. for his fourth meal of the day, raiding the refrigerator, which always contains a pitcher of apricot nectar mixed with flat ginger ale, quart bottles of cola, chocolate-chip cookies, and mayonnaise, which he will eat out of the jar with a tablespoon. 'Sometimes I wonder,' he said one such morning, yawning, heading back to bed, 'whether I run high mileage so I can eat like this, or do I eat like this so I can do high mileage?' Whatever the reason, his dimensions are 5 feet 8½ inches, 128 pounds, and 9E and flattening!"

However, having said that you can eat anything, we should add that there are some special dietary needs of runners that are worth taking account of.

The basic carbohydrates, simplest in chemical form, and therefore easiest for the body to process, are *glucose* and *fructose* and *galactose*.

# Table 7
## Carbohydrates

| Basic* | Bonds | | Mixture* | |
|--------|-------|---|---------|---|
| Glucose | Sucrose | Glucose and fructose molecules | Honey | Glucose and fructose |
| Fructose (fruits) | Lactose (milk) | Glucose and galactose molecules | | |
| Galactose | Maltose | Two glucose molecules | | |
| | Cellulose† | Long chains of glucose molecules | | |
| | Starches | Long chains of other basic carbohydrates | | |

* Basic and mixture carbohydrates are quickly absorbed, bonded carbohydrates take longer.
† Cellulose cannot be broken down by humans, so it provides fiber content for intestinal regularity. It is contained in lettuce, whole grains, cabbage, etc.

Then come combinations of these. *Sucrose* is a chemical bonding of glucose and fructose and therefore enters the bloodstream more slowly. Honey is a mixture of glucose and fructose rather than a bonding. Thus honey can be absorbed as rapidly as fructose. There are other combinations shown in Table 7.

The starches not only contain the basic energy of carbohydrates but they also carry the many minerals and vitamins needed in the daily diet. Because they are relatively complex structures they are absorbed relatively slowly (but much faster than fats) and should form the major source of dietary carbohydrates. They are found in cereals, grains, vegetables, and fruits.

There has been some conjecture that since fructose, in fruits and juices, is quickly absorbed into the bloodstream, it is a quick energy pick-me-up. However, there is no basis for this, especially since there is, as Chapter 4 shows, a long chemical process to go through between food getting to the bloodstream and its conversion into a usable form in the muscles. Glycogen in the muscles would be converted in preference. Nevertheless, be an experiment of one. If you feel like drinking juice before a race, try it. It is unlikely to harm you and you may *feel* better even if nothing physically advantageous results.

The body does require protein, about 0.8 grams per kilogram of body weight or something like 30–50 grams per day for a runner. However, since the average American diet is so high in protein (over 100 grams per day) this minimum need is never a problem. Any meat would more than satisfy a runner's needs for protein.

A danger arises when you have been running for some time, because you may find almost without noticing it that you are tending to avoid heavy, indigestible red-muscle meats. This occurs simply because runners find it uncomfortable to feel full, especially at the next run, when meat eaten nearly 12 hours before may still be in the large intestine. There will be a tendency to move toward a purer carbohydrate diet simply because the easier digestibility makes for easier running. You may find yourself edging toward vegetarianism. If this happens you will still get plenty of protein from the vegetables and milk products that you have, but you may find an imbalance of amino acids that should be corrected. Nutritional vegetarianism involves more than just giving up meat.

Earlier we spoke of the amino acids and what they were contained in. The four varieties which it is necessary to plan for can, as we said, be obtained in eggs. But they can also be obtained by combining other foods, in a balanced meal. Furthermore it is necessary to balance the meal rather than the day because all four amino acids must be consumed within about 30 minutes to be able to act in combination. They are not effective alone. However, this is easy to arrange, since if foods from the following four complementary groups are taken they will provide a balanced complementary set of amino acids. The four groups are:

- grains
- milk products
- nuts and seeds
- vegetables

Thus combinations such as bran muffins and milk, or a spicy mixture of millet and beans, or a dish made from rice, spinach, cheese, and mushrooms, will provide for the proper balance of amino acids. At the same time you are eating an easily digestible food without the drawbacks of red meat. Table 8 provides the protein and caloric content of some of the more common foods. Consult one of the numerous paperback books for a more extensive list of foods, including those with brand names.

Fats are also necessary to the runner, of course. They are principally carriers of the necessary vitamins A and D, and they make for a better texture and flavor in cooked foods. They do also satisfy you after a meal. However, as we have pointed out before, almost every diet will contain enough fats and one doesn't have to go out of the way to get them. Vegetables contain fats; nuts, olives, and avocados are particularly rich.

While a runner is training he loses a great deal of water as sweat, especially in hot weather, and at the same time he also loses essential minerals. It is necessary to replace the minerals in the proper balance as well as the fluid.

Dr. Cooper, in his aerobic studies, studied the changes and found that after sweating and strenuous exercise, sodium levels increased because of dehydration, potassium levels in the blood increased since it was released from tissue cells in the muscles which were broken down by the hard exercise, and calcium levels stayed about the same. Since the sodium concentration rose there was no need (as had been thought) for the runner

63

## Table 8
Nutritional values of common foods and beverages*

### HIGH PROTEINS

| Food | Quantity | Proteins (gm.) | Carbohydrates (gm.) | Calories |
|---|---|---|---|---|
| CHEESE | 1 oz. | | | |
| Cheddar | | 7 | 0.6 | 110 |
| Cottage | | 3.8 | 4.5 | 30 |
| Edam | | 5 | 1.1 | 100 |
| Muenster | | | 1.0 | 100 |
| Swiss | | | 0.5 | 100 |
| CHICKEN | 4 oz. | 26.7 | 0 | 155 |
| EGGS | 1 | 6 | 0.3 | 80 |
| FISH | 4 oz. | | | |
| Cake | | 4 | 9.4 | 300 |
| Cod (broiled) | | 30 | 0 | 200 |
| Flounder | | 32 | 0 | 220 |
| Lobster | | 20 | 0 | 155 |
| Shrimp | | 28 | 10 | 130 |
| Trout | | 28 | 0 | 240 |

### HIGH CARBOHYDRATES

| Food | Quantity | Proteins (gm.) | Carbohydrates (gm.) | Calories |
|---|---|---|---|---|
| CAKE | | | | |
| Chocolate | 1 slice | 2.4 | 50 | 200 |
| cupcake | 1 pc. | 2 | 31 | 200 |
| CANDY | | | | |
| Butterscotch | 1 oz. | 0 | 24.3 | 110 |
| Chocolate | 1 oz. | 2 | 15.9 | 145 |
| Fudge | 1 oz. | 1 | 17.5 | 120 |
| Gum drops | 1 lg. | 0 | 8.6 | 50 |
| Toffee | 1 pc. | 0 | 7.8 | 34 |
| COOKIES | | | | |
| Chocolate chip | 1 pc. | 1.5 | 7.8 | 50 |
| Fig Newton | | | 11.4 | 60 |
| Macaroon | | | 14.3 | 80 |
| Saltine | | 0.3 | 2.1 | 20 |
| Sugar wafer | | | 3.6 | 20 |

*This list has averaged the values for foods. They are accurate within about 5 percent.

| Food | Serving | | | |
|---|---|---|---|---|
| Tuna (in water) | 4 oz. | 32 | 0 | 150 |
| **MEAT** | | | | |
| Beef (lean) | | 28 | 0 | 230 |
| (with fat) | | 30.7 | 0 | 450 |
| Ham | | 22 | 0 | 270 |
| Hamburger | | 28 | 0 | 320 |
| Lamb (lean) | | 29.3 | 0 | 220 |
| (with fat) | | 29.3 | 0 | 350 |
| Liver, beef | | 30 | 6.9 | 260 |
| Veal | | 30.7 | 0 | 280 |
| **MILK** | 1 cup | 9 | 11.8 | 160 |
| **SPIRITS** | 1 oz. | 0 | 0 | 80 |
| **WINE** | 4 oz. | | | |
| Port | | | 14.0 | 190 |
| Red | | | 0.5 | 100 |
| Sherry | | | 4.8 | 190 |
| White | | | 0.5 | 95 |

| Food | Serving | | | |
|---|---|---|---|---|
| **FRUITS AND VEGETABLES** | | | | |
| Apple | 2½" diam. | 0 | 16.9 | 80 |
| Banana | 7" long | 1 | 34.5 | 90 |
| Beans | | | | |
| Green | ½ cup | 1 | 4.8 | 20 |
| Lima | ½ cup | 6.5 | 14.6 | 80 |
| Wax | ½ cup | 1 | 3 | 22 |
| Corn | 1 ear | 3 | 21 | 70 |
| Fruit salad | ½ cup | 0 | 23.8 | 100 |
| Orange | 3" diam. | 1 | 17 | 75 |
| Pear | 2½" diam. | 1 | 23.9 | 100 |
| Potato | 1 small | 3 | 21 | 70 |
| Potato chips | 10 2" | 1 | 10 | 120 |
| Raisins | 1 oz. | 0 | 15.5 | 80 |
| Tomato | 1 med. | 2 | 9 | 40 |
| **GRAINS** | | | | |
| Bread | 1 slice† | 2 | 12 | 60 |
| Cereal | 1 cup | | | |
| Puffed kinds | | 2 | 9.6 | 50 |
| Sugar coated | | 2 | 35 | 150 |
| Others | | 2–10 | 10–40 | 100–200‡ |
| Muffin | 1 English | | 17.5 | 140 |
| Noodles | ½ cup | 3.5 | 18.5 | 100 |
| Oatmeal | 1 cup | 5 | 13 | 130 |
| Pancake | 4" diam. | | 11.8 | 70 |

† 20 slices to a 1-lb. loaf.
‡ See the nutritional information on the packet.

65

Table 8
Nutritional values of common foods and beverages (*cont.*)

## HIGH CARBOHYDRATES

| Food | Quantity | Proteins (gm.) | Carbo-hydrates (gm.) | Calories |
|---|---|---|---|---|
| Rice | ½ cup | 2 | 22 | 110 |
| Spaghetti | ½ cup | 2.5 | 22 | 85 |
| ICE CREAM | 1 cup | 6 | 32 | 255 |
| JAM | 1 oz. | 0 | 18 | 75 |
| JUICES | | | | |
| Grapefruit | | 0.5 | 11.5 | 50 |
| Orange | | 3.3 | 13.5 | 60 |
| Tomato | | 1 | 5.2 | 24 |
| BEVERAGES | | | | |
| Beer | 8 oz. | 0.7 | 11 | 100 |
| Cola | 8 oz. | 0.7 | 9.3 | 100 |
| Cordials | 1 oz. | | 6 | 110 |

**Photo 11**
Cold drinks on the March run. Michael Wigal of Athens, Ohio, grabs a cup of water 11 miles into the 1978 Athens Marathon. (*Photo by Mark Rightmire*)

to take salt tablets. In fact, a low-salt diet is better and improves athletic performance in hot weather.

Cooper also found that magnesium was rapidly depleted even though it is in the same cells as potassium and might be expected to increase in the blood. But much magnesium is sweated away, and much is passed out in the feces. This is one reason why marathoners are rarely constipated; the magnesium acts as a cathartic by drawing fluid into the intestinal tract just as Epsom salts would. However, this loss of magnesium is important to athletes, since lack of this mineral can cause cramping of the muscles.

It is the reason why after a marathon, during the night, you may experience involuntary cramping of leg muscles. Thus magnesium must be replaced and perhaps emphasized before long-distance racing to alleviate the eventual loss.

Some commercial drinks such as Gatorade, Body Punch, and ERG combine the fluid that the body needs with some combination of minerals. They almost all include some glucose to give at least the sensation of a quick energy replacement. However, unless you obtain some psychological benefit from relying on these drinks it is as well to realize that the glucose isn't readily available to the body during the race. Furthermore, the drinks usually contain no trace elements and only small amounts of minerals— much less than is contained in orange juice! Nevertheless on balance we feel that replacement drinks do have a greater benefit than simple water alone.

Thus for mineral balance, Gabe Mirkin, a physician as well as a marathoner, recommends:

- for *potassium*, a varied diet of fruits and vegetables
- for *magnesium and trace elements*, varied nuts and whole grains
- for *calcium*, a small amount of milk products
- for *sodium*, a restriction of salt in cooking and eating, relying only on the natural salt available in the foods.

Percy Cerutty followed this sort of nutritional regimen for the athletes that he coached, though he emphasized potatoes and leafy vegetables for calcium instead of milk. The first meal of his athletes' day consisted of a bowl of raw and rolled oats, raisins, sultanas, nuts, and fresh fruit, thus fulfilling all the needs for potassium, magnesium, and trace elements. Calcium intake was provided by lunchtime vegetables and cheeses, together with soup or salad. At the evening meal, protein requirements were satisfied by fish, liver, or chicken and occasionally some beef. He kept beef to a minimum and was opposed to the then accepted athletic training of pre-event steaks. We now know quite well that steak is wrong, but in those days, in the '50s, he was ahead of his time.

## Carbohydrate loading

The interviewer asked, "Did you have a special diet?" and the response was, "No, I maintained my general diet, which is 60 percent carbohydrate and 20–25 percent protein and fat." "What about carbohydrate overload?" And the 1976 Montreal Olympic Marathon gold medal winner, Waldemar Cierpinski, replied: "I only heard about that after the race. When they interviewed me in Montreal, I knew nothing about it. Since then I have examined it, but I don't think it is good for everyone."

Thus whatever else we know about carbohydrate loading, we do know that it isn't *necessary*, at least not for one Olympic gold medal winner.

However the attraction at least for us lesser lights is that it *may* help. Most marathoners go through some form of carbohydrate loading before a race. Frank Shorter (1972 Olympic gold) is somewhat disparaging of the process, but he still feels that it is worth some 3 minutes' improvement to him.

From Swedish studies of long-distance skiers, it was found that high levels of carbohydrates taken before endurance events could improve performance. Since, as Chapter 4 will show in detail, action energy is derived from a conversion of muscle glycogen, which comes from carbohydrates taken in food, the result of these studies seems reasonable. Moreover, runners felt that if the body was first depleted, it could possibly be super-loaded.

Thus in the week before a race many marathoners will go through a sequence designed to deplete the muscles. Then they take in enough carbohydrates in the right form in the last three days before competition to supersaturate the muscles with glycogen. The hope is to go to the line with the highest possible loading of energy fuel. The sequence would go approximately like this for a coming Saturday marathon:

1. *Preceding Sunday:* The runner will take a "depletion" run of something like 15 to 20 miles, essentially to exhaust the muscles of available glycogen. From this run onward the runner will try to keep the muscles depleted by de-emphasizing carbohydrates in his diet. The evening meal might be limited to a fish or egg dish, possibly meat. Potatoes and bread and candy should be avoided, and possibly cheese can be used as a snack instead of fruit.

2. *Monday and Tuesday:* Both days are much the same. The runner should try to run close to his normal training distance at an easy pace, with a high-protein diet. Carbohydrates should not be cut out altogether; 60 grams a day is a minimum quantity. More can be taken if the runner finds the relatively high-protein diet very uncomfortable. Beware late Tuesday, since the high protein and slight hypoglycemia from which you might be suffering can lead to severe irritability. This is the time when you feel like kicking the dog or even the kids. On occasion we have known wives to tell the children to stay away from Daddy because he's nearing the end of his depletion phase!

3. *Wednesday:* This is the day the runner has been waiting for, since the running has become increasingly a labor. Even short slow runs are very difficult. Today is the end of the depletion phase, so after a short run sometime in the morning, the diet can change to a carbohydrate loading. You may feel weak at this point, and you will be much thinner! If you haven't fully depleted, then the run today could be a longer one (10 miles).

There are a couple of things to be careful of. First, the diet is a change of emphasis, not a complete reversal. Meals should de-emphasize meat, eggs, and cheese and instead there should be an increasing amount of noodles,

69

rice, fruit, vegetables, cookies, bread, pastas, and pancakes. However, since during the first three days the runner will have lost weight, maybe as much as 5 pounds, now is not the time to gain too much weight. Second, it is important, while eating carbohydrates, to take in plenty of fluids so that the carbohydrates can be stored in the muscles and not just passed through the body. Wednesday after the last run this process can begin, but be cautious and avoid the urge to stuff at the start!

4. *Thursday and Friday:* Again these two days are very similar. The emphasis on carbohydrates should be combined with plenty of fluids. No running should be done so that the active muscles can rest, recover, and simply store the glycogen. The danger here is that because of the inactivity and the release from the stringency of the depletion diet and the discipline of the past months of training, it is easy to overeat. During the loading phase about the same weight should be added that was lost during the depletion phase. A couple of pounds excess will not harm the race, but the runner has to remember that this is a loading phase, not an overloading phase! Perhaps the runner can best while away this unexpected and unusual free time by reading running books to get psyched for the coming marathon.

It is usual on Friday to indulge in a last meal of spaghetti or pancakes, as much to seal the race entry as to finish the carbohydrate-loading phase with a last thrust! On the night before the Boston Marathon, the Italian section of the city is full of lean emaciated runners, well out of place in their T-shirts and casual Nikes and Addidas foot gear. They are all asking for the best spaghetti house in town. We have often wondered if the restaurant owners understand why they do their best business on the night before Patriot's Day!

5. *Saturday—race day:* Now things become very personal. The carbohydrate-diet schedule is over, and many marathoners may not eat after the evening spaghetti meal again until after the race to empty the digestive tract. Others eat something if the race is not until midday, but this breakfast is usually limited to muffins and jam, or pancakes, orange juice, or some toast—all carbohydrate foods. Whatever you choose, it will soon become your own personal tradition, a part of pre-race preparations that you may not like to vary.

Table 9 provides a detailed carbohydrate-loading schedule for a Saturday race. For a race on another day, a Sunday, or Monday like Boston, you can move the schedule accordingly.

Proof of the effectiveness of carbohydrate loading is not available. The original 1939 studies by Hansen and Christensen simply compared skiers who had three days of either high-carbohydrate or high-fat diet. The carbohydrate eaters could work twice as hard as their colleagues. This has been substantiated by later workers in the '50s and '60s. Bergstrom and Hultman related changes in muscle glycogen content to different diets and found that high-carbohydrate diets did provide high glycogen values, and

70

## Table 9
Carbohydrate loading schedule*

| Day | Proteins | Carbohydrates | Fluids | Remarks |
|---|---|---|---|---|
| Day −6 | Normal | Low† | As needed | Run long and minimize carbohydrates thereafter from the evening |
| Day −5 | Normal | Low | As needed | Run slow |
| Day −4 | Normal | Low | As needed | Run slow, beware of irritability; weight may have dropped several pounds |
| Day −3 | De-emphasize | Emphasize‡ in snacks | Plenty, mainly with food | Start diet change after last run, say at noon |
| Day −2 | De-emphasize | Emphasize | Plenty, still with food | No running; beware adding weight |
| Day −1 | De-emphasize | Emphasize | Plenty, still with food | No running; evening meal of spaghetti or pancakes is traditional |
| Marathon day | None | Optional, very light | Yes. Plenty from 15 minutes before the gun and on! | Breakfast is a matter of personal choice, but it is better to go to the line without food in the lower intestine |

* This is a 2½-day depletion–2½-day loading schedule.
† Carbohydrates should not be totally avoided.

‡ Beware overloading and excessive weight addition.

71

moreover the resulting work capability was higher. They did their tests on a bicycle or a treadmill and showed that between the extremes of diet the possible endurance could vary by a factor of three! With a low-carbohydrate but high-protein diet there was only 0.6 percent glycogen in the muscle fiber and the maximum work time was 57 minutes. With the opposite, a high-carbohydrate and low-protein diet, the glycogen loading was 3.5 percent, with a work time of 167 minutes. This was confirmed by Karlsson and Saltin, who tested runners in groups and found several minutes' improvement over a 30-kilometer race for the same runners with reversed diets. Carbohydrate eaters averaged 135 minutes against normal eaters, who averaged 143 minutes. The same occurred for two groups. Carbohydrate loading is based on fact, though this is not yet so for the depletion phase of the pre-marathon–week diet.

Costill at Ball State University has shown that more glycogen could be stored in muscle fiber after very heavy exercise. That seems to be the limit of evidence which has led to the depletion phase followed immediately by the loading which we hope supersaturates the muscle glycogen.

The depletion phase is very exhausting, and there seems to be some evidence that damage might be done. Certainly at the end of the depletion when the runner is weak there is considerable danger of catching a cold when the resistance is down, or even of physical injury on the road itself. It is certainly an uncomfortable phase to go through. This may be the reason that many runners, particularly the better ones, are avoiding the depletion phase and simply going through the 2½- or 3-day loading phase alone. Their daily training mileage of 15 to 20 miles leaves them consistently well depleted anyway. There seems little point in going through depletion for benefits which may be merely hypothetical. Both Shorter and Rodgers avoid the depletion.

The carbohydrate-loading regime is not recommended anyway for first marathoners, for diabetics, or for others who may have a medical problem. Once the marathon has been completed, then you may care to experiment with mild carbohydrate loading for subsequent ones. We personally find the last three days before a race very pleasant and slightly indulgent after the rigors of self-discipline. As you find the body responds well, greater loading can be used.

When all the information is in and the studies are complete, it may be that the principal value of the carbohydrate-loading and formalistic running schedule of the final week before a marathon is in making the runner completely aware of the coming race. Throughout the week almost everything you do is aimed at maximizing performance on the final day, everything you read talks of other marathoners and their experiences, everything you feel is related to how well your body is going to be at the gun. It is a very thorough psychological preparation! At the gun, everything leads to a release—the mind is ready, the fuel is loaded, how can we fail?!

## Pill popping

Simply because runners are trying to maximize performance they are prone to take drugs in the form of "nutritional supplements." The very short message is that if they are not prescribed by your doctor for some personal disability, then pills can at best provide a placebo effect. At worst they can be harmful.

In earlier parts of this chapter we have discussed vitamins and pills. Those containing synthetic vitamins are the commonest form of drugs used by athletes. The earlier discussion did note that if you had a fairly well-balanced diet then you would have no difficulty in getting sufficient vitamins and minerals. Too many people, let alone runners, feel that if something is good, then more must be better. It is not so, and indeed there is danger of very grave damage in excess of *some* vitamins.

*Vitamin E* is a fashionable source of income for pill manufacturers. Considerable studies have been done on the vitamin and it's interesting to note the results:

· After 16 months on a Vitamin-E-free diet no volunteer could be rendered deficient in the vitamin.
· No disease state is known to be improved by Vitamin E.
· Despite studies on cyclists, runners, wrestlers, and footballers in the U.S.A. and in Europe, E supplements have provided no measurable increase in either strength or endurance.
· Two studies showed it to be detrimental in large doses.
· There is no evidence that it is toxic to the body.

So the best that can be said is that it won't poison you! Yet many are quite willing to take Vitamin E supplements.

Claims are made for Vitamin C. Even one Nobel Prize winner who is in this sense acting outside his range of expertise recommends Vitamin C as protection against the common cold. However, the only evidence for this appears to be the claims made by pill manufacturers. Vitamin C supplements are in much the same category as Vitamin E.

The latest fad among runners is bee pollen. It is supposed to have everything as well as being attractively "natural." The advertisements rely heavily on the fact that it is used by top American and foreign athletes, that it contains Vitamin E (see above), and that it is "cold-processed" for hive freshness. Very wisely, no claims are made for any beneficial effect. An athlete's pack runs at $15. No wonder the American athlete is said to have the highest-priced urine in the world.

In summary, unless your doctor identifies a deficiency in your physiology and prescribes a diet supplement, you are much better off without them.

## The personal approach

What you finally choose to eat is a personal approach. Some bodies will accept some foods that others reject. Sheehan has pointed out that those of us from northern climes have no difficulty with milk products, while those whose bodies have a southern nutritional ancestry cannot deal with the lactose and should avoid milk products if they have difficulty.

Then again, many runners find they become more and more vegetarian over the years and should be careful to balance their new foods to ensure they get everything they need. For example, if you fail to ensure enough iron in the diet, then iron-deficiency anemia may well result. Chapter 6 has a graphic account of the trials that can follow this problem without the runner necessarily being able to connect it with his diet. The problem is easily solved once diagnosed, but care over a balanced diet is an important preventive to trouble.

This discussion does not recommend vegetarianism for everyone. Some of us like meat and are quite happy with hamburgers and steaks. However, it is true that in the hours before a race, meat is not well digested by the human and so all it may be giving you is a taste bud satisfaction. That may be fine, but you should know that the old idea of feeding athletes with steak and eggs before a competition *is* a fallacy. Even the hidebound traditionalist football coaches have done away with this pre-race diet in most cases.

Finally, the press is delighted to report the horrendous diets that top runners apparently have. Many times they don't, but the normal diet doesn't make news, whereas oddities do. An extreme example of this was before the 1976 Olympic marathon when, on television, Erich Segal misrepresented Shorter's diet with a discussion of the enormous quantities of everything Frank said that he *might* have for breakfast on the day of the race. If we followed Segal's advice we might never lumber past mile 5! So although earlier we reported Kenny Moore's interview with Rodgers, that is not advice to go and buy yourself a jar of mayonnaise and a tablespoon.

Eat what practice has shown you suits your particular metabolic makeup. As a runner aiming at an efficient marathon you should also be aiming at keeping the weight down, so make what you do eat count. Know what the foods do, and enjoy the fact that your weight won't increase; the miles you cover will still let you indulge yourself in the foods you like.

# Chapter 4
# Putting It to Yourself
## The Effect of Stress
## on the Body

Running a marathon—exerting yourself continuously for about 3 hours without rest—is not an everyday occurrence. The body is stressed beyond what it is usually called upon to accomplish, and it reacts by changing some of its functions within limits to cope with the additional stress. However, the real challenge of the marathon is that for most people the run is just long enough in both distance and time that these limits would be reached without proper preparation. If this happens, either the body begins to hurt or it effectively relieves the stress by making the runner stop.

The previous two chapters have talked about training options and changes in diet with a single purpose: to provide you with the proper preparation to move the limits which the body might reach beyond the end of the race. They are still there, of course—apart from a very few rare individuals, you aren't going to be able to run forever—but you should be able to run 26 miles 385 yards in a reasonable time for your age without reaching these stress limits.

Nevertheless, the marathon *is* a strain and you *are* putting it to yourself. It's well to know what happens to your body and how your body reacts so that you understand the reasons for the diet and the training and can anticipate some of the effects. It is not nice to be surprised by Mother Nature!

Although we have spoken of stress, this stress isn't necessarily harmful. In fact, many studies in the past few years have shown that this stress is beneficial to the body rather than damaging, especially in terms of protection from heart attacks. Early studies dealt with the relative protection provided to college rowing crews and longshoremen, but the most important study is a recent one on Harvard alumni.

Dr. Ralph Paffenbarger started a long-term study back in 1962 and 1966 when he surveyed 36,000 Harvard alumni, asking about their jobs, health, and exercise regimes. Of those asked, 17,000 responded. Then in 1972 he sent further questionnaires to these respondees and has since analyzed and then published the results in mid-1977. The results were definite and positively endorsed strenuous exercise.

75

Since the first contact, about 600 of the alumni had died, and these were found to be principally those who were nonexercisers. This study, however, did more than confirm other studies of the value of some exercise; it went further in showing that the exercise had to be strenuous to provide significant protection. There was in fact a threshold which marked the line between exercise which protected and exercise which was too light to help.

The threshold turned out to be exercise which would burn about 2,000 calories weekly, or in running terms, about 20 miles per week run at a pace of some 7–8 minutes per mile. Harvard alumni who exercised less than this had 64 percent more heart attacks than those who sweated more. In fact, if every one of those surveyed had undertaken this level of exercise, statistically 166 more would have avoided heart attacks: a very significant number out of 600.

In his study Paffenbarger also looked at other risks like high blood pressure, smoking, overweight factors, and family history and concluded that the protection supplied by the strenuous exercise was independent of these factors. Thus he concluded by recommending running, swimming, and such things as basketball and handball for some three hours a week.

So even though marathon running and the training that precedes it is tough, it is nice to know that not only are you doing what you want to do, but you are getting the beneficial by-product of healthful protection.

This chapter, then, will deal with the technical details of stress adaptation, our energy balance, fluid balances, and the effect of altitude. Eventually it is worth understanding what is going on, but at a first pass, if you are not technically inclined then you may want to skip to the section Racing Ourselves later in this chapter.

## Stress adaptation

Training methods all use the principle of stress adaptation. If the body is stressed too much, it will break down and stop working. However, if it is stressed to its limits and then just a little bit more, it can adapt to this small increase in stress by increasing its capability to cope, and it becomes "trained" to do a little more than it could before. The ultimate limits have been moved a little further out.

A principal way in which this helps distance runners is in the adaptation of the cardiovascular system. Before you begin running, the cardiovascular system of heart and lungs is "trained" to cope with the rigors of modern life. Breathing, taking in oxygen through the lung walls, and transporting that oxygen to muscles enables modern man to get up in the morning, drive to work or school, and possibly engage in a little manual activity before returning home to sit in front of the TV. Climbing the stairs becomes one of the more energetic pursuits, and the body copes with this

76

additional stress by making him pant to take in sufficient oxygen for the extra work.

However, you are a runner, so things are a little different. You already know that the stairs don't make you pant so much; running has already pushed your limits out by making your body adapt to the more energetic running activity. It has done this by making you capable of taking in and using more oxygen: Breathing becomes deeper, more oxygen is transferred to the blood, and the blood is moved along more efficiently. The heart volume and stroke increases. It beats with a steadier and slower beat. More blood vessels develop in the muscle to increase the flow of oxygen. The extra stress has made the cardiovascular system grow more efficient. As you run farther each day you can feel this adaption working—it is easier over the months to do what was quite tiring earlier.

This cardiovascular adaptation has been measured in the laboratory by testing a variety of volunteers on the treadmill. There are a number of measurements that one can make, and a principal one involves the volume of oxygen consumed during the exercise ($\dot{V}o_2$) measured in milliliters per kilogram body weight per minute (ml/kg.min). This measurement accounts for the weight of the person in kilograms and the duration of the exercise in minutes, and if the person is working at maximum effort then the measurement is $\dot{V}o_2$ max. These measurements are made by having the volunteer wear a breathing mask which measures how much air is inhaled and how much carbon dioxide is exhaled, allowing oxygen usage to be simply calculated, while the volunteer is running on a driven treadmill at some constant speed and/or inclination which has been shown to be his maximum. Usually other things are measured at the same time, like pulse and electrocardiac signals, so the volunteer ends up being taped and wired to pieces of apparatus in a weird science fiction manner.

Figure 5 shows maximal oxygen intake values ($\dot{V}o_2$ max) measured for a number of volunteers of various ages. Both normally active (or sedentary) men and marathon runners were involved in the testing, and one can see that even a 50-year-old runner had a capability of 65 ml/kg.min compared to a "normally active" 25-year-old who could only achieve a value of 48 ml/kg.min. World-class runners average about 77 ml/kg.min, ranging from 71.2 ml/kg.min measured for Frank Shorter to a high of 84.4 ml/kg.min for Steve Prefontaine.

Not only is the runner able to take in and use more oxygen but he does so more efficiently. By stress adaptation the body learns that hard activity is going to be something it has to live with and the heart pumps more deeply but also more slowly, so that a runner's pulse will reduce after a few months of training. From a normal-population value of 72 beats per minute runners will often find their pulse becomes as reduced as 40 or even 35 beats per minute. Clearly the body is making some pretty radical changes! No wonder doctors who were used to treating "normal"

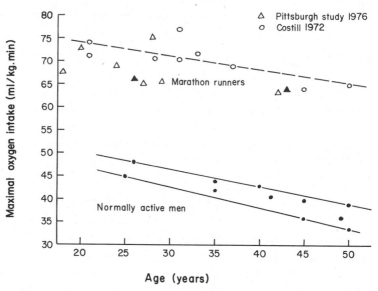

**Figure 5**
Maximal oxygen intake ($\dot{V}O_2$ max) versus age and occupation.

populations sometimes viewed the EKG of a runner with some anxiety. In the past runners have been advised *not* to run because their bodies showed these "abnormalities."

Clarence De Mar, the famed Boston runner, was warned not to run in 1911. He did so anyway and broke the record by some 3 minutes. However, in those days he was sufficiently worried by the doctor's advice that he didn't compete again for the next eleven years, and then tiring of being "sick" he ran again and won in 1922, 1923, and 1924, was second in 1925, third in 1926, and won again in 1927, 1928, and 1930. He was still running in Boston long after his doctor died!

However, there is one other factor involved in cardiovascular adaptation beyond an increase in maximal oxygen usage and a change in the heart's working pace. A marathon runner who has adapted by long-distance training is able to run longer at a higher percentage of his maximal oxygen usage than can a shorter-distance runner. The best distance runners can run with up to 90 percent of $\dot{V}O_2$ max, and they can thus excel over less well-adapted runners who might even have larger $\dot{V}O_2$ max values. Derek Clayton had a fairly average aerobic capacity at 69.7 ml/kg.min for marathoners, but he could run at 86 percent of this for long periods. He still has the fastest marathon time on record at 2 hours, 8 minutes, and 34 seconds! This endurance effect probably explains why Shorter at 71.2 ml/kg.min can win a gold medal at Munich and a silver medal at Montreal.

Aerobic capacity, or the capability of a runner to inhale and use oxygen, is a function of more parameters than just oxygen intake and pulse rate. To start with, the lung volume capacity has a bearing on how much gas can be processed in each breath, and the number of breaths depends on the strength of the respiratory muscles. Both improve in distance runners simply by adapting to the stress of training, and a maximum breathing capacity for a runner might be of the order of 210 liters per minute as opposed to 125–160 for normal males. This includes the fact that the lung capacity can have increased by as much as 20 percent.

The lungs provide a large surface for the transfer of oxygen through the walls of the capillaries to the hemoglobin of the blood, in exchange for the waste carbon dioxide which is being moved out. The distance runner also has a greater amount of hemoglobin and thus more oxygen can be carried by the blood in the red blood cells.

Then, as we have seen, the runner's heart has also adapted so that it has become larger and more efficient in its pumping stroke. The stroke volume can have almost doubled to 200 milliliters compared to less active persons with a stroke volume of between 100 and 125 milliliters. With this size of stroke volume the runner's heart can afford to pump much more slowly when at rest to supply the same amount of oxygen required as in the non-runner. This is why the pulse rate can effectively halve, for a resting workload. However, when performing strenuous activity the runner's heart can now pump blood at double the rate for an equivalent pulse rate.

The adaptation occurs during the stressful activity, and runners not only have this large vital capacity, but they can sustain it for long periods. In other words, *endurance* capacity has been gained. As we've seen, the runner may sustain large oxygen usage, 80 to 90 percent of maximum, for hours at a time, and this involves the heart also working at 80 to 90 percent of its maximum over the same period. And yet when the stress is removed after the race is over the heart can recover very rapidly down to a resting rate in a few hours. In fact, the quicker the recovery the better indication of a well-trained athlete. After a marathon it should be down again in less than 24 hours.

Once the hemoglobin of the red cells is saturated with oxygen, the blood is pumped to the muscles engaged in the activity. There the number of capillaries may have been increased by as much as 100 percent as a result of training. At this point the necessary oxygen is transferred to myoglobin, an oxygen-binding pigment of the muscle. The myoglobin stores the oxygen and in turn passes it on to the mitochondria. It is in the mitochondria that the body aerobically metabolizes foods, or the end products of foods, into energy-producing molecules. We will refer to this energy-conversion process shortly. Fortunately even this last part of the oxygen transportation process is improved in distance runners, since the levels of myoglobin are also increased by nearly twice normal levels, providing a greater transfer of oxygen and some additional temporary storage.

The study of the adaptation which causes all these changes is why volunteers are subjected to treadmill tests under close monitoring and scrutiny. The factors measured include:

- ventilation or breathing rate
- maximum oxygen usage ($\dot{V}o_2$ max)
- respiratory exchange ratio or ratio of $CO_2$ to oxygen
- pulse rate

In addition, stroke volumes can be estimated, while blood tests can measure hemoglobin content and other vital parameters. Furthermore, other studies have been able to show the cardiac-system growth in trained distance runners. Clarence De Mar's heart was said to be very large, with a huge aortic artery.

It is also worthwhile noting that this adaptation of the cardiovascular and the pulmonary systems can be developed at very slow training speeds as long as the exercise is of a reasonably long duration. In one group of runners training at slower than 8 minutes per mile but in long training sessions of 2 to 8(!) hours, seldom at more than 50 percent of their maximum oxygen uptake, all the runners developed exceptionally large aerobic capacities.

It is possible to have these measurements taken simply in a stress test under medical supervision at a number of centers and laboratories around the country if you are interested in your own physical-adaptation characteristics.

The message this gives us for training for a marathon is that we can allow the body to accommodate or adapt slowly to the stresses we place on it, and so achieve a cardiovascular performance that would not have been possible before.

### Our energy balance

The energy requirements for a marathon are very considerable. Within 2½ to 3 hours the body will expend some 2,600 calories, more than a full day's requirements for an average sedentary person. Since it is impossible to ingest and digest this amount of food during the race, this energy is taken out of storage from muscle glycogen and from fats.

The most available store is the muscle glycogen, a complex chain of glucose molecules, which is stored in the active muscles. This is converted by glycolysis and two other chemical processes into useful molecules called ATP (adenosine triphosphate) in which the chemical bonds are convertible to energy. Figure 6 illustrates the sequence of events.

The glycogen in the body is obtained from our food glucose in a number of different forms. Starches in bread contain long-chained glucose molecules, whereas honey contains a broken-down mixture of glucose and fructose. Then in some sweet foods such as cane sugar the glucose and fructose are bonded together as sucrose. In any case the body uses

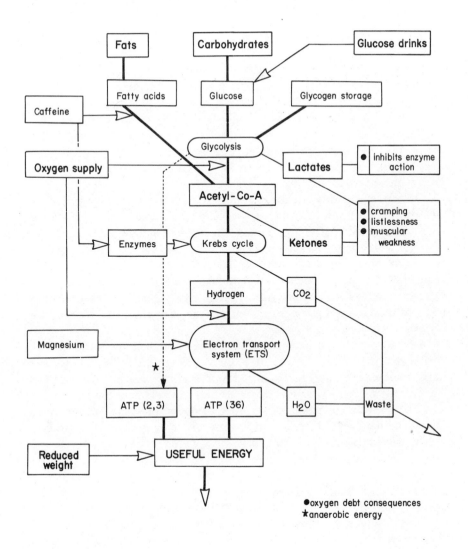

**Figure 6**
Stages in energy production.

this food by breaking down the glucose by enzyme action in three steps, the first of which is glycolysis.

During glycolysis the glycogen and glucose molecules are converted first to pyruvates with the release of two ATP energy molecules. Then *if* there is enough oxygen present the pyruvates get converted into two Acetyl Co-A molecules, which go on to the next step in the Krebs cycle. If there is not enough oxygen the pyruvates would become lactates (a form of lactic acid), which makes the cell environment more acid. If it becomes too acid for the enzymes to work there is a very well-known effect: The muscles feel weak and they can eventually cramp and generally hurt. Thus we have to have sufficient oxygen available to provide energy conversion at the right rate.

In the next step, the Krebs cycle, a similar process occurs. The Acetyl Co-A becomes a citrate and is degraded with enzyme action to carbon dioxide and hydrogen. The hydrogen carries electrons through the electron transport system (ETS), where finally the electrons are used in creating ATP (thirty-six more molecules) from an intermediate phosphate and the hydrogen recombines with oxygen to form water. The thirty-eight total ATP molecules formed from the original glucose molecule represent the energy produced.

One other negative effect can result. Since we also need oxygen at the end of the ETS cycle, if there is insufficient the whole sequence can back up and the Acetyl Co-A molecules can be converted instead into ketones, which result in ketosis, again producing listlessness and muscular weakness—both undesirable in the course of a marathon! So it is very clear again that this energy conversion requires large supplies of oxygen at the right time and rate to ensure that we have an adequate supply of energy in those muscles doing the work. Hence the importance of training the cardiovascular system.

Before leaving Figure 6 there is another very important effect to notice. Although the principal source of food is the carbohydrate intake stored in the muscles as glycogen, this stored food is insufficient to last the runner for more than approximately 2 hours. This is why races longer than 20 miles are so different from shorter ones, since the body has to start using fats in the muscles. These fatty acids are used through the same process, although glycolysis is not required. However, the process is much slower; fatty acids are a poor substitute for carbohydrates because it takes longer to release and process them. Thus if we exhaust our glycogen reserves at 20 miles we are liable only to be able to process fats and thus produce energy much more slowly. We would "hit the wall" and suddenly decrease in speed. Chapter 7 will explain graphically what this means.

Actually the use of fatty acids starts right away, as Figure 6 shows, but unless the body is trained, very little fat is converted until it is really needed.

A word of caution, though. We need to use the fatty acids, but that doesn't mean that a fat person can run a marathon better than a skinny one. On the contrary, the fats involved here are those in the muscular fibers, not those heavy rolls on the surface flesh. We have learned too that even slender women have a greater proportion of fatty acids in their muscular makeup than men and they are apparently better suited to run longer distances because of their apparent large stores of convertible energy. This is, as yet, still a hypothesis, but certainly women do very well in the ultra-marathon distances of 50 and 100 miles, and in the marathon itself rarely experience a wall.

With these physiological changes occurring, an untrained runner attempting a marathon, or one who is attempting to run it too fast, would go through the following sequence. He would first be able to run comfortably as his available glycogen was used up and as some fatty acids were being converted. Unfortunately he would then not be able to breathe well enough, and despite panting, his leg muscles would begin to feel weak, with some twinges of cramp as the lactic acids built up. Then probably as early as 12 or 15 miles, he might hit the wall and very rapidly slow down to a walk, until the increase of acidity in body fluids would produce such weakness and cramps that he would be forced to stop, probably long before the appointed 26 miles 385 yards. This happens to about one in every six aspiring marathoners. It is very painful.

### Fluid balances

Within the energy-conversion cycle an end product is water which has to be rejected as waste, and it will be eventually released as sweat. However, another product of the energy use by the body is heat, and a very major problem for all endurance athletes, especially distance runners, is the rejection of this heat from the body.

At the end of a marathon even on cool days a body temperature of 104°F is relatively common, and temperatures as high as 106°F have been recorded. Temperatures as high as 108°F might be fatal, so it is important to be able to reject heat as it is produced. This is done by sweating.

The blood and lymph systems transfer the blood from the muscles to shallow capillary systems just beneath the skin surface, where heat can be dissipated to the atmosphere. Simultaneously, water is drawn from the blood by sweat glands and released on the surface of the skin, from which it evaporates and cools the blood and lymph just below the surface. This is easier, of course, if the environment is dry and evaporation is rapid, but if you are running your marathon in humid conditions, without being able to splash cold water on the skin, the sweat will not evaporate and the heat cannot be rejected. The body then becomes overheated and resulting heat stress is a very severe problem. In a case like that, either cooling has to be obtained or the running pace must be reduced so as not to create so much heat. Heat-related problems are generally not recognized as severe until they occur.

In 1976, April in Boston turned out excessively hot. The temperature at the starting line was 116°F, and the air temperature for the first 16 miles hovered above 95°F. Those runners who managed to complete the run either decided from the outset to run more slowly, or they found eventually that the heat problems forced them to run more slowly at the end. In any case, times were poor, as Figure 7 shows. Despite the fact that the hospitable Boston crowds poured water on the runners from every type of container ranging from fire hoses to saucers, the curves showed that even the better runners slowed about 8 to 11 minutes overall, or 0.2

83

minutes per mile per degree F, over the previous year, 1975, when conditions were much cooler. At the other end of the pack, poorer runners slowed twice as much.

A partial answer is again stress adaptation or heat training, as discussed in Chapter 2. The body learns to sweat both earlier in the run and more. The water loss by sweating can be very considerable, reaching as high as 8 to 10 pounds per runner during a hot marathon. The 4,200 runners at the 1978 Boston race lost a total of over 10 tons of fluids through sweat!

Unfortunately the runner isn't always aware of the problem, and without even feeling thirsty he can run himself into heat exhaustion and collapse. Thus it is important to drink early and often during the race to try to maintain the body-fluid levels. Many of the drinks available, such as ERG, Body Punch, Gatorade, and the like, contain a variety of minerals and electrolytes which are also sweated from the body. Even very fit runners who are well adapted to high temperatures and even high degrees of dehydration are affected by loss of such electrolytes as ions of sodium,

**Figure 7**
Effect of heat on finishing times at Boston Marathon (1975 and 1976). *Note:* Curve B for full entry modifies the actual entry Curve A by the addition of a number to account for runners absent at the Olympic Trials.

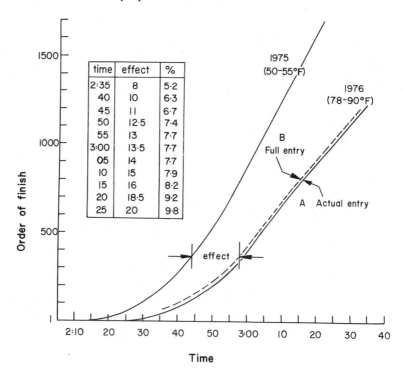

| time | effect | % |
|------|--------|-----|
| 2:35 | 8 | 5·2 |
| 40 | 10 | 6·3 |
| 45 | 11 | 6·7 |
| 50 | 12·5 | 7·4 |
| 55 | 13 | 7·7 |
| 3·00 | 13·5 | 7·7 |
| 05 | 14 | 7·7 |
| 10 | 15 | 7·9 |
| 15 | 16 | 8·2 |
| 20 | 18·5 | 9·2 |
| 25 | 20 | 9·8 |

potassium, calcium, and magnesium. These electrolytes are used in the functioning of the nerves for the contraction of muscles, and thus a depletion of these trace minerals can also produce the symptoms of cramping. The exact importance of these minerals is not well known, nor is the effectiveness of the proprietary drinks. Nevertheless, most runners seem to agree that potassium and magnesium need to be replaced in the longer races.

There is some evidence now that concentrated sugar solutions in the stomach do not get absorbed by the blood as rapidly as more dilute sugar solutions. The concentrated sugar acts as an inhibitor against absorption. Thus although it might appear that if you drink a sugary fluid you are about to get an instant lift, it now appears that you may be able to transfer more sugar by drinking a fluid with less sugar in it. It is absorbed more quickly, and the amount of sugar that reaches the bloodstream is larger in the short term. This is worth bearing in mind when you choose a drink to be handed to you by helpers.

Whether or not fluids with electrolytic additives and/or sugar are available or not, it is important to replace fluids. In theory the reduction of plasma volume could impair exercise performance, but there is some evidence which says that the fluid comes also from intracellular spaces, and many top-rank runners appear to be able to run just as well in a dehydrated state. The phenomenal Jack Foster, who ran 2:11 when he was 41, apparently has little trouble with heat. In 1976 he won his Olympic Trial at 80°F with 2:16 and then finished the Inferno at Boston in fourth place with 2:22:30. He was 44 at the time. However, you and we are not Jack Fosters and in our case it is most important to replace the fluids as early and as often as one can.

Current International Marathon Rules prohibit the taking of fluids for the first 11 kilometers, and thereafter they may be taken regularly at 5-kilometer intervals. Unfortunately the runner really needs the fluid early before he even feels remotely thirsty. The American College of Sports Medicine recommends taking a pint or even two of preferred fluid just

15 minutes before the race. Earlier than this and it will reappear as an embarrassing call of nature, but 15 minutes is just enough time to get the fluid in and then use it in the race. This will tide over the body until the official aid stations start.

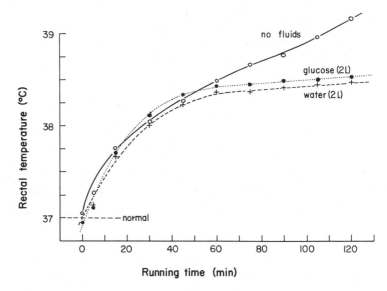

**Figure 8**
Effect of fluid replacement on body temperatures with time.

Tests have shown that even with the aid of a drinking bottle the runner is simply unable to take in the same amount of fluid that he is sweating. In marathon tests even though the subject was losing 9–12 pounds few runners could drink more than a pint. If forced to ingest more it became uncomfortable, and at the end the liquid was still in the stomach and had not been used beneficially. So the message is to take whatever you can, early in the race, even if it is a cool day. Figure 8 shows the effect of fluid replacement on the rectal temperature in 2-hour treadmill tests.

### The effect of altitude

Ever since the 1968 Olympics in Mexico City, the effect of altitude on distance running has been of considerable interest.

Earlier, the beneficial effects of stressing the body to invoke greater efficiency in the cardiovascular system was noted. The body was pushed just a little into an area where it had difficulty in coping, and it did manage to adapt to the additional stress. Much the same thing happens at altitudes above 5,000 feet, because the air pressure is lower and oxygen

diffusion through the lung walls is poorer. Moreover, the air itself is poorer in oxygen content. Again the body accommodates to this by improving cardiovascular usage of what oxygen it can get after training in higher areas.

Thus although running at altitude will leave you gasping even after moderate activity, after a period of bodily acclimatization and adaptation running gets back to normal. However, when the runner returns to compete at sea level the theory goes that his performance is comparatively improved. Thus most Olympic long-distance runners train at altitude, and many choose to live there. Colorado has become somewhat of a haven for marathoners: Frank Shorter (Olympic medalist in 1972 and 1976) now lives there and benefits from training there.

### Racing ourselves

A race is very different from running around the block or down the lane on the weekend, and certain differences start even before the sound of the gun. Almost everyone has some apprehension, ranging from "Will I win?" to "Will I finish?" This fear causes the release of adrenaline;

blood floods into the muscles, leaving the skin and vital organs. We become a little pale and the stomach doesn't feel too well. Butterflies in the stomach!

All this is quite natural, and a warm up helps to stretch muscles and tendons and also to get the oxygen transport systems working and on line for the coming effort. The oxygen is loaded into the blood and the runner is ready.

The gun goes off and there is a sudden acceleration to race pace. You can't even help it, because the tide of runners carries you forward, probably a little faster than you really meant to start. So for about 2 minutes or 400 to 600 yards, the body works overtime. ATP production climbs as the oxygen already in the blood is used to meet the new demands in energy, but very soon this blood oxygen is gone, and even though the heart and lungs are working as hard as they can, there will be a sudden drop in blood oxygen, and in the glycolysis energy-conversion cycle lactates are temporarily produced, which make the legs feel leaden. Then after 2 minutes the cardiovascular system recovers from this oxygen debt and the cramping lactates are oxidized away. The runner begins to feel better and he has reached his racing pace.

Many runners prefer to avoid this racing shock of accelerating by going through the process before the race. Just before that gun, many will run even quite hard to bring the cardiovascular system up to speed and ready to rid the muscles of any excess lactates as soon as they are produced. Running a couple of miles before the 26 miles 385 yards is not as odd as it looks on race day!

Most of the physical changes resulting from prolonged running beyond 20 miles are inevitable, and although stress-adaptation training helps, the racer is going to experience some of the effects. If he races faster, then all the bodily changes are accentuated and he is heading for difficult times before the finishing line. This is why Zatopek, the 1952 multiple gold medalist in the 5,000-meter, 10,000-meter and marathon, said: "We are different in essence from normal men. Whoever wants to win something runs 100 meters. Whoever wants to experience something runs the marathon."

### Psychological stresses

Because the marathon produces such inevitable physical stresses, it requires an exceptional amount of mental fortitude to cope with the psychological stresses which also appear.

The first stage of the race is friendly. Running is easy and not much different from the miles of training over recent months. It is companionable, and for the first 5 miles, one tries to find another runner moving at the same pace. Although some are silent runners, when you run with another, conversation generally flows easily. He may be a German-born tennis instructor living in Toronto, an Army brain surgeon, or a company executive. This is when new friends are made. It is also when the race can be "won" or "lost," since the physiological changes are all speed-dependent and an exact pace needs to be struck for the most efficient marathon. The other runner can help in maintaining the right pace and the right peace of mind. The pace may not vary by more than a few seconds each mile, especially when two runners pace each other.

The second half of the race comes beyond 20 miles when signs of bodily changes appear. Muscles begin to ache and show each weakness; other runners too are showing signs of fatigue. Now friends are not simply conversationalists but companions in adversity. The mind begins to question the value of the whole enterprise: "What am I going to get out of it?" "Wouldn't it be great to stop and rest a little?" "I don't have to prove myself, so who would care?" Each question has to be answered: "Stopping and resting won't help, whereas there's not much farther to go, and *I* would care later if I stopped now." These arguments go on with ever-increasing severity through the rest of the run. As E. C. Frederick says: "It's a rare person with the fortitude and mind control to force himself or herself to finish a marathon when not properly trained for it. Even highly trained persons undergo much soul-searching and must dig deeply into their bag of tricks to endure those last 6 miles."

"I wanted to quit, but you come all this way, you tell all the people at home that you're coming, and you push yourself," said Paul Kraus of Pennsylvania after the 1977 Boston run. A fellow finisher said that the last 5 miles had been almost a constant debate about whether to stop, and it is worth noting that the last 5 miles at Boston are largely downhill.

Companionship can help in this battle, but even surrounded by a crowd of 3,000 runners, each runner becomes an island in the psychological battle to overcome the physical hurts, and to finish. This second half of the race progresses from mild discomfort to a survival struggle.

### We are what we think we are

It is in this psychological battle that perception of success is most important to the runner. If he or she is passed by another recognized as comparable in ability, the pace will sag noticeably, whereas if the runner catches and passes someone of equal stature (or better still, someone who should be faster), then the performance will improve. Sometimes this improvement is a significant increase in pace because of the boost in confidence. It seems most important to all of us that we believe we are doing well, even though we may only be doing comparatively well. One runner said, "At Boston in 1977 I passed a struggling member of the Irish National team who, I knew, had come in 39th in the Montreal Olympic Marathon. Although it was really the Irishman who was 'dying,' my pace noticeably recovered and I felt fresher." When

89

marathoners were surveyed for the most significant effect in a good or bad marathon result, this comparative performance was cited as the dominant inspiration.

It happens to the very best. Describing the 1977 Boston Marathon, the premier marathoner of the United States, Bill Rodgers, writing under the title "The Marathon Can Always Humble You," related how he was concerned as Jerome Drayton, the eventual winner, dogged his footsteps through the halfway point at Wellesley, but then after Drayton passed him, "I soon knew I wouldn't finish. There was no reason for me to keep going. I have no desire to slog it out in the old tradition of the marathoner. . . . that was the message I was receiving in my heart and brain." This was from the phenomenal winner of New York, Amsterdam, Kyoto, Waynesboro, and Fukuoka in the same year.

Fortunately if you know that perception plays such a large role in how well you do then it is possible to rationalize the effect and minimize it by setting new goals which don't involve other runners. Another runner in the Paul Masson event in 1978 was doing badly in the final miles, being passed by a number of runners, including some of his friends whom he should have been beating. In the last 6 miles, sixty-seven other racers passed his agony. However, he knew that he should ignore the relative performance, and he began to measure his struggles by counting: stops, intervals, and paces. Eventually he finished, having lost several minutes, but in other circumstances this perception of failure could well have resulted in a DNF (did not finish) epitaph. Half the battle is knowing the problem.

Since the runner often has to battle for survival, either because of a mistake in pacing, heat conditions, or lack of preparation, his strength of will is sometimes all that will carry him through. Witness one competitor at the 1975 Masters Olympiad in Toronto who was struggling to finish even after 15 miles and during the last 5 to 8 miles could not recognize anyone. He nevertheless finished in a blur of incomprehension, and as his foot crossed the white line drawn on the road, he felt all supporting strength leave his leg muscles. Yet if the line had been drawn 200 yards, or maybe even 2 miles, farther, he would still have finished. The only thing that carried him through the last miles was mental resolution.

This resolution has many factors: the need to prove oneself to others, the need to prove oneself alone (especially in the first marathon), or perhaps the impossibility of the alternative (a "meat wagon" ride with other failures!). The debate that the runner has will use all these arguments. He may even play games, such as running only as far as the next milestone, and the next, and the next. Even while he argues in this way and recognizes the foolishness, a marathoner also recognizes that the arguments work! Lack of motivation can be disastrous.

At the 1976 Skylon International Marathon a small boy, aged about 12, when he stopped exhausted just short of the finish, refused to be removed from the course even though he had to support himself by holding onto a tree. He had sufficient self-motivation to prove himself—and finish he did. In the same race an older man stopping for a drink at 25 miles with a mere 2,000 yards to go found himself in a critical argument on the wisdom of continuing. Fortunately he did, because otherwise his self-recrimination would have been as intense as the joy he actually felt in succeeding.

When it is clear that the runner will be able to finish, quite often he will resume the competitor role. So for the last several hundred yards, despite all previous agonies, you may see runners attempting to sprint to beat another finisher. After all, it is a race, isn't it?

The body can be adapted by stressing it in training, but training the mind to provide the necessary motivation is still in its infancy, still being tried and tested. Pre-race "inspirational" reading of running literature and talking to other runners is part of "psyching" oneself. In a marathon it appears to be essential. The doctor for the East German team at the Montreal Olympics said of the marathon winner, Waldemar Cierpinski, "He also kept himself fit psychologically as instructed." It is clear that the best performances are produced on those occasions appropriately described by marathoner Ed Bingham. He said, "My mind and body finally came together on that particular day." Someday in the future we may know how to train the mind as we presently train the body. For the moment it is half the battle to know how we are putting it to the mind!

After a marathon, remembrances of pain very quickly fade. In about twelve days motivation returns, although physical fitness may be recovered much earlier. Miki Gorman, the 1977 Boston women's winner and a one-

**Photo 12**
"I am satisfied that I have spent my energy worthily." Zeus Perewinkle shows the effort needed for a hard 26-mile run in the Mayor Daley Marathon in Chicago, 1977. (*Photo by Dennis Trowbridge, Journalism Services*)

time world record holder, said, "The pain I felt in this race can only be compared to the pain of childbirth." Fortunately, also similarly to childbirth, it is not until 20 miles into the next marathon that you suddenly remember what the second half was like before!

### Young in years

Bill Rodgers can finish the Boston Marathon in a record 2:9:55, at an average pace of 4:57 for each and every mile! How does he do it? Jack Foster of New Zealand, who is 14 years older than Rodgers, took only 83 seconds longer (3 seconds a mile) when he achieved his best at 41 years. Rodgers was 27. Then Arthur Taylor of Canada only took 2:27:17 to average 5 minutes 37 seconds at age 50.

There is the clue: the age factor. Because the marathon produces such inevitable physical stresses and requires a certain amount of mental strength, age is a small barrier. Even though speed may diminish with age, physical endurance and strength of will do not. Marathoners continue running well into their 60s and 70s: youths of many years. This maturity helps the runner to cope with the psychological strains ahead.

Many things go downhill with age. Probably the optimum age for the sprint is in the early 20s, and tables published by Higdon show that a 40-year-old would show a slowdown of 8.1 percent whereas a 50-year-old would show a slowdown of 16.0 percent. However, in the marathon, where the optimum age is much later, the 40-year-old suffers only a 4.5 percent slowdown and a 50-year-old a 14.5 percent slowdown. In throwing and jumping events, youth is even more preemptive over age than in the sprints. Many of these figures, however, were produced before the current boom in marathon running, and so they may be misleading.

A decade ago a 40- or 50-year-old runner would almost certainly be a person who had returned to the sport after a long layoff. Times of 3 hours would win masters group events. Now the 40-year-old runners are those who were 30-year-old runners and have never given up the sport.

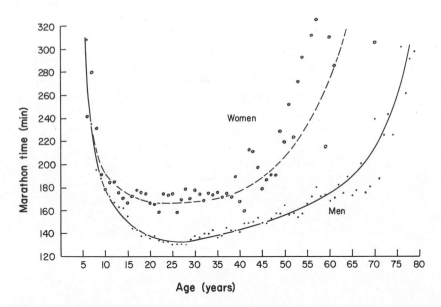

**Figure 9**
Effect of age on marathon performance (U.S. age-group records, 1977).

Their times are much better, and now it takes times under 2 hours and 40 minutes to win masters races. This would make the curve on Figure 9 even flatter with age.

Figure 9 shows the effect of age on marathon times by plotting the current age-group records. The 60-year-old runners can compete very well with 10-year-old runners—that's part of the attraction of the sport. The 10-year-olds may have less endurance, while the 60-year-olds suffer in the joints, but it evens out over the course of 3 hours.

Figure 9 also shows the women's records as the higher curve. Girls up to about 10 are of the same ability as their counterparts on the boys' curve, their lack of strength being made up for by their better natural running style. However, for ages above 10 the man's strength tells and men's age records are superior—at least up to now. Since women were prohibited until very recently from running with men by such backward agencies as the AAU, they haven't had the same opportunity for improvement. Even now in 1978 women are not allowed to run more than 1,500 meters in Olympic competition on the grounds that it would not be good for them! Indeed, since domestic races have been opened to women entrants, and since the number of women racers has increased, the times have been improving: In 1974 the world record was 2:43:54 by Jackie Hansen, but in 1978 it was reduced to 2:32:30 by Waitz of Norway. By 1978 eleven women had recorded times under Hansen's. By comparison, the men's world record hasn't changed since 1969. Thus the two curves

# Table 10

## Marathon slowdown with age*

Percentage decline in ability from the optimum performance age

| Age | Decline (%) | Age | Decline (%) |
|-----|-------------|-----|-------------|
| 35 | 1.3 | 58 | 24.8 |
| 36 | 1.9 | 59 | 26.1 |
| 37 | 2.4 | 60 | 27.5 |
| 38 | 3.0 | 61 | 28.9 |
| 39 | 3.7 | 62 | 30.3 |
| 40 | 4.5 | 63 | 31.8 |
| 41 | 5.3 | 64 | 33.3 |
| 42 | 6.2 | 65 | 34.8 |
| 43 | 7.1 | 66 | 36.3 |
| 44 | 8.0 | 67 | 37.9 |
| 45 | 9.0 | 68 | 39.4 |
| 46 | 10.1 | 69 | 41.0 |
| 47 | 11.1 | 70 | 42.5 |
| 48 | 12.2 | 71 | 44.0 |
| 49 | 13.3 | 72 | 45.6 |
| 50 | 14.5 | 73 | 47.1 |
| 51 | 15.7 | 74 | 48.8 |
| 52 | 17.0 | 75 | 50.3 |
| 53 | 18.3 | 76 | 51.9 |
| 54 | 19.6 | 77 | 53.5 |
| 55 | 20.9 | 78 | 55.0 |
| 56 | 22.2 | 79 | 56.6 |
| 57 | 23.5 | 80 | 58.1 |

* These data were the result of analysis by Ken Young, Director of the National Running Data Center, Tucson, Arizona.

on Figure 9 are moving closer together, especially as more older women are running and each year new age-group records are established.

As we noted above it is possible to predict slowing down with age (Table 10), but it is not yet clear to us what bodily changes determine this slowdown. Unfortunately most studies have been performed on aging people who did not undergo vigorous exercise, and it's clear that exercise modifies the conclusions. Principally, however, it is clear that muscles and other cellular matter lose mass and elasticity both in the muscle fibers and blood-vessel walls. In other words, the older person becomes stiffer. As we've seen before, stretching to relieve this stiffness is a vital part of training, the more so in older athletes.

If you are—and you must be since you've reached this deeply into this book—an aspiring marathoner, it is well to remember two things: first, that age is not a large factor in competitive marathons (17-to-37-year-olds are on a par), so you can look forward to many years of the sport; and second, the personal challenge which enlivens the psyche and accelerates the body's metabolism can make those years very rewarding.

One older runner noted that it would be nice to be able to be 20 again, but since that was not possible, then the next best thing to that was to be able to beat the 20-year-old in his next marathon.

### Mending with rest

We have been discussing the traumas of physiological and psychological responses triggered in the body by putting it through the stresses of a 26-mile-385-yard race. What place does rest play in the scheme of things?

Chapter 2 showed that rest was an integral part of training for the marathon. This is so because there are other benefits of rest which contribute to the adaptation effect that training is trying to induce. Rest is not just an absence of hard work.

Resting for two or more days just immediately before the marathon enables your body to replenish its stores of muscle glycogen, especially if you have decided to load with carbohydrates. Moreover, it replenishes your need to run. After extensive running if one is deprived of it for a little while there is a feeling of loss, a withdrawal symptom, as if the act of running was an addiction. Indeed many writers have described "run-aholism" as a form of disease! Nevertheless these two days of rest are as much a psychological need as they are a physical need. After them you feel like going to the starting line simply to get moving.

We phoned two friends on the night before a marathon in which the wife was to run her first, and we asked how things were. The answer was that everything was all right except for the boredom. They couldn't go

out to run! The rest they had taken was doing its job, making them ready to take to the roads.

After a race, especially the marathon, the body has suffered considerable stress, a depletion of reserves of energy that must be made up, and even, in some cases, damage to the muscles or tendons that must be repaired. There will be a material imbalance in the body, the blood lacking some constituents with an excess of others engendered by the exercise. These physical changes need repair, and a period of rest is necessary. Rest in this context means either abstinence or at most gentle running of a few miles a day.

Much has been written on how much rest is necessary. It clearly depends on the individual. We have known runners who are quite capable of races on successive days or many crammed within the space of a few weeks, but these are clearly the exception. Most of us need longer. On the other hand, there are the opposite extremes which recommend a factor of 20 before engaging in another marathon: $20 \times 26.2$ miles' training before the next one. Somewhere there is a happy medium which must be found by personal experimentation.

Graham, the older author, has found that his body recovers in somewhere between five to ten days. After this time it is capable of undertaking the same stress again. On the other hand his mind is not—it takes a little longer to recover, twelve to fourteen days. After that time he feels like running competitively again. It is as if the psyche needs more time than the quadriceps.

It must be a very personal thing, dependent on the stress level of the first event. In two marathons eight days apart, Graham found his body able to do the job almost at the same effort, but his mind was a little afraid of the undertaking. The very uncertainty defeated the physical ability. However, on two occasions with marathons fifteen days apart, in each case Graham's mind was confident and able to support his body. The muscles were capable of a good effort in the second race (one of them a best result ever), but the end of each race showed an uncharacteristic slight deceleration rather than the usual acceleration, so there was a little missing.

The best piece of advice is to monitor your own body and take the rest you need from what you feel. Also, keep tabs on your resting pulse, perhaps by taking it each morning before rising. If it is within a few beats of remaining constant, then you can continue to run your miles, but if it increases by, say, 10 percent or remains a little elevated after a marathon, then this is a good time to back off and rest. One has to carefully distinguish the events of the previous evening, of course; Graham has noted that convivial refreshment will also keep his pulse going, and on those days a little *extra* mileage clears the head! But certainly being aware of your body and listening to the messages that are sent is good advice.

# Chapter 5

# All Dressed Up

The marathoner must pay more attention to running gear than the fitness jogger because of the extensive time spent in training. He or she requires protection from the pounding on the pavement as well as from the elements. Minor flaws can create major distress over the duration of several hours. Hence, selection of running shoes and clothing should not be taken lightly. We are always amazed at the large fraction of entrants at marathons who are improperly dressed (and we're not talking about color combinations!). In this chapter, we'll give advice on selecting running equipment that will make your year-round racing and training more efficient and comfortable. In addition, since foot plant and injuries are often related (as you'll see in Chapter 6), careful attention in shoe selection is important. Because shoes are by far the most important piece of equipment, we'll start with them.

### Shoe selection

Even as recently as five years ago, the serious runner was quite limited in his selection of footgear. Almost none of the shoes was as comfortable and functional as the current models marketed by the bigger, more progressive companies of today. The running market was not large (except for perhaps track); hence little consideration was given to the needs of the road racer. All this has changed dramatically in recent years. The running-shoe business is now a $500-million industry. The current popularity of jogging as well as road racing has produced a very profitable market. Today's runner is bombarded with hundreds of styles of running shoes. Even the dime stores and discount houses are selling shoes for running. The major manufacturers bombard the running literature with fancy full-color ads extolling their latest models. You can find shoes which are claimed to "store up energy and give you more thrust during toe-off" or which provide "increased heel stability." Furthermore, the publishers of these magazines have taken to rating and evaluating shoes as a service to their readers. These assessments have ranged from a detailed set of laboratory tests, measuring such characteristics as sole flexibility and shock absorption, to the personal impressions of the reviewer. Even with this "help," the runner may still feel a bit lost in selecting a shoe for racing or training. For this reason, we feel there is a need to say a few words about shoe selection with the particular needs of the marathoner in mind.

Our aim is not to recommend a specific shoe or brand (in fact, we will not refer to manufacturers' names), but to provide you with the information necessary to select the pair that best fits your personal needs. We will divide our discussion into two parts—one dealing with training shoes and the other with racing flats. Since these types of shoes have different functions, their selection is based on different criteria.

## Training shoes—day by day

By far the most important (and perhaps the only) factor in choosing a pair of training shoes is how they feel to you (not to some magazine writer). If they are comfortable and allow you to train at your desired intensity without injury or irritation, then they are the shoes for you—even if they cost only $9.95 at your local discount store. However, generally a shoe of this quality ought to have several important design features, which we will discuss briefly. If you keep these factors in mind when shopping for your next pair, you are likely to minimize some of the headaches in the trial-and-error procedure.

In selecting shoes, always examine the shoes yourself. With the proliferation of running, a store which carries a selection of shoes is generally not far away. It is a risky gamble to purchase shoes sight unseen through the mail. While in the store, assume the clerk knows nothing. Then you won't be disappointed! In most instances his knowledge of running is quite limited, and he'll know even less about marathoning. Hence, you should be prepared when you go to purchase shoes. Know the factors that are important in selecting a training shoe. Combining this knowledge with your personal preferences and needs will hopefully result in the selection of a pair of shoes that is right for you.

When trying on a new pair of shoes, put on both shoes (you don't hop on one leg, do you?). It is often remarkable how different the feel of the left and right shoes can be. Remembering that foot plant varies with speed, you should recognize that a shoe which feels comfortable standing or walking may feel very different running. Hence, take a run around the store (you must, as a runner, be past the point of self-consciousness). Try to predict what the shoes will feel like after several hours on the road. To do this, you need to take your test run on a hard surface. Since most shoe stores are carpeted, you may need to jog outside the store or in the stock room.

Naturally, correct size is important. If the shoes are too small, black toenails can result (see Chapter 6). Shoes that are too large can lead to blisters and more serious injuries caused by a lack of support. Be sure the socks you wear when trying on the shoes are similar in thickness to those you wear in training. If you don't wear socks, and state health laws require them to try on shoes, wear very thin nylon dress socks, or women's hose. And if you wear orthotics, by all means insert these in the new shoes.

In addition to general comfort, the following items are important points to be kept in mind when selecting a pair of training shoes.

CUSHION   Shock absorption, particularly in the heel, is of primary importance in selecting a shoe for long-distance roadwork. Adequate cushioning is essential to minimize overuse injuries which can result from the high mileage of marathon training. Each runner has his own perception of what cushioning he requires. It is possible to have too much give in the soles. The true test of adequate cushioning is in the running. This is why you need a trial run around the shoe store—on a hard surface, since even a paper-thin racing flat will have great cushioning on a rug. Remember that you need more cushioning in training shoes for the miles you'll cover.

Shock absorption is achieved through sole construction. The soles of nearly all training shoes on the market are multilayered. Generally, the outer sole is of a tough, durable material, while the other layer(s) are softer and provide most of the cushioning. The latest trend in shoe manufacturing is the addition of numerous studs or projections on the bottom of the shoe. While these undoubtedly add to the cushioning, keep in mind that these nubs can wear down relatively quickly. By 100 miles, the studs on the heel can be completely worn off. If you repair your shoes as described later in this chapter to prevent this wear, then you are effectively reducing some of the cushioning provided by the nubs.

FLEXIBILITY   To some extent, there is a trade-off between sole flexibility and cushioning. Shock absorption is generally achieved through increased sole thickness, which makes the shoe more difficult to bend. A lack of sole flexibility overstresses the shins, Achilles tendons, and calves. When testing out a new pair of shoes, concentrate to see if there seems to be some extra effort required to push off. Toe-off should come naturally without a conscious effort to bend the shoe. This quality is very difficult to assess from a 20-yard jog in a shoe store. Generally the symptoms of an overly stiff sole are first noticeable by a tightening in the shins, or sore ankles and calves during a long training run. Another way to check for sole stiffness is to hold the heel of the shoe firmly in one hand and bend the shoe at the forefoot. If this requires a lot of force, the sole may be too stiff. You can compare different models of shoes to get a relative feel for flexibility. If by some chance you get stuck with a pair of rigid-sole shoes, try putting two or three cuts through the tough outer sole across the forefoot to increase the flexibility.

99

HEEL LIFT   Heel lift is the difference in height between the heel and the ball of the shoe. This factor is another critical one in injury prevention. Shoes with inadequate heel lift put excessive strain on the Achilles tendons. A minimum of ⅜ inch is necessary in training shoes for those who are susceptible to tendon strain.

HEEL CUP   A firm heel counter which surrounds the heel can provide some stability for the heel on foot plant. It supports the heel and reduces wobbling or excessive heel rotation. It is absolutely necessary in a training shoe, which may be used to cover a variety of uneven surfaces. A good heel counter is rigid and extends all the way around the back of the shoe, completely encircling the heel bone.

There are other variables of shoe design which are more of a personal preference. For instance, many of today's training flats have a flared heel, supposedly to provide added stability on impact and to minimize the inward rotation of the foot. We find runners' opinions varied on the need for a flared sole. There is some evidence that very wide flared heels may actually cause, rather than prevent, injuries. Similarly, there is no unanimity of opinion on rounded heels, although such shoes now dominate the market.

Another feature often oversold by shoe manufacturers is the arch support. The ones in nearly all shoes currently on the market are worthless. They feel comfortable but actually provide no support. If you require a good arch support, you will generally have to purchase a more substantial one and replace the foam pad which comes with the shoe.

Finally, examine the quality of construction of the particular pair you intend to purchase. With the increase in running-shoe production, the quality control of some manufacturers has slipped. For $30 to $40 you deserve a nondefective product. Be sure the stitching is sound on all interior and exterior seams. Run your fingers carefully throughout the entire inside of the shoe to check for loose flaps of material or threads, which could cause blisters. Be sure the insole and arch support are properly secure and that there are no unusual bumps or wrinkles. Finally, check to see if the sole is firmly glued to the upper all the way around the shoe's outer boundary.

Some shoes are provided with speed lacing—the laces are threaded through plastic loops instead of the more usual holes. This is supposedly added to even the tightness automatically up the instep. Sometimes it can do the opposite by tightening the bottom and loosening up at the top. Again the choice of speed lacing is a personal one.

Another point to consider if you use training shoes for trail training is lateral strength. Some shoes have a leather surround on all sides of the nylon upper, whereas others have an unprotected junction between nylon and sole and thus less lateral strength for turning and twisting runs.

Chapter 8 relates a shoe failure that resulted from the lack of this protection.

One quality which you cannot test in the store is durability. With the wide selection of training shoes available, several models are likely to fit your personal needs rather well. Hence, it is to your advantage to select those which will last the longest. Running shoes are no small investment. A marathoner who can manage only 500 miles on a pair of training flats could end up spending over $300 per year on training shoes alone! We also recommend periodic sole repair and maintenance to increase shoe life (more about that later in this chapter).

Finally comes the amount you plunk down to purchase your shoes. As you are probably well aware, the prices of running shoes are sky-rocketing. The current boom in jogging can only worsen things as it becomes "in" to be a runner. We think the tremendous profits being made by shoe manufacturers are outrageous, and hope that someday competition within the industry will bring prices down. Having said that, however, we must emphasize that you should not try to pinch pennies when buying running shoes. Our experience has been that you pay for what you get (and how!). There are few bargains to be found in your local discount house. The few bucks you may save by buying an inferior shoe are not worth severely blistered feet or, worse yet, an injury.

Once you have discovered a favorite shoe, then it is generally safe to order future pairs by mail. Some runners prefer the convenience, and often they can save a few dollars on the price. However, keep in mind that a size 8 from one manufacturer is not the same as a size 8 from a competitor. Furthermore, different models from the same manufacturer can vary widely in fit. Thus, you really should try on each new style you purchase.

### Racing flats—the special occasion

Because of the length of the marathon, many runners wear their normal training shoes during the race, obtaining maximum comfort by running in shoes to which they are accustomed. Training shoes also afford the maximum protection from the stresses of racing the 26-plus miles. Both of us ran our first couple of marathons in training shoes, and we think it is probably a good idea for the beginning marathoner, unless you are a very experienced road racer who is used to racing flats. However, after you become an experienced marathoner, you may want to make a change. You may find your performances leveling off and be searching for a way to get out of a rut. You might try switching to a lighter shoe.

Most racing flats currently available are considerably lighter than the average training shoe (roughly 25 percent). This couple of ounces can make a dramatic difference. Many runners feel as if they are wearing no shoes at all when wearing racing flats. This reduction in weight can be a significant saving over the long duration of the marathon where energy reserves are critical to performance.

In gaining the advantage of reduced weight, you must sacrifice something. This is generally a reduction in cushioning and support. Racing-flat soles are significantly thinner. In addition, the heel counter may be omitted or cut back, and the heel lift is generally much less than in training shoes. In a sense, you accept the slightly higher probability of injury in exchange for an improved performance. But this is what racing is all about: gambling; taking risks to discover your personal limits.

Of course, the additional risk of injury is not so large that you should avoid trying racing flats. The increased chance of injury during races is a result more of the intense stresses that are imposed than of a temporary reduction in protection. However, this does not mean you should train regularly in racing flats either. If you run for prolonged periods without proper cushioning and support you may leave yourself open for an overuse injury.

Weight is not the only consideration in selecting a shoe for racing marathons. Although you are willing to give up some cushioning to reduce shoe weight, this does not mean that racing flats should have no shock absorption. Unless you have an extremely tough frame, some cushioning is necessary; otherwise, the road shock will destroy your rhythm and offset the advantage of reduced shoe weight. Fortunately, manufacturers have recognized the need for some cushioning, and the hard, paper-thin soles of several years ago have for the most part been improved or replaced without necessarily adding weight because of the new materials available.

Flexibility is another important feature of a good racing shoe. In general, flexibility is greater than with training shoes simply because soles are thinner. However, some brands of racing flats, whose outer soles are hard rubber, can be surprisingly rigid.

The presence or absence of a heel cup in a racing shoe is a personal preference. Many marathoners feel the need for this support over the 26 miles. However, because of the faster race pace, you are usually running more on the balls of your feet, with the heels receiving relatively less impact. Hence, the need for a solid heel counter is not as great as in training when the heel takes the brunt of the load.

In summary, as with training shoes, overall comfort is the most important factor in shoe selection. If they feel good and don't cause you blisters or other problems, then you have found your brand.

### Make do and mend

Because running shoes are a sizable investment for a marathoner, it is to your benefit to maximize their useful life. There are two

102

**Photo 13**
A marathoner's weekly shoe-repair session. (*Photo by Cindy Brown*)

approaches which you can take. One is resoling when the wear becomes excessive, and the other is to prolong the sole life as much as possible by keeping the soles repaired. We favor the latter approach. If you don't keep your soles repaired, the wear after a few weeks of high mileage can significantly affect the motion of the foot during the gait cycle and make you more prone to injury. Periodic maintenance minimizes this change in foot plant and rotation during the gait cycle. In addition, with the cost of most commercial resoling services in excess of $12 per pair, it is less expensive to do the job yourself. We've found that regular attention to sole condition can more than triple the life of the shoe. In fact, the uppers will often wear out before the sole reaches a state where further repair is not practical.

To repair and maintain worn shoes, most runners utilize either hot glue or a commercially prepared adhesive which comes in a tube. Whichever you find works best, keep these points in mind.

- Don't let the soles wear down significantly before repairing them. Get after them at once. Also, repair shoes frequently so the original outer sole wears as little as possible. Thin layers of additive hold better and thus wear longer than thicker ones.
- The adhesive should restore the surface of the shoe as close as possible to its original shape. Don't build up glue or put on extra layers of material as this may produce some imbalances.

### Shirts and shorts—more than just fashion

Although shoes are by far the most important article in the runner's wardrobe, the other clothing does merit some consideration. The explosion in running popularity has hit the clothing business as well as the shoe industry. Now one no longer needs to run in those old, tight, cotton high school gym shorts.

As with shoes, there is a particular need to pay attention to the clothes worn in races. Light weight and comfort are of primary importance. Most marathons require runners to wear a shirt (if for no other reason than to attach a number). For racing tops, we prefer lightweight, porous nylon singlets. The armholes should be deep to avoid chafing of the underarms. Color is also a very important factor in hot-weather racing. A light color is preferred, since it reflects (rather than absorbs) sunlight. In the 1976 Olympic Marathon, gold medalist Waldemar Cierpinski was virtually unrecognized early in the race because he abandoned his country's traditional blue jersey for a white singlet. Fishnet tops are also preferred by many experienced marathoners for summer races. These provide the maximum possible cooling but still give you something on which to hang your number.

To further reflect the heat, many runners also don a lightweight white cap (like a painter's hat) or drape a handkerchief over the head. A head covering wards off some of the sun's rays, and you can put ice cubes beneath it during the run to further cool the head and neck. Graham successfully uses a handkerchief pinned to the back of the sweatband to protect his neck from the sun.

Shorts for racing should not be binding or interfere with the stride. For this reason they are generally brief and may be split up the side. Several major companies have come out with a brief/short combination which makes underwear or an athletic supporter unnecessary. These are rapidly catching on in popularity (although one of us still prefers to use the jock in racing). Nylon, again, is the preferred material as it does not become heavy and sag when wet, and it dries more quickly than cotton— an advantage for training clothes as well.

Another concern of many women marathoners is the selection of a bra for racing and training. Many female runners have difficulty finding a bra which provides comfort and support. More than with any other article of clothing the selection of a good bra is by trial and (mostly) error. Your best bet is to ask other women runners for their suggestions.

Because of the marathon's duration, chafing can be a real problem. You are likely to be suffering enough from the stresses of running the marathon without adding the burning pains of chafed nipples or groin. For this reason, the clothes you select for the race should not be brand-new. They should be washed several times and tested out on some long training runs. Finally, for an extra layer of protection, apply some petroleum jelly to the critical areas just prior to the race.

For racing purposes a good singlet and pair of shorts can be expensive (in excess of $20). However, for everyday training where the runs are not as long or intense, and there is less concern about weight, one need not pay so much attention to detail. For moderate temperatures, a cotton T-shirt and shorts are fine. (As you become a marathon veteran, you'll have no shortage of T-shirts in which to train!) As the mercury climbs, you may want to discard the T-shirt, at least during training runs. Remember, however, that an exposed skin absorbs more heat than a loose white shirt.

Socks for racing and training are up to you. There is no consensus as to what is best; you can find numerous runners at each race with full socks, half socks, or even none at all. Some prefer thick absorbent socks, others like thin nylon ones. The choice is entirely up to you. If you wear socks, be sure the ones you purchase have no loose material or lumps around the stitching in the toe. Such flaws can produce very painful blisters during long runs. As with the other gear for racing, never tackle a marathon in a new pair of socks. Always use a pair that you know are comfortable, and check the old reliables to be sure they aren't wearing too thin.

### Out in the cold

(Southern California readers may omit reading this section!!)
Successful marathoning requires a year-round commitment. To maintain the aerobic base necessary for the marathon, you can't go into hibernation each winter. Particularly if you want to do well in the spring marathons, you need to get those miles in during the winter. If you dress properly, the winter weather should not hamper your training significantly. In fact, much of the time, long runs are easier to get in, since the concern for fluid replacement is not as great.

How you dress depends, of course, on your own personal tolerance for cold. For example, we generally stick to T-shirt and shorts down to about 45°F. Below this we add a nylon windbreaker and perhaps some cotton gloves. Around freezing, a stocking cap may be added. Only when the mercury nears the 20°F level (or on very windy days) do we add protection for the legs.

While your personal preferences may vary, there are some guidelines to follow when training in severe winter weather. For subzero temperature and/or wind-chill factor conditions (see Table 11), it is especially important to protect the head and torso, since this is where nearly all of the body heat is lost.

Use several layers of lightweight clothing rather than heavy, bulky garments. The layer next to the body should be absorbent and non-irritating. Its purpose is to wick the perspiration away from your body so your skin doesn't become drenched with sweat. Fishnet underwear or a cotton T-shirt works fine. Over this you may add a long-sleeve insulating T-shirt (like thermal underwear). Turtlenecks are especially good as they protect the neck as well. If it is really frigid many runners

105

## Table 11
### Wind-chill factors

| Wind (mph) | Temperature (Fahrenheit) | | | | | | | | | | | | | | | | | | | | |
|---|---|---|---|---|---|---|---|---|---|---|---|---|---|---|---|---|---|---|---|---|---|
| | 40 | 35 | 30 | 25 | 20 | 15 | 10 | 5 | 0 | —5 | —10 | —15 | —20 | —25 | —30 | —35 | —40 | —45 | —50 | —55 | —60 |
| **Calm** | | | | | | | | | | | Equivalent chill temperature | | | | | | | | | | |
| 5 | 35 | 30 | 25 | 20 | 15 | 10 | 5 | 0 | —5 | —10 | —15 | —20 | —25 | —30 | —35 | —40 | —45 | —50 | —55 | —65 | —70 |
| 10 | 30 | 20 | 15 | 10 | 5 | 0 | —10 | —15 | —20 | —25 | —35 | —40 | —45 | —50 | —60 | —65 | —70 | —75 | —80 | —90 | —95 |
| 15 | 25 | 15 | 10 | 0 | —5 | —10 | —20 | —25 | —30 | —40 | —45 | —50 | —60 | —65 | —70 | —80 | —85 | —90 | —100 | —105 | —110 |
| 20 | 20 | 10 | 5 | 0 | —10 | —15 | —25 | —30 | —35 | —45 | —50 | —60 | —65 | —75 | —80 | —85 | —95 | —100 | —110 | —115 | —120 |
| 25 | 15 | 10 | 0 | —5 | —15 | —20 | —30 | —35 | —45 | —50 | —60 | —65 | —75 | —80 | —90 | —95 | —105 | —110 | —120 | —125 | —135 |
| 30 | 10 | 5 | 0 | —10 | —20 | —25 | —30 | —40 | —50 | —55 | —65 | —70 | —80 | —85 | —95 | —100 | —105 | —110 | —120 | —130 | —140 |
| 35 | 10 | 5 | —5 | —10 | —20 | —30 | —35 | —40 | —50 | —60 | —65 | —75 | —80 | —90 | —100 | —105 | —115 | —120 | —130 | —135 | —145 |
| 40* | 10 | 0 | —5 | —15 | —20 | —30 | —35 | —45 | —55 | —60 | —70 | —75 | —85 | —95 | —100 | —110 | —115 | —125 | —130 | —140 | —150 |

**LITTLE DANGER**

**INCREASING DANGER (EXPOSED FLESH MAY FREEZE WITHIN ONE MINUTE)**

**GREAT DANGER (EXPOSED FLESH MAY FREEZE WITHIN 30 SECONDS)**

* Winds above 40 mph have little additional effect.

will add a wool sweater or flannel shirt. This is then topped off with a nylon windbreaker. Avoid rubberized or vinyl jackets, as they do not breathe and will trap all of the moisture inside. Several new all-weather suits are now on the market which feature a vented back flap which supposedly enhances the removal of moisture from inside the clothing. Some runners still prefer the traditional sweatshirt. However, they are rather bulky and can become quite heavy as they absorb perspiration.

Protection for the head is also essential, as the majority of the body's heat loss (40 percent) is through the head and neck. For this purpose a wool stocking cap is excellent. Unlike some synthetics, wool retains some of its insulating qualities when wet, because of the oil in it. For very frigid conditions a ski mask which covers the entire head and neck with small openings for the eyes, nose, and mouth is excellent. For further protection, you can even cover your mouth and nose with the ski mask and breathe through the mask. The exhaled air actually warms the mask and keeps your face warmer.

Although the extremities are not as important with respect to total body heat loss, they are often very sensitive to the cold, and of course there is always some danger of frostbite. When it gets too cold for cotton gloves, switch to woolen mittens or perhaps several pairs of wool socks. For the legs, generally only one or two light layers of protection are necessary. The important thing is to find something which inhibits the stride the least. Runners' preferences vary. The traditional sweat pants are popular, but they are rather bulky and can be a significant source of drag when running on windy days. Other popular items are long thermal underwear, leotards, and pantyhose (even for men!). These reduce the drag from the wind, but occasionally bind and chafe and are not always as warm as sweat pants. Finally, there are the lightweight nylon pants of the new all-weather suits. We've never used these, but from what we hear they may be the best leg protection available; they combine warmth and protection from the wind, light weight, and comfort, while reducing drag. However, the currently available all-weather suits are very expensive, the pants alone costing $20 to $30. Their durability is questionable; hence, the added comfort may not be worth the extra cost.

Dressing for a cold-weather marathon can be a real problem. Here the runner is torn between minimizing the weight of clothing and maximizing warmth. The duration of the marathon complicates matters even more. There is a very real danger of hypothermia for the runner over the latter stages of the race—particularly if he has gone out too fast. Over the last few miles, he may be soaked with sweat, his glycogen supplies are depleted, and he is slowing down, thus generating less heat. It is very easy to become chilled. For marathons in subfreezing weather, we recommend a very cautious early pace. In fact, unless you are a very experienced marathoner, an all-out PR effort under such frigid conditions could be

**Photo 14**
Start of the first marathon run in Delaware, the Delaware National Guard Marathon. Dan Rincon (No. 2121) leads the pack. Winning time: 2:30:02. (*Photo by Delaware National Guard*)

dangerous. Pay close attention to your body's signals, and always try to have access to warm dry clothes immediately upon finishing.

In selecting clothes to race in, keep the layering concept in mind. However, you might not require quite as much protection as for your long slow training runs. Photo 14 illustrates some of the types of clothing worn during cold-weather marathons. Note that most of the runners have multiple layers of thin clothing on the upper body. The bulky warm-up suits are the exception rather than the rule. Leave them at the start or abandon them shortly afterward.

## Purchasing running equipment

Formerly, running equipment could be bought only in general sports stores where the average clerk knew as much about the marathon as he did about climbing the Matterhorn. Thus aspirants were enticed to buy fashionable shoes based more on the number of stripes than on any quality of fit, use, and wear. Even today the buyer must beware.

However, there has been a fortunate development recently for long-distance runners: Stores are being opened by running practitioners who know what they are speaking about and, moreover, they are willing to provide good advice. The Phidippides chain started by Olympian Jeff Galloway and Bill Rodgers' Running Center in Boston are cases in point.

As an example, Rodgers' store retails running equipment, some selected manufacturers' products, and its own full product line of clothing. However, the center does more. It caters for its public in a knowing and socially conscientious manner by educating, assisting, and advising embryonic long-distance runners. The center runs free public clinics with formal speakers on particular races, nutrition, health, training methods, exercise programs, and the like. Together with doctors and trainers who are in attendance, they cater to the runners' needs. Fun runs are held periodically from the center, and they are used to advise runners on better running, the use of equipment, and remedies for common problems.

Bill Rodgers looks on running as a part of our life-style, growing rapidly certainly, but here to stay. He wants to help runners enjoy their sport with a minimum of trials and tribulations. To this end, passing on his experience is a most effective and altruistic effort. If you can attend such an outlet as the Bill Rodgers' Running Center then you should have no difficulty in choosing suitable long-distance running equipment. Every man and woman on the staff is a runner and knows the subject from the ground up. If you do not have such a center in your neighborhood, then you should either ask for the assistance of a more experienced marathoner or proceed warily to test your potential purchases.

# Chapter 6

# Trials and Tribulations

If you are a marathoner who is biomechanically perfect and always uses sound judgment in your daily training, then this chapter is not for you. However, nearly all of us are probably lacking in one way or another. Thus we are prone to injury.

When peaking for a marathon, we are very close to that razor's edge between competitive sharpness and injury. The nearness of the approaching race, while a boost psychologically, can often be a hindrance physiologically. The difficulty is that the anticipation and excitement of the upcoming marathon often causes us to push a little too hard or too far. Your enthusiasm may lead to a cold, or worse still an injury, in those last few weeks. All those injuries your competitors bemoan just before the start of the race may not all be alibis. They just may have some basis. Derek Clayton (2:08:34, world's best marathon time) has said, "Due to my severe training, I have had many injuries, three of which have put me in the hospital."

The majority of the runner's injuries result from overstressing—either doing too much or going too fast, or both. As we mentioned in Chapters 2 and 4, marathon training's basic principle is stress adaptation. You improve your condition by stressing the body and then allowing a recovery period during which the body increases its adaptive capability. The problem with many runners is that they don't know the limits of their adaptive capability and sooner or later overstep their bounds.

In addition, different parts of the body respond to training at different rates. In general, cardiovascular conditioning increases rapidly with distance training. The heart and lungs develop a capacity for aerobic work that far exceeds the capacity of the feet and legs to take the continued pounding on the pavement. Hence, the top half of you is ready for 100 miles per week, while the bottom half is screaming "Whoa!" at 50. The result is often some sort of overuse injury.

### Overuse signals

Various writers have recommended listening to the body in an attempt to forecast the moment at which overuse is imminent. The pulse

111

has been identified as one possible signal of overuse. The recommendation goes that if you take your pulse each morning before rising then you will have a good idea of what level the resting rate usually is. Then if it ever rises 10 percent above this, it is a possible sign of overuse and it would be better to cut back on mileage for a few days until the pulse has regained its usual level at rest.

Unfortunately this signal may not be adequate for all individuals. We have found that in some cases the pulse is not very significantly changed even by having run a marathon the previous day, let alone just training mileage. On the other hand, the variation is as much as 10 percent after a convivial drinking party the night before. However, the pulse test might work for some people and it is probably worth trying.

Since overuse caused by long slow distance is more a total overstress on the body, the first sign of overuse is likely to be exhibited by the weakest link in your own body's makeup. This may or may not be shown by the pulse. Only you will be able to find out by stressing a little more and watching for signs of breakdown, recognizing them for what they are, and then backing off to confirm your diagnosis. Thereafter they will be a valuable tool in training.

As an example, Graham finds that as the mileage is elevated to about 100 miles per week for more than a couple of weeks, apart from a little general tiredness which can be expected, small skin eruptions appear as pimples on the neck and under the chin. These are very innocuous and go away almost immediately when mileage is cut back. If on the other hand they are ignored and mileage is not reduced, then slightly more severe signs can occur. Usually then he will contract a cold, possibly quite mild but very difficult to get rid of, and very damaging before a race. He has learned from experience to reduce the intensity of his training as soon as those first small pimples appear.

The sign will be something else for you. It is up to you to discover what it is.

Tom Osler in his pioneering booklet *The Conditioning of Distance Runners,* published as long ago as 1967, well identified general symptoms of overuse. He listed five:

- persistent leg soreness
- lowered general resistance to ill health
- lack of motivation and an I-don't-care feeling
- sluggishness or heavy-leggedness following a workout
- poor coordination, lack of sprightliness

All the signals are quite mild, and as long as they are recognized early and heeded, then no lasting damage is done. However, if they are not heeded, then the leg soreness or poor coordination will lead to an injury, or else the lowered resistance may result in a serious cold or illness.

Observe the signal, back off, and retreat to slower gentle running. It is important to keep a good flexible mental attitude toward training with no rigid schedule that you feel you *must* complete, or else. In this case, once the signal has been detected, you *must not* continue on the same schedule. Along this line, experienced marathoners often cut back in their training in the final week or two just before an important event. This provides some built-in protection against overuse injuries which anticipation can bring on.

The importance of resting has been noted elsewhere (Chapter 2). Part of its value is that it helps to anticipate overuse injuries. If you can find the right combination of training and rest for your body, then you're a long way toward enjoying successfully completed marathons.

### An ounce of prevention

In addition to heeding your personal warnings of overuse, there are some things you can incorporate into your everyday training to further reduce the likelihood of injury. If you are preparing for your first marathon and just trying to improve your endurance base by increasing your mileage, a good rule of thumb is to increase your distance by no more than 10 percent per week. If you find yourself becoming fatigued at this rate, try stepping up by plateaus. Add 10 percent one week, and hold that level until it becomes comfortable. Then tack on another 10 percent, and so on until you reach your goal.

Another preventive measure is to use the hard/easy approach discussed in Chapter 2. This applies to long slow distance trainers as well as those who rely on speed work. Learn to vary the distance from day to day.

Also get in the habit of warming up and cooling down. Allow a few minutes for some of the stretches illustrated in Chapter 2 and begin each run at a very slow jog. This increases the blood circulation to the muscles and gradually loosens up stiff ligaments and muscles. A sudden transition from inactivity to a full stride can strain a tendon. As a matter of interest, we've found many marathoners require 2 to 4 miles before their joints are loosened up and they feel like flowing into a full stride.

Similarly, a proper cooldown after the workout is important. This is more often neglected than the warm up, as there is generally an urge to use all available time to accumulate miles. If you have just completed your run at a brisk pace, perhaps creating a small oxygen debt, movement should not abruptly cease upon completion of the distance. Get in the habit of finishing each run with a jog of ¼ mile, gradually coasting down to a walk. Never come to a complete stop after a run, or worse yet lie down. We know runners who have passed out from this.

Finally, always wear good training shoes and keep them in good repair. If you're heading out for a 20-mile workout, don't slip on those 1,200-mile racing flats with the worn-down heels. Shoes are a very important factor in injury prevention. Always be sure your training shoes have good cushioning, adequate heel lift, and a stable heel counter. Follow the guidelines in Chapter 5 in selecting a training shoe, and keep the soles in shape with a periodic application of glue. Almost all of your training should be run in training shoes. Avoid racing flats except for perhaps the occasional interval session or time trial. Give your feet and legs all the protection they can get.

## A pound of cure

So now you're hurting. Before panicking, objectively analyze your current situation. This analysis may reveal that self-treatment is all that is needed, and thus you need not waste time and money visiting the doctor. Even if professional help must be sought, this evaluation is essential background for the diagnosis and specification of treatment by the doctor. Try to determine how and why the injury occurred. Some common causes are:

- sudden increase in training mileage
- transition from slow to fast running
- transition from flat running to hill work
- change in running surface (grass to roads)
- change in shoes.

A well-kept training diary can be helpful here.

Can you run on it? Does the pain get better or worse as you run on it? If it improves with running, it may gradually disappear if you take it easy for a few days. If the pain worsens during the run and afterward, it may be caused by inflammation of the damaged tissues as the body increases blood flow to the damaged area. In these cases, continued running can be harmful. Although "rest" is the runner's most despised four-letter word, sometimes it is necessary. If your injury has forced you to cut back to 2 miles a day at a slow jog, you are probably better off taking some time off and allowing the injury to heal rather than adding to the damage by continuing to run. That slow mile or two is not giving any significant benefit, and your overall training is probably better enhanced by a rest period which would speed recovery, thereby getting you back to normal mileage sooner. If the pain is so bad you are forced to limp, by all means do not continue to push it. By favoring the injured leg, you are overstressing the healthy limb. The resulting imbalance may lead to additional complications.

For most common runner's injuries, muscle, tendon, and joint disabilities, the immediate recommended treatment is ice and elevation. The application of cold constricts the superficial vessels, thereby limiting swelling and reducing pain. It also numbs the nerve endings, which gives added relief. Harry Hlavac (sports podiatrist and author of *The Foot Book*) also notes that as the cold sensation penetrates deeper, it causes a reflex

114

dilation of the deeper vessels, which brings in healing cells and removes damaged cells.

If you are forced to take a rest to cure the injury, then application of heat to the injured area may be beneficial following a day or two of ice therapy. Heat dilates the blood vessels and increases circulation to the injured area, and that may increase the rate of healing. There is some disagreement over the benefits of heat treatment. Several authorities recommend continued cold treatment and avoidance of heat therapy. You will have to experiment to discover what works best for you. Our experience has shown that heat is of the most benefit for large-muscle injuries (like the calves or quadriceps). For injuries of the joints and tendons, continued application of ice often works better. In any event, you should know that heat produces local swelling and may do more harm than good for disabilities like tendonitis which are aggravated by swelling. In general, don't use heat therapy if you are continuing to run.

### Blame the feet

Hand in hand (or should we say foot in foot) with overuse injuries are those which occur as a result of some musculoskeletal deficiency. It has been stated that more than 30 percent of us have a basic deficiency in the structure of the feet. Most of these go unnoticed, as the body compensates for them in day-to-day activities. However, the increased intensity of running can cause these difficulties to manifest themselves in many ways. Very often they don't show up where you'd expect, but in other areas, particularly the knee.

A normal foot can be described as one where the heel is perpendicular to the ground when the person is standing upright. The lower leg is roughly perpendicular to the floor. The metatarsal heads (the bones directly behind the toes) are all in contact with the surface. An abnormal structure is one where this perpendicularity does not exist. Figure 10 illustrates a normal foot structure as well as some common deficiencies. A very common and easily recognizable example is "bow leg," or tibia varum. In this case the line through the heel tends to lean out from the center. So even to lie flat the foot would have to be rotated inward.

Even for normal feet there is a significant degree of difference in gait between walking and running. In walking, the feet are placed, right and left, quite far apart, so the point of balance swings from side to side (Figure 11). In running, the feet are placed almost directly in line. The faster one moves, the more the point of balance moves directly ahead. In order to get the feet into this inner running position, they must twist over more in reaching inward. (The podiatrists call this "pronating.")

The foot has two basic functions when running. Upon contact with the ground it acts as a shock absorber, allowing the foot to accommodate

115

any unevenness in the surface. During the propulsion or push-off phase the foot serves as a rigid lever thrusting the body forward. While the bio-mechanics of the foot during running are quite complex, you can get a good idea of the movement of a normal foot from Figure 12. This illustration shows a view of the foot from the rear at various stages in the gait cycle. You can see that the normal contact point is on the outside of the heel. The heel bone itself is tilted inward, as indicated by the dotted line. As the body moves forward, the foot turns in and flattens out. This inward rotation, which is accentuated by the narrower running gait, accompanied by the forward movement, is termed "pronation." After the ball of the foot has contacted the ground, the foot then switches function and becomes the lever propelling the body forward. The force comes mainly through the inside of the foot (the first two metatarsal heads). Note that the heel bone has rotated out and then back in during the entire cycle. The normal angle encompassed by all of this movement is approximately 4°. During this twisting or rolling of the foot, the knee is forced to rotate. It is easy to see this if you accentuate the foot roll for your-

**Figure 10**
Illustration of normal foot structure (upper left) and some common deficiencies.

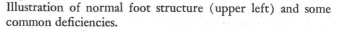

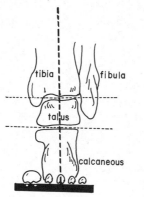
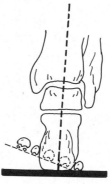

Normal        Forefoot varus

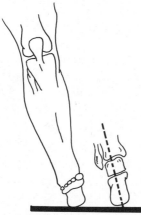
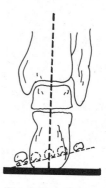

Forefoot valgus

Tibial varum

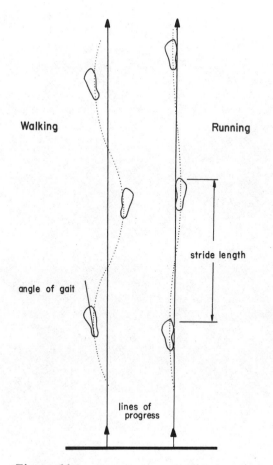

Walking

Running

stride length

angle of gait

lines of
progress

**Figure 11**
A comparison of gait patterns for walking and running.

**Figure 12**
Heel movement during the gait cycle.

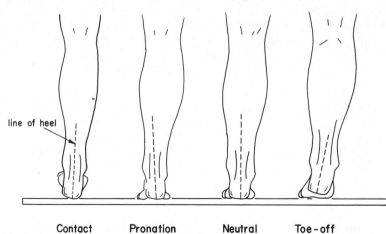

rear view

line of heel

Contact    Pronation    Neutral    Toe-off

self. The knee rotation may be easily accommodated, but if the foot pronation is excessive the resulting excessive leg rotation may give rise to knee problems.

As a result of this gait cycle, striking first on the outside of the heel and pushing off finally on the inside front of the toe, these points are the normal places of wear on running shoes. Different wear patterns on the soles of your shoes indicate that you have some difference in gait or foot placement from the norm.

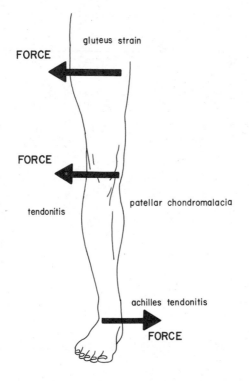

**Figure 13**
Forces exerted on the leg during pronation. Some common running injuries resulting from excessive pronation are noted.

The structurally deficient or weak foot produces problems in that its motions differ from the norm. A very common problem is excessive pronation or inward roll of the foot before toe-off. In such instances, the angle of rotation of the heel bone exceeds the normal 4°. This movement increases the forces which are transmitted up the leg, causing the joints and connective tissue to receive more than their share of stress. Figure 13 illustrates the direction of the major forces resulting from excessive pronation of the foot.

### Support thy feet

If you suspect that you have an injury that is a result of some structural imbalance, you might save yourself some money by attempting first some self-treatment. Very often runners who are plagued with bow legs or excessive heel rotation can cure their knee problems by placing a thin wedge along the inside border of the heel of the shoe (see Figure 14). This works so well for many runners that one major shoe manufacturer has built a wedge into its top line of training shoes. You can make the wedge of surgical felt or cork, covering it with some shock-absorbing insole material if necessary. The wedge has to be tailored to your own

**Figure 14**
Position of heel wedge for runners with injuries from excessive pronation (example: right foot).

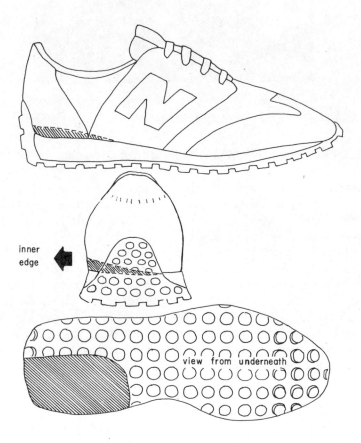

inner
edge

view from underneath

**shaped felt pad fitted inside of the heel of the shoe**

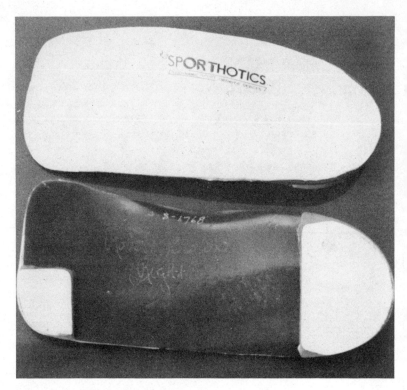

Photo 15
Orthotics. (*Photo by Skip Brown*)

needs. Find out what works by trial and error. However, it is best to begin with a minor correction and progress to larger angles if necessary. A good starting point is to make the maximum height of the wedge (on the inside of the heel) about ⅛ inch. Conventional arch supports which can be purchased in most drug stores can also provide some relief to the runner plagued by excessive pronation.

However, more and more runners are seeking professional help in dealing with their injuries. The key is in getting the right advice. Unless you know an orthopedic man who is an expert in treating runners' injuries, avoid them like the plague. In most cases they are used to treating older people with deteriorating bones or joints, or injuries caused by a sudden trauma. The torn cartilage of the halfback is a far cry from the usual runners' overuse injuries. Furthermore, orthopedic surgeons are tremendously expensive, and it can take months to get an appointment. The specialist to see is a podiatrist—preferably one knowledgeable in sports medicine. You can generally get an appointment within a week (especially if he has an interest in runners), and at least at this writing, the examination fees are not expensive. Before recommending any corrective device or treatment, the podiatrist will generally perform a complete biomechanical evaluation of the feet and legs in both weight-bearing and non-weight-bearing conditions. He will determine the precise angles of the bones, and the rotation encountered in running.

If the podiatrist determines that a foot support can be of some benefit, a casting of the foot in a neutral position is made. With this mold and the data from the biomechanical evaluation, a device is constructed that essentially fills the void between the ground and the runner's neutral foot position. This is called an "orthotic."

Orthotics are simply custom-made supports which fit into your shoes and support the foot throughout the gait cycle. They do not correct the structural imbalances of feet, but simply allow the foot to function in a more normal manner. Just like eyeglasses, they compensate for deficiencies rather than correcting them. Since they are not truly supports (the muscles and tendons still do all the work), they do not result in a weakening of any area. A commercially available pair of orthotics is shown in Photo 15. In addition to the custom-made arch support and contour designed for the individual runner, there are also heel posts and forefoot posts to control the foot movement from touchdown to toe-off.

The total cost of getting fitted with orthotics varies widely, depending on the podiatrist's fees, the type of device (rigid or semirigid), and the company that manufactures the orthotic (only rarely does the podiatrist do this himself). We know of costs between $85 and $200 for this service. Hence, selection of a podiatrist is not a decision that should be made lightly (and it may pay to shop around if you have the luxury of several to choose from). However, if orthotics are the only way to reach the training mileage required for the marathon, the serious runner will pay almost anything.

There are some other things you should know about orthotics. First of all, they don't fit in all shoes. Because of the added heel lift provided by the heel post, orthotics tend to raise the heel up and out of the shoe. Hence, you may have excessive slippage of the heel upon toe-off. You can alleviate this to some extent by removing the insole of the shoe so the device sits farther down in the shoe. If this doesn't work, you may have to change shoe styles to one with a deeper heel. Your heel may feel a bit wobbly, as the heel cup in the shoe has less control. Often this is more of a mental perception the runner has as a result of the added heel lift of the orthotic, and real reduction in stability is insignificant. Again, insole removal or a change in shoe style is the solution.

In addition, orthotics generally require a slightly larger shoe, as they effectively increase foot width by a size or two. Unless you happen to prefer one of the few brands that come in variable widths, you may have to buy a half-size larger shoe to accommodate your orthotics.

Other problems often encountered with the transition to orthotics are abnormal pressure in the arch, and blisters. If these persist, then a follow-up visit to the podiatrist is necessary for some adjustment. However, you should keep in mind that many users experience some difficulty in getting used to their inserts. Sometimes it takes several days of walking with them in your shoes before running can be tolerated. The break-in period can take several weeks. If you're not back up to normal mileage in a month, you probably require some adjustments.

Finally there is the question of racing in your orthotics. Some runners (especially the top competitors) are willing to risk the lack of foot control in favor of saving a few ounces in important races. Before you make this decision, you should be aware of the disadvantages. Most commercial orthotics are quite light, and thus you truly are not saving much weight. The combined weight of your racing flats and the orthotics is still less than that of your training flats. Furthermore, if you have been training consistently with the orthotics and suddenly remove them, the lack of support may throw your stride off just enough to offset the benefit of the weight reduction. Finally, you don't need to be told that racing a marathon is more severe than any of your training sessions. Hence, the reduction in foot control, especially as the runner tires and runs more on his heels, greatly increases the probability of injury. This is particularly true for the Achilles tendons. Combining the reduction in heel lift from the orthotics' removal with the reduced heel elevation of most racing flats results in more stretching of the Achilles tendons. Thus you are risking tendonitis or perhaps calf-muscle injuries from racing without your orthotics. Although the preceding text may seem rather negative, we think you should be made aware of the risks involved in racing without orthotics. If you decide to give it a try, select a short race rather than a marathon as an experiment. The chance of an overuse injury is less, since the race is shorter, and it will allow you to get a feel for racing without the supports to see if your cadence will be disrupted.

The following sections discuss some of the more common specific problems which plague marathoners. The reader who desires more details on specific injuries or information on the less common problems should consult Harry Hlavac's *The Foot Book* or other books listed in the back of this book.

### Runner's knee

Surveys of distance runners' injury problems have reportedly found that the knee is the most commonly injured area. Runner's knee is a catch-all term applied to all types of ailments affecting that joint. Generally it refers either to tendonitis or chondromalacia. Chondromalacia is an irritation of the cartilage underneath the kneecap (patella) which occurs when the patella does not glide smoothly in its designated groove. True chondromalacia results in a sharp, stabbing pain directly under the kneecap. It is most noticeable on hills. Other than in running, pain often appears when walking up stairs, or squatting.

122

The knee is the largest joint in the body and functions solely to produce forward movement. Any movement other than straight ahead can cause damage to the supporting tissue. The stability of the knee and resistance to abnormal sideways movements is provided primarily by the quadriceps and to some extent the hamstrings. Distance runners almost never suffer from a lack of hamstring strength. The quadriceps are another matter. It's that imbalance problem again! Strong posterior muscles, weak frontal muscles.

Other causes are either structural deficiencies or overuse, or, most likely, both. As we noted earlier, the foot is generally the culprit. In this case, overpronation or flattening causes the lower leg bone to twist inward (see Figure 12). This transmits a torque to the knee, causing the kneecap to be pulled off center and interfere with one of the chondyles (or knobs) on the thigh bone. Repeat this several thousand times during a run and you have inflammation.

In treating chondromalacia or tendonitis, the important point is to heed the early warning signals. Early treatment can spare you a long disabling knee injury. If knee pains persist over a couple of days, you likely have a more serious problem than just the occasional aches and pains of training. The initial treatment should be to reduce training to where the pain is absent or significantly reduced. This generally means cutting out the hills. In addition, try to run smoothly. Slow jogging is more jarring to the knee and may be more painful than a smoother, faster stride. Also try to avoid running on roads with a sharp crown. This forces abnormal pronation of the foot on the high side of the road. If such roads are unavoidable, keep the injured leg on the outside of the road. As a matter of interest, changing sides of the road has relieved many cases of runner's knee pain. Ice sometimes brings relief and should definitely be used if there is any swelling. Aspirin may also provide some pain relief as well as assist in the reduction of swelling. In no case should a cortisone shot be accepted without a proper diagnosis, as this simply masks the problem and doesn't provide a cure in any way.

You should also begin preventive medicine at once. Concentrate on strengthening the quadriceps. As we noted earlier, this will help stabilize the patella and prevent lateral movement. If the pain is severe, begin with straight leg raises. Lie on your back, tighten the quadriceps, and raise the leg. Hold for 15 seconds or so, then relax. Repeat this exercise several times. After a day or two, begin adding weights slowly. If your knee is not overly painful when flexed, a better exercise is to perform the weight-lifting exercise illustrated in Photo 16. Start with about 10 pounds. Lift the weight slowly to the horizontal position. Hold for about 10 seconds, lower the weight, and rest for a few seconds. Repeat until your quads begin to tire. You can add more weight as you gain strength.

If your knee isn't cured by several weeks of this treatment, your problem might be one that requires some correction of the foot plant.

You can first attempt the remedies noted earlier—heel wedges and arch supports. If that fails, a trip to the podiatrist is warranted. Never go first to a surgeon for knee problems. There have been cases of rash surgery or even internal surgical diagnosis that were unwarranted and provided no cure. Surgery should be a last resort—it is almost never needed by a runner with a runner's injury.

It is possible for the knee problems to be quite temporary. Very often a first marathon, especially if the training has been inadequate, will result in very sore knees as a primary injury. This is more due to the prolonged and unexpected knee stresses encountered than to any fundamental deficiency. Therefore if your knee soreness comes after an extended run it is worth taking things easy and gently starting to run long slow distances again to see whether the problem goes away as the muscles and tendons heal. It is not worthwhile rushing off to a podiatrist when knee and foot pain or discomfort occurs immediately after a period of prolonged stress, especially if training has been poor. However, if knee or foot pain persists for a week or ten days, then professional advice may be called for.

Photo 16
Knee extension. Weightlifting exercise for strengthening quadriceps muscles. (*Photo by Cindy Brown*)

## Achilles tendonitis

Ever since Homer related the tragedy of Achilles' death, when Paris wounded him in his one vulnerable spot, his heel, we have known of the peculiar susceptibility of the tendon which joins the calf muscle to the heel bone.

Injuries to the Achilles tendon rate high among runners' common ailments, second only to knee injuries (14 percent versus 18 percent with injuries serious enough to halt running). Unfortunately this tendonitis can be more wretched, since the cure is very slow and there is some reason to think that once you have had Achilles tendonitis then you may always have it. It is therefore very important to avoid it in the first place.

Since you are aiming at the marathon and to some extent changing and increasing your running habits, it is as well to list possible causes of Achilles tendonitis before discussing remedies. It is principally due to lack of flexibility in the leg muscles, which is then aggravated by the application of some particular stress. When we train we are shortening the trained muscles, and they can transmit stress to the joining tendons. The Achilles is particularly susceptible because of the strength that is developed in the calf muscles. In addition, excessive pronation of the foot without proper support by the shoe can also transmit additional stresses to this tendon. Either way, we are our own worst enemy by not doing something about the problem *before* it occurs.

As you add mileage in the pre-marathon period, and as the leg muscles are trained, the tendon and calf should also be stretched to allow for the additional loads they will have to carry. This stretching (see Chapter 2) has to be done before and after your training to have most effect. Don't wait for tendon pains before beginning a stretching routine. Your training shoes are also important in preventing Achilles tendonitis. Be sure they have adequate heel lift (see Chapter 5). In addition, the heel of your shoe should provide proper support and not allow the heel to wobble. Since the tendon is vulnerable during sprinting and while running up hills, if your new marathon training calls for either of these you should increase the stretching, and be prepared to back off on both activities if any tendon discomfort appears.

Joan Ullyot has dramatically and accurately described a diagnosis of Achilles tendonitis, which is worth quoting: "Inflammation usually appears insidiously over a period of days. The area is usually tender (try squeezing an inflamed Achilles tendon and you'll see what I mean). Aspirin characteristically brings dramatic relief within 15 minutes. Inflammation tends to feel better on motion, worse after prolonged rest. If you get up in the morning and have trouble limping to the bathroom, and yet can get along quite well around the house after a while, your problem is diagnosed."

Often this injury is therefore not very well cured by rest, since movement lubricates the tendon sheath. However, the problem will only get worse unless the cause is removed, so it is best to cut out any interval training or hill work, keeping the runs short and at a gentle pace. Stretching of the calf and tendon should be instituted, but not to the extreme where pain is felt.

For mild Achilles tendonitis, take aspirin to reduce pain and inflammation, keep running gently, and reduce the specific loads of mileage, hills, and intervals (the last two entirely) until the pain has gone. You might add a heel lift of about ⅛ inch inside your shoes to relieve some of the strain on the Achilles tendon. If caught early this remedy might take two weeks.

However, if the pain is ignored then the tendonitis can get worse, all the way to tearing of the tendon fibers and possibly even a complete break in the tendon. The cure may then require surgical repair and a long period of rest and rehabilitation.

This extreme problem is unlikely to happen to you, since as a runner the pain would force you to reduce your activity if you tried to persist through the milder injury stages without remedy. In any case, even before pain, it is worth making only gradual changes to your training regimen to avoid tendonitis. If at any stage you intend, for example, to start some speed training on a track, don't imagine that you can run 60-second quarters right away without something giving. In this case it may well be the Achilles tendon. At the first sign of pain, use cold to reduce the inflammation during the first half-hour after exercise. Then for future training sessions take the advice we have outlined above.

Treat Achilles tendonitis as one of the more serious of injuries that you can contract as a runner. It certainly cut our Trojan War hero's sporting career short!

### Cracking under the stress

Stress fractures are another injury which is not uncommon in marathoners. Stress fractures are small hairline cracks in the bone which usually result from the continuous pounding of road running. The majority of stress fractures occur in the foot, with the metatarsals (the bones which form the ball of the foot) the most common location. There is generally no specific trauma that triggers this injury. The pain increases gradually and grows to be more severe with increased training. The pain is deep beneath the skin and very sensitive to pressure. As the condition worsens, there may be some local swelling. A stress fracture can only be verified by X-rays, but in the initial stages of the injury, the crack may not be observable.

If you have symptoms of stress fracture, treatment should commence at once, using ice on the sore area. Ullyot recommends the use of a felt pad to relieve some of the pressure on the injured area and an elastic bandage to hold the foot bones together. Running should be cut back drastically. If the pain worsens, a rest period is in order and you should consult a podiatrist. The important thing is to begin the healing process at once to keep the fracture from growing into a bone break. Stress fractures heal much faster than broken bones.

## Foot problems

As you would expect, foot problems also rank high on the list of runners' complaints. These can range from heel to toe, and can have such exotic names as plantar fascia or be as simple as a blister. The foot is a complex structure of twenty-six bones and numerous ligaments and muscles which interact in the running process. The biomechanics of foot movement are quite complex when examined in detail, and the numerous abnormalities in foot structure and function would require a separate volume to treat in sufficient detail. To give specific advice on any single injury could be misleading, because of these complex interactions. However, for many of the injuries related to structural deficiencies and overuse, the general principles described earlier are advisable. Reduce training and avoid hills and speed work. Use ice on the inflamed area, and institute a program of stretching and strengthening exercises to reduce muscle imbalances. If you suspect your injury is due to a structural problem, home-made wedges and arch supports can be tried. However, if these self-cures don't produce relief, your best bet is to consult a sports podiatrist. There are a couple of common problems encountered by most marathoners at one time or another which are simple to treat. These are discussed in the following sections.

## Blister bugaboo

All of us have seen those depressing photographs taken in the basement of the Prudential Center after the Boston Marathon, where runners are lying on cots having their feet attended by the staff of podiatrists. The scene reminds one of a Red Cross tent on a battleground. Most of these doctors are treating that most common of injuries—the blister.

Most marathoners experience blisters at one stage or another, whether from new shoes, the heat, or just a crease in the socks. Most are very minor inconveniences, and only rarely are they serious enough to restrict training. A blister is simply a separation of the layers of skin as a result of friction. Other than in the marathon itself, if you feel one coming on, it is best to stop and try to remedy the situation at once. Large blisters are more difficult to treat, and those that burst open are more susceptible to infection.

In treating blisters, first clean the area well, using soap and water and

127

then an antiseptic. If the blister is small and causes no pain it is best to ignore it. Chances are it will dry up and vanish in a few days. If it is larger than ½ inch and in an area that makes running painful, you can puncture it with a sterile needle, draining the fluid and leaving the overlying skin in place. Before running again, apply some sort of protection. A Band-Aid is good for smaller blisters. However, if a blister is large or painful, a protective doughnut of moleskin surrounding it will relieve some of the pressure. Cover this with a bandage as well. Take care not to let any adhesive tape come in contact with the skin on top of the blister; leave the dead skin in place as long as possible to provide protection for the new growth underneath. If the area of redness around the blister starts to increase in size, an infection could be developing and professional treatment should be obtained.

To avoid blisters in the first place, always break your shoes in with short runs—especially your racing flats. Never start a marathon with a brand-new pair of shoes, even if you've worn that size and style for years. You're likely to find a slight defect in the stitching which may ruin an otherwise good race. Indeed, so that racing shoes are not a shock to the feet, we always take a short training run a couple of days earlier in the shoes in which we will run the marathon. This enables the feet to feel the racing flats ahead of time. This practice is a good one even for tried and tested racing shoes.


## Blackened toenails

Rather grandly, this injury is given the name "sub-ungal hematoma" by the medical profession. However, this badge of marathon runners is simply a sign of bleeding leading to a blood clot below the toenail, and it can be fearfully painful.

It is so prevalent among marathon runners that Jack Scaff, organizer of the Honolulu Marathon, suggested that in view of the new popularity of marathon running, he would expect someone soon to be marketing a new, chic toenail polish color of black and blue! Then true runners wouldn't be quite so noticeable around the pool.

The remedy, of course, is simple. It is important to wear racing shoes with sufficient room so that in the rush of the race the toes still have sufficient clearance when the feet are driven forward. The same effect is not so critical during training, when the urgency and drive of the race are absent, so it is possible that you may need shoes a half-size larger for racing. In addition to sufficiently large shoes, keep your toenails quite short so that they don't take any impact. This is one of those things to be added to your preparatory checklist before a marathon. Finally, for additional protection you can wear comfortably thick socks to provide some increased shock absorbency.

With these preventive measures you should not injure your toenails.

128

However, if you do, there are certain reliefs you can provide. You should not touch the affected toenail for 24 hours in order to allow the fluid to accumulate. By this time the pressure of the fluid will sometimes be causing quite intense pain and you will have to keep things away from a very sore appendage. Now, however, we have been able to quite painlessly relieve the pressure, drain the fluid and possibly blood, and ease the pain miraculously in one simple operation. This procedure is simple and works quite well for us, but one must get a doctor's advice or instruction before proceeding.

We take a sterile needle (put first in hot water and then in an antiseptic) and gently insert it down beneath the nail to the blood clot. It sounds as if this action itself should be painful in the extreme. It isn't at all and the needle can be inserted so slowly that even if there were pain you could simply stop. We have always found the tissue to be inert. The needle forms a drainage hole through which the fluid and blood can be squeezed after the needle is removed. Finally, clean with more antiseptic. The pain you had been having from the pressure of the fluid will vanish immediately. You may have to repeat this procedure the next day if more fluid or blood accumulates, but twice is usually quite adequate.

You can, of course, have this done by a doctor. In this case the same process is carried out, although then it is usual to bore a tiny hole through the nail into the affected area. Personally, we like our own solution.

If you don't relieve the accumulation of fluid, or do it too late, then besides the immediate pain, you will also lose that toenail eventually. You may, of course, lose it anyway if the original damage was severe enough. However, losing a toenail is no tragedy. It doesn't look very sightly, since it will become discolored and eventually it will be forced out as a new nail grows beneath it. In about two months you will simply be able to remove the old nail without any hurt being incurred.

This is a small injury with no serious consequences, but it is much easier to avoid than to bear the pain of the sore toe for a day. We have never thought much of being in the fashion and so we do all we can to keep our toenails pink!

### Bumps and bruises

Another problem often encountered during training is a bone bruise. This results from a sharp blow to the foot, often caused by landing on a stone. The seriousness of this injury depends on the degree of damage to the periosteum, or covering around the bone. Generally there is just some inflammation and soreness which may require a protective heel pad for the next few days. Use ice to relieve the pain and swelling. However, if the periosteum is broken, a bone spur may develop. If the area becomes red and a lump develops at the injury site, you should consult a podiatrist.

129

# A stitch in time

Stitches, or severe side pains, are a common complaint of the beginning jogger or novice runner. Only rarely are they a problem for marathoners. Stitches are simply spasms in the diaphragm or lower abdomen which produce sharp intense pain. Breathing hurts, and the runner can be forced to slow down, or even stop, if the pains persist. In addition to the immediate pain, the soreness following the initial cramp may persist into the next day, thus affecting future runs as well. They generally result from improper breathing technique, or a sudden change in respiration rate.

The concept of "belly breathing" has recently been publicized in the running literature as if it were some new scientific discovery. But in fact, most experienced runners breathe this way naturally (or at least when running near race pace). The phrase "belly breathing" was coined to emphasize the motion of the abdominal muscles when breathing. Very simply, when inhaling, the diaphragm pulls downward to suck air into the lungs. Concurrent with this motion, the abdominal wall moves outward. The reverse action occurs when exhaling. However, most nonrunners do just the opposite. They suck their tummy in when inhaling. This reduces the volume of air being drawn into the lungs. This habit can carry over as a person takes up an exercise program, like running. However, as one advances to become an experienced competitor, this habit unconsciously vanishes, as it is grossly inefficient in oxygen uptake.

This is not to say that marathoners are immune to stitches. They can strike even the best at any time. Two common causes of the stitch are a sudden change to anaerobic running, and leaning back while running down hills. In both of these situations, the diaphragm and abdominals are strained more than normal, and may be more prone to spasm. If you are an experienced runner and still suffer from such pains, you might do well to pay attention to the following aspects of your training.

As we noted in Chapter 2, efficient downhill running form attempts to keep the body perpendicular to the road surface. Leaning back wastes energy (it actually slows you down), as well as making you more susceptible to the stitch. The added stretching from leaning back coupled with a high respiration rate (especially if you have just finished climbing the other side of the hill) is a common cause of abdominal muscle spasms. Hence, avoid the urge to lean back and relax on the downhills.

If stitches plague you in races, it may be your training program that needs to be modified. If you train exclusively on long slow distance, then the increased respiration of racing may trigger the stitch. A remedy for this problem is to incorporate some anaerobic running into your daily training. This need not be as rigorous as intervals, or hill workouts. Just a few bursts periodically during your long runs may be all that is necessary.

On rare occasions, runners may experience pains in the chest, some-what higher than the location of a stitch. These are usually just a slight straining of the chest-wall muscles. However, if it is a pressing sort of pain, it would be wise to consult your doctor, just to ensure that there is no heart involvement.

## That aching back

Often when the marathon aspirant increases his mileage, he gets it in the back. Lower-back pain (often referred to as sciatica) is a common complaint among beginning marathoners who are just venturing beyond the 3-mile-per-day training level. Sciatic nerve pain can also cause pains in the hip as well as continuous sharp pains shooting down the leg. Lower back pain is frequently a symptom of muscle imbalance. In this case, it is usually the overdeveloped lower-back muscles versus weak abdominal muscles.

For most runners, this is rarely a lengthy, disabling injury. In gen-eral, the treatment is twofold—strengthen the abdominal muscles and stretch the lower back. Bent-leg sit-ups are the best abdominal-strengthen-ing exercise we know. Note that we said *bent-leg* sit-ups. If you keep your legs straight you are actually using the lower-back muscles to help pull you up, and the benefit to the abdominals is less. Two of the best stretch-ing exercises for the lower back are toe touchers and the backover (see Chapter 2, Photos 8 and 9).

If the preceding treatment is ineffective, the problem may be more than muscle-strength imbalances. You may have a structural imbalance in the legs (one short leg), or a slight pelvic tilt which is producing the back pain. In this case, professional help is required.

## GI blues

A marathoner's physical problems are not all confined to the appendages of motion. Runners can also be plagued by a plethora of other ills, most notably in the gastrointestinal tract. These are generally a result of the stress of marathon training disrupting the body's normal functions. Items such as milk, meat, and coffee, which normally cause no difficulty, can become a source of discomfort as the training level increases. Each runner has his or her own peculiar problems with different foods and eat-ing habits and to list them here would be indigestible. The only advice we can offer is to experiment and find what foods suit you best and what ones bother you. We do recommend that you do not try drastically dif-ferent food the night before a marathon. Stick with foods to which you are accustomed. For more on special dietary needs and pre-race diets, consult Chapter 3. If you have a truly persistent problem that repeatedly

131

hinders training, we suggest consulting a physician. For these types of problems, hopefully, his advice will not be to stop running.

The tension and anxiety just preceding a race can also trigger problems which are unnoticed in training. Such difficulties as upset stomach or diarrhea on race day are more frequently due to nerves than food. For this reason, we generally fast for at least 10 hours before the race.

## Too hot to trot

Hyperthermia, or an elevated body temperature, can be deadly. Several runners have died as a result of not heeding the body's warning signals and overextending themselves in hot-weather races. Heat-related injuries can affect *any* runner in *any* kind of shape during a race or even an everyday workout.

Heat injuries are often divided into two degrees of severity. The first stage is heat exhaustion, in which the runner may actually collapse because of excessive fluid loss. The symptoms are pale, clammy skin and normal to subnormal skin temperature. Replenishment of body fluids is the recommended treatment. The problem can become life-threatening if it advances to a heat-stroke condition. In this second stage, the skin is dry and red, and at an elevated temperature. Other symptoms of impending heat stroke are nausea, dizziness, and difficulty in breathing. Speech is likely to be incoherent. Treatment for heat-stroke victims should be immediate lowering of the body temperature by immersion in cold water. If this is not done immediately, brain damage or death can result from the elevated body temperature.

Unfortunately, unless you know what to look for, you may run into heat exhaustion without even knowing it. Because of the extreme danger of heat stroke, it is important to recognize the symptoms of the onset of heat exhaustion and treat them immediately. If you feel any of these symptoms during a workout or race, you should try to obtain fluids at once, and then find a cool, shaded spot to rest.

Replacement of fluids during a race is essential! Chapter 4 discusses fluid balances in more detail, but for completeness the key points to be kept in mind when racing marathons are as follows:

- *Prepare for fluid loss before the race*, by drinking 10 to 20 ounces of fluid within 15 minutes of the start. This provides a hedge against the perspiration losses to come and ensures that the body has not been partially depleted during pre-race sweating.
- *Drink fluids frequently during the race*, 3 to 6 ounces every 15 minutes, if possible. Never pass up an aid station. Stop if you must to ensure that you get several ounces of fluid at each aid station.
- *Splash water all over your body* during the race to aid in cooling. Your clothing is also important, as discussed in Chapter 5.

The best prevention is acclimatization to hot-weather running. Physiologically, this does three things:

- Circulation to the skin is improved, thus enabling the body to reject heat more efficiently (a marathoner sweats easily).
- The body's perspiration capacity is increased to allow for the additional cooling required in hot-weather running; and the sensitivity to sweating is increased so that perspiration begins at a lower temperature (a marathoner sweats earlier).
- The electrolyte loss in the kidneys and through perspiration is reduced.

For those of us who train regularly in the summer heat, acclimatization occurs naturally. By July, we are used to the heat, and while it may slow us down, we know how our bodies react to this added stress and can adjust our training programs and race pacing accordingly. The real danger from heat occurs in the spring, where temperature changes may come on suddenly. Such an instance was the 1976 Boston Marathon, where after a relatively cool spring in the Northeast, the runners were confronted with temperatures in the 90s on race day. Most of the runners were not heat-acclimated and suffered tremendously during the race (as illustrated in Chapter 4). This experience taught both of us a lesson. You should begin preparing yourself for such instances by heat training in the early spring. Even though it may still be cool outside, you can heat-train by wearing extra clothing which insulates the body and creates a hot miniclimate within the clothing. Of course you should be careful when doing this on long runs in cold weather, as the water loss may soak the clothes and thus leave you shivering. Heat training can be miserable on warm spring days, as the added clothing can turn even the easiest run into a laborious effort. However, it may well pay off should a hot day coincide with your spring marathon.

You should not heat-train every day in the spring. The body must be allowed to adapt gradually to the heat stress. In the early phases of heat training the body can require more than 24 hours to replace the lost fluid and electrolytes. Hence, three days a week is adequate. Studies have shown that during continuous training in the heat, runners become acclimated in seven to ten days. It takes somewhat longer if you are heat-training in cold weather on alternate days. Our suggestion is to begin some sort of heat training in early March to be prepared for scorchers like Boston in 1976. If you are not heat-acclimated and the marathon turns out to be on a warm day, we would recommend not racing that day unless you are a veteran of many marathons, and even then, ease off on the early pace.

Once the hot weather arrives, be sure you replace the fluids and electrolytes lost through sweating each day, to avoid a gradual depletion which may influence the daily training. One way to avoid a gradual dehydration during summer training is to keep a record of your morning weight. If it drops more than 2 pounds over 24 hours you may still be dehydrated from the previous day's run. Although most of us replace the sodium losses through salting our foods or eating seasoned snacks, the replacement of other trace elements like potassium, magnesium, and calcium is also very important. Be sure your diet contains foods which are high in those minerals (see Chapter 3 for some food ideas). Avoid taking concentrated tablets of these minerals (such as salt tablets), as they require significant water to assimilate and if insufficient fluid is ingested they can further upset the fluid/electrolyte balance.

## It may not be old age

The following is a personal example of a common handicap which Graham encountered and was able to diagnose and overcome.

Since starting competitive running in late 1974, he had been quite proud of his over-40 performance, especially since it steadily improved at all distances from the mile to the marathon. Naturally, training mileage of long slow distance increased, and there was a very direct relationship between this mileage and improved times. Monthly mileage increased from 100 to 300 miles, and 10-kilometer times correspondingly improved by some 6½ minutes, or more than a minute per mile.

However in the second half of 1976 he had difficulty in maintaining those times despite relatively constant milage. At the time he feared that this might indicate that age had at last caught up with him. Runners he had happily beaten in races months earlier were now careening past him in race after race. It was a most dispiriting period. His running diary contains comments like "Legs OK—spirit not!" and "No specific aches or pains but my legs were tired."

One curious fact, though, was that marathon performances did not show quite the same disastrous trend. In late 1976 he had a series of five good sub-3-hour marathons, including a personal record right at the nadir of the poor 10-kilometer results. In fact his marathon pace turned out to be *better* than the pace in short races! It almost looked as though he would have to prepare for 10-kilometer events with pre-marathon routines. The main problem, however, seemed to be loss of motivation.

After a little respite in the winter of 1976–77, a small rejuvenation, things got even worse by midyear and it looked as though he was back to pre-1974 shuffling. Mentally, running was a pain. He began stopping on hills during training runs and rationalizing that he didn't need to suffer. At Boston, though he managed a respectable 3:04 overall, he did quit three times at 15, 17, and 20 miles, and only the thought of the meat-wagon alternative drove him back on the course. The crux came when he began to tolerate low performances, stop on hills during races, and then even welcome a rest without a hill in sight.

134

Then in August in a regular medical checkup he was diagnosed as having a low hemoglobin count, down about 30 percent from what it had been before running. This is much more than the usual relative count reduction experienced by distance runners because the plasma volume has increased with exercise. Thus after a series of tests to rule out possible internal bleeding it became apparent that he had iron-deficiency anemia, probably due to changes he had made recently in his diet.

From his childhood he had been a meat-eater, but since taking up running after a "rest" of some nineteen years he had drifted away from muscle meat, since he disliked the "day-after" feeling resulting from slow meat digestion. He became more and more of a practicing vegetarian from mid-1976 onward. In 1977 he recognized at last that he was a vegetarian, even to the extent of ordering the blah versions obtainable on regular airline flights.

Vegetarianism, however, is more than just avoidance of meat. What he had not done was to arrange a balanced vegetarian diet with the proper intake of nutrients, including proteins and, in his case, iron. So after diagnosis he added lots of leafy vegetables and vegetable protein to his diet, and he also took an iron supplement. Successive blood tests showed a return of the hemoglobin count to previous levels. Iron supplements, however, should not be taken without first consulting a doctor.

While this was going on, he continued running at the same rate and, amazingly, after about a month a quite sudden improvement occurred. His motivation returned. The old killer instinct was back in the race, and many times he didn't even notice hills that he had stopped on several times a few weeks earlier. His 10-kilometer times reduced to where they would have been on the basis of training effect alone without the dietary hiatus. In one month he established personal records in all distances between 2 miles and the marathon, and he went on to race five marathons in five months in late 1977, all under his previous PR of late 1976! You can imagine the ̃exhilarating effect it had on his self-confidence. The effects are shown in Figure 15.

In discussing the problem with other runners he found that it was a relatively common problem and not necessarily associated with age. He found young and older, men and women, with the same anemia problem, and they all seemed to have had the same depressing period of uncertainty and performance loss, followed by an exhilarating restoration of ability.

If you go through such a patch of low motivation and tired running, it just may be that you have the same problem. It would be worthwhile to have a blood test—a good clinic can have a short diagnostic test done in 15 minutes. If you have recently changed your diet, then you ought to review Chapter 3, and don't make the mistake Graham made. To emphasize what it says there, it is particularly important to supply the body with the correct balance of minerals: calcium, phosphorus, iron, and iodine. Iron is at issue in the case of anemia.

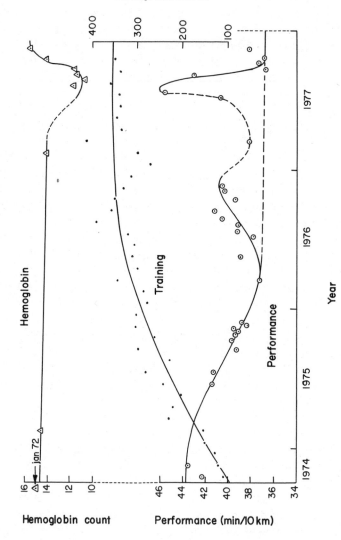

**Figure 15**
Effect of hemoglobin level on 10-kilometer race performance.

Although we know quite well that many women are anemic for physical reasons, it turns out that 10 to 12 percent of men in the United States also suffer from an anemic condition. Good sources of iron are green leafy vegetables such as lettuce, turnip greens, chard, cabbage, and spinach, and dried peas. Raisins, nuts, dried fruits, and prunes help for snacks. Check with your physician to ensure that any low hemoglobin problem is connected with diet, rather than a physical problem such as an ulcer. In that case, changes in eating habits will require expert advice and the ulcer will require treatment.

In the meantime, take heart—a curious sudden drop in performance may be curable. It may not be old age!

### Running noses

Having discussed the most common, and some uncommon, physical problems of distance runners, we need to consider the most ordinary of illnesses—the common cold and the flu. While running may make you a much healthier individual, it does not provide immunity to such viruses. In fact, when you are training heavily in marathon preparation, your reserves to combat infection are reduced, and you may be *more* susceptible to illness. Beware of the signals of overuse and heed their warning, particularly in the winter when colds and flu are more prevalent.

While we all respond differently to these infections, we can provide some observations based on our experiences. If we contract a cold, we find that the symptoms are not as severe as those of the nonrunning population. Only rarely does a cold cause us to miss a day of running—although we do reduce the distance and intensity. In fact, gentle running with a cold seems to help as it often relieves congestion and sinus headaches. Nevertheless, even though the symptoms are not as severe, we find they often tend to drag on as a minor annoyance and discomfort for many days. This is probably caused by the fact that we continue to train with colds. After the initial days when the symptoms are the worst, the training gradually returns to its normal level. Thus, in our anxiousness to get back to full steam, we are not allowing the proper recovery period to completely dispose of the infection. Generally, however, relapses are not a problem, and the annoyance of a running nose for a few days is offset by the mental satisfaction of getting in the normal mileage.

Running when you have the flu is another matter. Our personal guidelines are: if you have a fever, it is best not to train. There is evidence that overextending yourself while you have the flu can lead to heart problems—the last thing we need. In each of the last several years, a parade of flu viruses has invaded the U.S.—the Hong Kong, the swine, the Russian—you name it! With each new virus there seems to be a massive immunization program. We have not taken any flu shots, and our experience has been excellent. On the rare occasions when the bug strikes, we

# Table 12
## Injury checklist

| Injury | Treatment | Effect on running |
|---|---|---|
| BLISTER (Separation of skin layers by fluids) | Cold compress, followed by sterile drainage; relieve stress to affected area | Insignificant, depends on the location and pain |
| BURSITIS* (Inflamed fluid protective sac) | Protect area after removing the source of irritation | A few days |
| CONTUSION OR BRUISE (Damage to blood vessels beneath skin surface) | Cold compress in first 24 hours, heat application thereafter | Insignificant to a few days |
| DISLOCATION* (Bone separation at a joint) | Immobilization and support, physical therapy | 2–4 weeks |
| FRACTURE, COMPLETE* (Complete bone break) | Immobilization and support | 6–8 weeks |
| FRACTURE, STRESS* (Partial crack in bone) | Support and much limited activity | 6–8 weeks |
| NEURITIS* (Nerve pinching or irritation) | Relief of interference; no cortisone unless the pain is severe | Days to weeks with slow buildup in recovery |
| PERIOSTITIS (Bone bruise) | Protection of area; may require professional attention | Days to few weeks |
| SKIN CALLUSES (Thickening of skin for protection) | Correct the reason for the need of protection by better shoes or proper orthotics | Insignificant |
| SPRAIN (Ligament tear) | Apply ice to area and then immobilize (may need professional treatment) | Days to weeks |
| STRAIN (Muscle or tendon tear) | Apply ice to area, use support as necessary | Days to weeks |
| SUB-UNGAL HEMATOMA (Blood clot under nail) | Drainage of blood and fluid, protection of nail from pressure | None to 1 or 2 days at most |
| TENDONITIS (Inflammation of tendon sheath and, in extreme cases, calcification) | Cold compress in first 24 hours, heat application thereafter | Reduced running to tolerable discomfort/pain level; no hills or sprinting |

* Professional advice is mandatory in these cases.

don't find the disability to be crippling. Since we first began marathon running, neither of us has acquired such a bad case of flu that we were forced to spend a week in bed. Our theory is that the excellent conditioning acquired in marathon training allows us to combat the virus more effectively (once the strain of running has been removed). While we recover more quickly from the flu, the disease does significantly offset training. We accept this and listen to our bodies in returning to normal training levels. Even though the number of days when running is missed entirely may be few (often only one), the aftereffects of the flu are quite evident. Generally, an overall weakness and lack of energy persists for several days. While it is probably alright to run when the temperature has returned to normal, the activity should be restricted to easy jogging at a reduced mileage. Be wary of an overanxiousness to return to a full training load.

One year, one of us contracted a virus—almost a full flu—in the last two days before Boston. He decided to run anyway since it seemed wasteful to discard three months of mileage invested in the race. Race day dawned. The symptoms were minimal and on the line had apparently completely disappeared! The race was not a good one, probably due to a number of things including late race sun, but the cold/flu didn't reappear and apparently didn't effect the race. However the next morning the flu symptoms were back in spades and the sickness took its normal course! It was almost as if the adrenaline of the race had provided a one-day immunity.

Our advice is run gently with a cold, do *not* run with a fever. Take time to recover. At all times monitor your body in returning to training.

This chapter is not meant to be a complete guide to running-related injuries and problems. Its purpose is to introduce you to the basic concepts—particularly those of overstressing, muscle imbalance, and structural deficiencies—and to make you aware of the need to practice preventive medicine in your everyday training. We have just tried to present most of the common problems which marathoners encounter, the typical causes of these conditions, and what type of treatment is generally recommended. Table 12 (adapted from Hlavac's *The Foot Book*) summarizes the various injuries in order of their severity and lists some pertinent data about each condition.

# Chapter 7
# **The Great Day**
## The Race

All your training, all the miles that you have run over the past weeks, all your careful and restrained diet, and all the words you've read about the marathon, eventually lead to a single day: the day of the race.

For the past week it seems that the race has been in your mind constantly, even if you've run tens of marathons before. The slowing down of training ending with a couple of days of rest, and the changing diet and the carbohydrate loading in some form, have told your body that something special is about to occur. Thinking about it, talking to friends about their marathons or their intentions in this one, and reading about it have told your mind about its testing time to come. Then the day dawns, and it seems that still everything has to be done before the starting time.

### The ritual

Most marathon runners settle into an almost religious ritual on the day of the race. The same things have to be done, in the same order, and with the same careful attention to detail, as if performance will be drastically affected by one missed item. Thus the best way to explain what should be done on race morning is to explain what we do. Table 13 gives a bare-bones checklist of things to be done, though it can't communicate the mystical quality of the actual procedure.

Even for a noontime race start like Boston, the day begins early. There are clothes to be laid out and vital necessities to be gathered together, and of course the body has to be tested to see how it feels.

When you first awake, the ankles stretch to test whether any residual aches and pains remain, the knee is surreptitiously bent to test for the old injury, and if these first examinations are passed it is worth getting up. Then a quick visit to the toilet and back to do some preliminary stretching in more serious intent—leaning against the wall of the motel, and lying to stretch back and hamstrings, and then a few quadriceps exercises. Just a quick runthrough, noting that there is still an appalling amount of stiffness. Maybe later stretching will clear that!

If you are like us you may not eat at all on race morning, although others seem to do quite well on an early pancake breakfast. We are more

140

concerned with emptying the bowels, and if this is difficult because we are tense, we have even been known to drink glasses of hot water to get things moving before we leave the luxury of the motel toilet.

Dressing is very much a ritual. Dress is usually the tried and tested clothes that you wore last time. There may be variations for weather, so the weather is carefully tested too. A white T-shirt to reflect the sun's rays is a good idea. Comfortable shorts that don't rub, the old racing flats or possibly your most comfortable training shoes—all require final selection from the multiple clothes that you brought just in case. Socks, if you wear them, have to be very carefully applied, each one smoothed exactly over the toes, making sure that no crease remains to build into a crippling ridge later in the race. Then come those favorite racing shoes themselves, eased on into the right position: laces carefully tied so that they're not so loose as to let the shoe move but not so tight that they cramp the feet, which swell a little in the later stages of the run. Finally, you double-tie the laces so that they won't come loose some 15 miles down the road.

Then the necessities have to be gathered together. Possibly a bottle of some drink preparation for a final drink before the gun, a jar of Vaseline to coat the irritation points before starting, your pre-registration card, or in some cases your racing number and safety pins, the key to your room, and possibly a bag to carry the sweats and other things to the finish line; all have to be accounted for. Each race is a little different. At Boston, for example, Graham tucks a dime in the fold of his socks in order to phone home immediately after the finish from the basement of the Pru-

## Table 13
The pre-race checklist

| 1  | CLOTHES TO WEAR   | Shirt, shorts, jock/bra, socks, sweatband, gloves (smooth out those socks!) |
|----|-------------------|------------------------------------------------------------------------------|
| 2  | SHOES             | Don't forget to double-tie them                                              |
| 3  |                   | Race number pinned carefully on the front                                    |
| 4  | STRETCHING        | A little on awaking, and for 10 to 15 minutes before the race start          |
| 5  |                   | Food is optional but should be light and not within two hours of the race    |
| 6  | TOILET            |                                                                              |
| 7  | VASELINE          | Groin, armpits, and nipples                                                  |
| 8  |                   | Liquid in the last 15 minutes before the gun                                 |
| 9  |                   | Key to the motel tied into your shoelaces for security                       |
| 10 |                   | Do you need any money—phone or transport charges?                            |
| 11 |                   | Something to carry your belongings from start to finish; it should be labeled with your name and if possible race number |
| 12 | PRE-RACE WARM UP  |                                                                              |

dential Center. Also this is the only race in which he wears a stopwatch because of the difficulty of getting a final time at the end (intermediate splits, too!). Sometimes the mind seems to worry about these small things far more than the coming race. Perhaps that is its own safety mechanism.

Then finally before leaving the motel, that inevitable last chance at the toilet. Maybe the hot water has worked by now!

There is usually some form of transport to the start, and then you start to meet the other runners. All of them are lean, hungry, and above all, clearly the fittest people you have ever seen. In comparison, you feel weak, fat, old, incapable, undertrained, overtrained, ill: Choose your own excuse.

However, curiously you find in talking to these tigers that they are all suffering from some much more serious disability than yours. One is just recovering from a cold or pneumonia, another from a severe Achilles-tendon problem. One runner hasn't been able to run more than 60 miles a week ever since he broke his leg in the spring, while another caps this by saying that his back is so bad that this will be his last marathon before having to go to surgery. Fortunately for you, everyone is actually ill, so you shouldn't feel so bad after all.

You make sure your running number is not stiff enough to irritate during the run by bending and dog-earing it. You carefully pin your number on the front of the shirt, taking care not to hide the message that you may have on the front. We all want to be individuals, and the need to be recognized, even ever so transiently, by onlookers is very strong. (We make absolutely sure that the name of our running club, Human Energy, is clear and visible for all to see.)

Then the Vaseline is applied to the groin rubbing points, to the nipples, and possibly under the armpits, to avoid that excruciating late-in-the-race pain and possibly bleeding that comes with unrelieved rubbing. One runner we know of empties a full jar of Vaseline into his socks before the race, so much that it squeezes through the wool into his shoes when he crams his foot in as well as the Vaseline. He swears he never gets any blisters! However, we have never gotten a bad blister either, and we don't use any tape or Vaseline on the feet.

After these activities, you may have to line up for the toilet again. Boston used to hold the record for inadequate toilets; about eight for 2,000 runners, although this has improved slightly to about twenty for 4,000 plus. The lines at the toilets are conversational areas for comparing training regimes and results with other runners, so the time spent is not entirely lost. Then, of course, any woods or bushy country around the starting point will also be brought into play for last-minute relief. (One should be careful to avoid despoiling other people's property, of course.)

Eventually there is a call to the line. If it is a warm or humid day, it is worth taking a last drink within 15 minutes of the gun. Taken at that time it will not have time to reappear embarrassingly as a call of nature, but will contribute to your very necessary fluid reserves. It is time now to get rid of belongings, probably in a bag carefully labeled and given to an attendant to await you at the finish, and move to the starting line. The race will soon be on.

### The race

One of the difficulties experienced by new marathoners is getting caught up with the chase. They are astonished, when they hear the first-mile time, that they have run so fast. Now the difficulty is backing off and striking a pace which you can hold for the whole distance. It is very important not to go out too fast; it's just as dangerous as insufficient preparation. Both can lead to hitting the wall.

Your initial pace should be approximately 15 seconds a mile faster than your expected average for the whole distance. This means that if you expect to run a 3½-hour marathon, which is 8 minutes a mile almost exactly, you should start at about 7:45 a mile. If you expect to finish in 3 hours, or 6:51.9 a mile, you should start at about 6:35. Then again, if you feel that you are capable of 2 hours and 45 minutes or 6:17.6 a mile, then about an even 6:00 a mile would be an efficient starting pace. Of course this is a rule of thumb, but a workable one, especially when you are not yet experienced enough to know your pace.

Remember that in a marathon, running fast to start with is not money in the bank. Rather it is a short-term debt still to be repaid in the second half of the race, past 20 miles.

Figure 16 shows how marathons may be paced, both well and badly. The curve shows mile pace over the course of the 26 miles 385 yards from the faster start to the slowing down at the end. The curve marked "Maryland 1974" is a beginner's marathon, slowing down all the way with a little recovery over a period of downhill at about 8½ miles. The wall was hit at about 14 miles, although the gradual slowdown enabled the runner to finish in 3:38. The curve marked "Masters 1975" shows a classic wall at 16 miles because the runner started out far too fast. However, the curve marked "Skylon 1975" illustrates an efficient marathon, starting a little slower and having enough energy to pick up speed at the end. This one was run in 2:58. The unwise Masters 1975 curve, run with almost the same preparation, was finished in 3:17. The unwise start incurred a repayment of some 19 minutes!

Figure 17 illustrates two other cases. Mission Bay 1978 shows a reasonably paced run, although the start was slower than normal because of the crush of 4,500 participants. There was a steady middle portion and an acceleration toward the finish. It resulted in a 2:50 marathon. On the other hand, Paul Masson 1978 illustrates a race in which the runner carried out the same plan as in Mission Bay and managed it almost exactly for 20 miles. The times at 20 miles were only 10 seconds different. However,

143

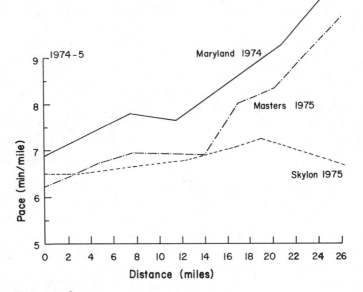

**Figure 16**
Marathon pacing for Maryland 1974 (beginner), Masters 1975
(unwise fast start), and Skylon 1975 (even-paced).

**Figure 17**
Marathon pacing for Mission Bay 1978 (even-paced) and Paul
Masson 1978 (insufficient recovery).

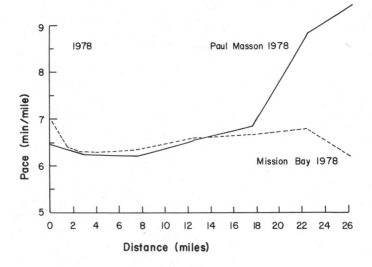

at Paul Masson the wall was hit in the middle of the final hill at 21 miles, and the pace decayed drastically as shown. The times included innumerable stops gasping to recover, during which time 67 runners passed. The perception of success was very poor! The final time, 3:04, showed that the second race had somehow incurred a debt of 14 minutes over Mission Bay 1978. The reason was not in the training, which had been 82 miles per week for Mission Bay and 81 miles per week for Paul Masson. The reason was that there were only eight days for recovery between the races and therefore the pace in Paul Masson was far too fast. A pace only 15 seconds a mile slower might well have resulted in a final time some 5 to 8 minutes better.

The initial pace is almost as important as the long miles of endurance training that you have banked against the race. It must be tailored to your expected finishing time, which itself must be estimated realistically, taking into account such variables as temperature, wind, recovery after any previous race, and physical well-being. That sounds like an intolerable task of prediction! You must start in your first marathon with prudence and learn your capabilities race by race. It is easier to speed up after a slow pace than to keep going at the same pace if you started out too fast.

Graham has learned to judge his pace by the depth of his breathing. In training, breathing is very light, but as the pace increases the breathing gets closer to a pant. Many marathons have measured the severity that goes with the correct rate. Then again, if you can manage to select a companion running at about the same rate, it is easier to maintain constancy when two of you can pull each other over the bad spots and ease off on the good. The companionship and conversation allow the rhythm to become automatic.

Pre-race stretching is most important. Each runner has his own ritual set of exercises, composed of those he usually does in training and those that have helped him before. They are very individual, because we all have different degrees of looseness in our various joints and muscles.

Graham uses a backover just before a race to assess what quality of race is about to come. If he is able to bring straight legs over his head while he is lying on the floor and thus touch the ground beyond his head with ease, it will be a good race. His back is supple enough. But if the legs don't come over easily, he knows more stretching is necessary to loosen everything.

Both of us use the wall-pushing exercise to stretch the calf muscles. This is the same exercise which stretches the Achilles tendons when used regularly and a very necessary one now to loosen these lower-leg components. We also stretch hamstrings by lowering the head over a stretched-out and raised leg. (Chapter 2 tells you much more about the needed stretching.) Most important, though, we both believe very strongly in a pre-race jog to get everything moving.

145

**Photo 17**
A matter of desperate inches. Brian Maxwell wins by 0.6 second after 26 miles in the National Capital Marathon at Ottawa, 1978, over Paul Bannon. Winning time: 2:16:02. (*Photo courtesy* The Citizen, *Ottawa, Canada*)

There are marathon runners who will lie immobile right up to the time when they are called to the start, on the assumption that they are going to need all their energy to finish the 26 miles 385 yards. They are not about to jog a mile or so and waste that energy. If they are that "finely tuned" to be able to do just that exact distance, then they should not be there at all. As we've seen in earlier chapters, the pre-race movement, a jog or even run, is needed to get the metabolism working and to start to oxidize lactic acids, which otherwise will make you feel stiff and tired in the first couple of miles. Thus usually both of us will run about a mile or a mile and a half just before the race, to mobilize the internal chemical processes and also to complete the stretching that we did earlier by some racelike movement. This is by no means wasted effort, since we are leading the body to an understanding of what it is about to be called upon to do for the next 2½ to 4 hours. It gives a final chance to test our clothes for comfort and our shoelaces for tightness, and generally clear the mind of dangerous doubts.

Brown, a younger and more competitive racer, has a different view of pacing which may have more application to you. It is generally agreed that the fastest times, as we have said, are achieved through even pacing. Nevertheless, to chop down a PR you are going to have to risk a little and push it in the early going, at least to test yourself once in a while. In order to know how hard to press, you must know your current condition. Brown tries to run just at the aerobic/anaerobic borderline, just below the pace which would create an oxygen debt. He tries to keep the upper body relaxed and to run smoothly. He listens to his body for signals of premature fatigue or strain. If he is laboring to maintain the pace, then he backs off on the throttle just a little. Generally when running an all-out marathon the effort is such that extended conversation cannot be held—too much talking would put you into oxygen debt. It is better in these cases to run your own race, concentrate on your pace, and monitor your body's signals. Running at a relaxed pace with other runners has to be left to training runs or the odd low-key marathon, after you have reached the competitive level. If you do run with a partner for most of the race, you may not be putting out your optimum. Save your visiting for a more social race where a PR is not of primary importance.

It has been said by Miki Gorman—and she should know, as a marathoning mother—that running a marathon is a little like childbirth. She meant that during the run sometimes the discomfort is beyond what you expected and barely supportable, and yet afterward the mind quickly forgets the pain and the effort and remembers only the finish and the feeling of achievement.

To try to capture the fleeting feelings of a first marathon, Graham constructed Table 14 virtually within hours of finishing the race. It is a graphic  description of the changes that a runner goes through. It is worth noticing the change between the way he thought the run was going at

# Table 14
## Maryland Marathon, Baltimore 1974—a personal description

*Weather:* Windless, sunny, low 30s°F

| INTERVAL (miles) | RUNNING RATE (min/mile) | PHYSIOLOGY Lungs | Legs | Other | PSYCHOLOGY |
|---|---|---|---|---|---|
| 0–5 | 7:12 | Excellent | Excellent (Foot pain at 7 miles goes soon) | Warming up | Excellent (Happy enjoyment) |
| 5–10 | 7:48 | | | | |
| 10–13.1 | 7:35 | Excellent | Very good | Sweating | Very good (Recognition of labor but no problems) |
| HALFWAY | (7:32.2) | | | | |
| 13.1–16.2 | 8:17 | Very good | Very good | | Very good (Belief in ability to finish) |
| 16.2–20.2 | | | | Hills at 15.7 and 19.2–20 miles defeated | |
| 20.2–22.2 | 9:25 | Very good | Good | Tiring | Good (Recognition of labor but confident) |
| 22.2–26.2 | Last mile approx. 10:40 | Very good | Fair (Knees sore) | Tiring and laboring | Poor (Survival—thoughts of walking!) |
| FINISH 0–26.2 | 8:19.7 | Excellent | Very good (One knee sore) | Total recovery in 3 weeks | Excellent (Completion running all the way!) |

POSITION: 297 out of 700  TIME: 3:38:20  TRAINING: 22.9 miles per week

149

16 miles and the rather desperate thoughts beyond 22 miles. The change didn't seem to correlate with physical feelings, although strength was generally deteriorating, but it was almost a mental trauma.

In this particular case, the runner was badly prepared, with only 23 miles a week and nothing longer than one 16-mile run. In your case things are going to be different, because you will have received sufficient training and will have started at a reasonable pace to avoid the wall altogether. You may not have to suffer your son running alongside over the last ½ mile, saying, "Come on, run, Dad!" when you think that's what you're doing!

With proper preparation, changes during the race are less violent and the runner becomes a racer. Table 15 illustrates a better-prepared race for Graham. This time, with an evenly paced race, the thoughts were always competitive, with eyes firmly fixed on the next runner who might possibly be overtaken. The worst point in this particular race was when the runner dropped his glasses only a mile from the finish. Knowing that he had a personal record time possible, there was a very quick debate as to whether to leave the glasses or waste valuable seconds in picking them up!

### What race to run?

That is the race, but how does one choose a first marathon? Should it be the most convenient in time or just location, or are there other criteria? A lot of runners seem to attempt their first on the basis of convenience, but that is surely not the best way to go about it.

Chapter 1 spoke a little about what makes a good race and came to a conclusion that one necessary ingredient is the friendliness of the atmosphere. We can, however, list another set of necessities and desirables which you may wish to consider in choosing a marathon to enter. Some of them may be of interest only when you have become more competitive in taking a last few seconds off for a personal record, while others may be of importance to the starter.

- *Pre-registration.* No one is anxious to line up for hours on race day just to get a packet of instructions or a number.
- *Pre-race facilities* for changing, for leaving belongings, and for inevitable visits to the toilets. There should be an adequate number of the last, otherwise we are back to standing in line on race day again.
- *A well-arranged start.* The raceway start should be wide enough to accommodate the number of runners, and the runners should be staggered according to performance. We have experienced races where thousands started in a road wide enough for ten to twenty, and others where runners were allocated a lead position if they had an AAU card! Fortunately there is a trend toward putting runners qualified by performance up ahead. It worked well in Boston in 1978.

## Table 15
Marine Reserves Marathon, Washington, D.C. 1978—a personal description
*Weather:* Wind (south), misty and low cloud, 50–60°F

| INTERVAL (miles) | RUNNING RATE (min/mile) | PHYSIOLOGY | | Other | PSYCHOLOGY |
| --- | --- | --- | --- | --- | --- |
| | | Lungs | Legs | | |
| 0–10 | 6:10.5 | Excellent (Breathing hard) | Excellent | Warming up and settling | Excellent (Feeling the competition) |
| 10–17 | 6:26 | Excellent | Excellent | Sweating hard | Very good (Looking for pacer) |
| 17–18 | 6:42 〈6:19.5〉 | Excellent | Very good | Glasses misting | Very good (Good rhythm going) |
| 18–20 | 5:44 | Excellent | Very good | Wind load | Good (Sharing wind loads) |
| 20–21.9 | 6:51.9 〈6:55〉 | Excellent | Very good | Glasses carried | Very good (Know I have a good time, pass people) |
| 21.9–26.2 | 6:56.4 | Very good | Good (Feet sore) | Little tired in last mile | Very good (Still in the competition) |
| FINISH | 6:24.5 | Excellent | Very good, no damage | Good (Fast recovery in 2 weeks) | Excellent (Competitive and a PR!) |

POSITION: 130 out of 2,656 (Masters: 10 out of 352)  TIME: 2:48:01  TRAINING: 81.6 miles per week

- *Adequate split information,* preferably at 1 mile and then every 5 miles. Too many splits and there is too great attention paid to time rather than to the body.
- *A marked course.* Each mile should be marked, in addition to the 5-mile intervals. Individual mile markings toward the end help, we find. Some courses are marked with paint on the road, rather than upright signs, and the numbers are difficult to catch. We don't all run with lowered eyes!
- *Accurate times.* A runner deserves at least two things without question: accurate distances (a certified course) and accurate times. It seems obvious, but probably about 25 percent of races don't manage it.
- *Clear directions.* One of the authors has several times missed his way on a race course, not always due to his being accident-prone. Most times the race course wasn't adequately marked or stewarded.
- *Good aid stations* starting at 5 miles (despite ancient Olympic rules which state no aid may be given before 11 kilometers). On hot or humid days it is vital to get water or some electrolytic replacement drink early. Sponge stations are desirable on hot days, and they're nice even on other occasions. The Canadian National Capital Marathon probably has the ideal aid and refreshment stands—splits given every 5 kilometers, drinks at the kilometer mark past the split, and then sponges at the kilometer mark past the drinks.
- *Medical assistance,* not too visible but dependable in an emergency, with attendants trained in the relief of heat exhaustion. (On one occasion the appearance of a vulturelike ambulance hovering close to Graham in a difficult run which had just become a survival struggle worked a remarkable revival in the legs. They were able to summon enough effort to escape the vulture and work their way home.)
- *A well-arranged finish.* There should be sufficient space past the finish line to accommodate any buildup in finishers. It is disastrous to have to stop ¼ mile short of the finish line because there isn't enough room to cross it. This has happened a few times lately.
- *Post-race facilities* for changing, showering, collecting belongings, and meeting friends. Putting on sweats with race-tired legs is difficult enough—at least there should be somewhere to do it.
- *Results available after the race.* At least the first twenty places should be available, as well as the first woman and master. One should not need to wait three months to find out how one fared. (At the time of writing we are still waiting for results from 5½ months ago from one race, and 4 months from another.)
- *Awards.* There should be some. A certificate is always nice to hang on the wall for your first marathon result. After that they tend to be superfluous. Unusual awards like mugs or merchandise are more acceptable than gaudy trophies and dollar medals.

- *Course interest.* Every runner has his or her preferences which could be taken into account in choice of a marathon. Point-to-point versus laps or an out-and-back? Scenery? Flat or rolling or hilly? Downhill or up?
- *Environment.* You can try to select weather by choosing a fall or spring race or a Northern one for coolness. On the other hand, you may prefer a warm race in the South. Take wind into account. Skylon is plagued with some headwinds, but one race we know in Ohio guarantees a tailwind by deciding which direction to run the point-to-point after the wind has decided which way to blow.
- *Restrictions.* Some events have restrictions: no one under 19; no men; only AAU members; and so on. Others are on a first-come-first-served basis and so require early application. You may prefer an open race.

This list is not comprehensive, but certainly these considerations should be part of the decision process in choosing a marathon. Sometimes an event will also have other associated activities which enter into it. Most organizers seem compelled to offer a seminar or clinic. These range from reasonably good to bad to excruciating, so ask a few questions first about the quality of speaker. Being a podiatrist or doctor or track star does not guarantee that the personage is also a speaker.

Having chosen a marathon, if it is a new one to you, you should study the course before the race. If it is possible a drive over the route is the best way to get the lay of the land. Pay particular attention to the location of hills and areas where you might make a wrong turn. Even in the highly organized races of today, it is still possible to lose your bearings and stray off the course. Note where the various mile marks are and the type of surface (asphalt, gravel, or dirt). Review the location of the aid stations where you can expect to get liquids. If you plan to have an aid team or friend out on the course to assist you, now is the time to find out where he should be located. There is nothing worse than expecting aid and finding out that by mistake you have to wait a further 5 miles for it. Finally it is a good idea to get some familiarity with the last 2 to 4 miles where in the race the road can appear very much longer if you don't recognize course landmarks.

### The competition

Marathoners have a wide variety of personal goals for each different race. Many are looking just to finish the event. Others are trying to pace themselves to a PR while a very small fraction are trying to place high in an open or age-group division. While you may at present be about to try your first marathon, it won't be long before you are in one of these other competitive struggles.

The competition within age groups is rarely the head-to-head battle it is in the open division. In very large races, unless you know your opponents, you may have no idea who is entered in what age group, and who your own particular opponents are. Hence, age-group competition is largely an after-the-fact occurrence. You run your best race and then sit back and see how you fared relative to others of your age, or youth.

Of course, on those occasions when you do find your opponents in the race, the competition can be as cutthroat and as agonizing as any front-runners' battle for the lead.

Although this book is not primarily directed toward the rare marathoners who are in competition seeking victory rather than a PR, a few comments about their strategy are in order. (Actually, we know very few marathoners who would make the distinction, since they aim for victory *and* a PR.)

In the open division, generally more strategy and tactics are employed. A common strategy is to go out fast, acquire a huge lead, and then hang on to win. Generally the desire to pursue is diminished if the leader can break contact with the rest of the pack. Of course the runner who tries this approach must have extreme confidence in his own capabilities, and be prepared for a potentially painful finish in which others may be catching him. Another method to break contact which is common is to throw in fast surges periodically in the middle of the race to break the pack. Frank Shorter tried this (unsuccessfully) in the 1976 Montreal Olympic Marathon.

Generally among the front-runners the race is one of attrition. You maintain the pace as long as possible, and the runner with the most endurance survives to win. Only rarely in major events does a world-class marathoner come from behind to place well or win. Some of the exceptions are the third-place finish of Don Kardong in the 1976 Olympic Trials, where he moved from around 20th to capture the final spot on the U.S. Olympic team, and the very similar finish put in by Jeff Wells in the 1978 Boston, where he just failed to win by the smallest margin in the history of the race.

There is some information to be gleaned from the strategies of these top performers. First of all, recognize that the race is one of attrition and select your initial pace wisely. Second, when passing other runners, move up quickly and quietly if possible. Pass them rapidly before they have a chance to respond. If you can open up a quick 20 yards and at least appear to be pulling away, your competitor may not have the desire to pick it up. If you pull up and run side by side for a time, his spirits may get a

**Photo 18** (OPPOSITE)
Finishers concentrating in the final yards of the 1977 Marine Corps Reserve Marathon. No. 2619 is co-author Graham with a finish time of 2:48:01. (*Photo by Colorbrite*)

psychological boost and you may well find him leaving you! Such surges are also useful in losing a runner who persistently runs on your shoulder.

An interesting aspect of gamesmanship was used on Graham in one race. A competitor asked whether it really took much more effort to run with his elbows stuck out like that! For the next few miles it really *did* take more effort, as he tried to keep his elbows by the sides of his body. This strategy is only recommended in desperate situations.

### Realism

Marathon veterans know that each race cannot bring a personal record. We should all recognize that, and not push to complete exhaustion on a day when you are feeling off or the weather conditions are adverse. One should aim to complete the race at a comfortable pace, leaving the principal effort for another occasion. However, there are usually one or two races each year which you can point toward for a personal record. Your training should be geared to these specifically selected races. Much of what we have been speaking about in the past few chapters should help to make those marathons especially successful ones for you.

# Chapter 8

# The Finish Line and More

The race is over! Emotions seem to be closely tied to physical sensations, and for a time everything is a curious mixture of opposites. There is an exultation that the race has been run and conquered, mixed with a relief that the legs can at last be allowed to stop moving. There may be a sense of newfound wisdom saying "Never again!" while other recesses of the brain are plotting next time's strategies. Part of you wants to lie down quietly to sleep in peace, yet some other ego would gladly dance a jig. One thing seems certain: It is a very rare runner that can taste the flavors of a marathon without wanting to drink again at the well.

Almost all of us (and of course there are exceptions which prove the rule) will soon be thinking about next time, despite the protestations from the body that it has done enough already.

Of course, you cannot go out and run another right away. There is a very important recovery period to go through before getting back to any consistent training. There are individuals who habitually run so many marathons that back-to-back events are quite achievable. Sy Mah and Craig Harms, both with over a hundred marathons to their credit, seem to find it easy. However, they are very rare individuals in the marathoning population. Most topflight marathoners like Shorter and Fleming will take a recovery rest.

### Recovery

Immediately after a marathon, there is a tendency to relax both physically and mentally from the discipline and regimen of the strict training that one had to go through in preparation. Diets are not necessary, and one certainly feels the right to "live a little." Most marathoners seem to eat excessively for this reason, and what weight has been temporarily lost during the run is quickly put back, in most cases with a little interest. Running in the first couple of days after tends to be slow, stiff, and quite an effort. Workouts should be kept easy and short as a result.

If the recent race was a hard one, the quadriceps will have been used and they will be very sore, especially when descending. Going downstairs can be very difficult, so it is not strange to see recovering marathoners coming down backward. It certainly helps, although it does attract a lot of curious looks.

Because of the sore quadriceps, in the early runs you should avoid running down steep hills. Arrange your loops so that you can run up the steep slopes and down the long gentle hills—exactly the opposite to what you should do to protect sore hamstrings after short fast races.

Very often during the marathon, you may have contracted a blister, made one toe sore, or possibly aggravated a local pain on one leg or foot. There will be a tendency to protect that point by putting more effort on the other leg or foot. It is most important during the recovery to recognize that *all* parts of the body are weak and require protection, so it is difficult to place additional stress on any part of the body without suffering a further injury. Make sure that you run evenly; don't favor one leg or foot. It is better to lay off altogether for a couple of days than to instigate a secondary injury.

The theme, then, is short, slow, steady, and very careful runs during the following week, leading very gradually back to a level of running not unlike the long slow distance recommended before the race. It should take about five to ten days to regain your usual mileage. Ron Wayne (four sub-2:20s in 1974) resumes after two days, but he attributes it to high-volume training *before* the race.

It is not only the body that has to recover, of course, but the whole being. Tests have shown that even after the very severe stresses of the 1976 Boston Marathon, the blood was able to regain its normal constitution in about five to seven days. The muscular ability (rebuilding and glycogen replenishment) takes longer, on the order of ten days. Assuming no physical injury, the joints and skeletal frame are not a limiting feature in this time scale. However, the mind can be. The will to run is the last thing to recover. As Tom Fleming said, "The body recovers faster than the head because the body forgets very fast."

Graham has found that it takes him about twelve days before the act of running gives the same physical joy as it did before. Usually sometime during a run on the twelfth day a spring will return to the legs as he feels good and *wants* to run farther, or faster, or freer than the day before. This is when competition returns and plans for the next race become real. At fourteen to twenty-one days after a marathon, another can be run as well as or in many cases better than the earlier one. This varies from runner to runner, of course.

Since recovery is very much an individual thing, it is recommended that you take note of, or even chart, the changes as they occur after the first marathon and use the information as a basis for recovery activities in the future.

Not long ago it was considered impossible to run more than two good marathons a year, not because of the difficulty in peaking for them so much as because of the need for recovery. Even today many publications

158

publish recovery charts advising no further racing until something like ten or twenty times the race distance has been accomplished in further training mileage. However, this is too "average" to be useful advice. It appears that once training has peaked the athlete toward a certain race, this peak may be held for upward of two months and several marathons can be run with almost equal efficiency. Fortunate runners can even achieve this peak twice in the year to take advantage of the spring and fall marathon seasons. Bill Rodgers is a good example of frequent marathon racing: in twelve months he ran five marathons, winning all five with four times under 2:13. He didn't seem to show signs of lack of recovery when he ran Boston at the end of 1978 in 2:10:13. Remember, however, that in his early years he did not run so frequently, nor with such even times.

All this is not to persuade you to run incessant marathons, but simply to note the current feeling that with good base aerobic training you need not take many weeks of recovery before the next race.

### Future targets

Very few runners can complete a marathon and not want to go back to see whether the time can be improved, so your future target, after the pain of the last few miles has subsided, is probably going to be another 26 miles 385 yards.

This time you will have something more definite in mind than just finishing it. You will almost certainly be setting a time target for yourself. It may be something quite vague, like anything better than last time (which has already become your personal record). It may, however, be a definite goal, like qualifying for Boston; currently sub-3 hours for most runners, and sub-3½ hours for masters over 40 and for women. On the other hand if you are above average you will have some finer goals involved: sub-2:50, sub-2:30, or whatever. The effect is the same—you will be immediately drawn to the idea of better training. At this point it is worth reading Chapter 2 once again.

One of the best ways of improving your time overall is to improve your pacing during the race. Generally a first marathon will have had some dramatic slowing down at the end, and this can be reduced with a little more endurance mileage coupled with the confidence of having completed the first one. Having done much to reduce this slowdown by increased endurance, further improvement will come by choosing a judicious pace. Even 5 to 10 seconds per mile too fast at the start can lose those same seconds and more at the end. One has to beware the foreclosure that quite often comes after a race has been mortgaged to early speed. It is very much a matter of experience, so you may find benefit in pacing off a more experienced runner in the early stages of the run. Chapter 7 discusses pacing in more detail.

159

Short races should not be neglected among your future targets. Races up to 15 kilometers or up to 10 miles can be valuable sharpening tools, giving you the speed that you will need in the longer races. They also give the variety that the body needs—otherwise there would be a tendency to relax into a comfortable "marathon pace" because the body simply doesn't know what it feels like to race and run harder and quicker.

## Ultra-marathons

Having conquered the marathon's mystique, having met the 26 miles 385 yards and vanquished them, there is soon some thought of other trials to surmount. Most clearly in running this means longer distances, or ultra-marathons.

In 1977 there were eight 50-kilometer races in the Unted States, a distance not much longer than the 42.195-kilometer marathon. However, in the same year there were sixteen 50-mile races and five 100-kilometer runs. Ample opportunities for those looking beyond the marathon existed. Moreover, apart from the 50-mile J. F. Kennedy Run-hike in Maryland, which drew 483 starters, participation in these events is not large, so that opportunity for an individual seeking escape from the thousands running the marathon is there.

In addition to these regular distance races, there are others of irregular distance simply because a starting point and an end point exist. The oldest of these is the South African Comrades "Marathon" of 55 miles from Pietermaritzburg to Durban. Then there is the London to Brighton 52.5 miles in Great Britain, the 72-mile race around Lake Tahoe, and the 3-times-100-kilometer towpath race along the Chesapeake and Ohio Canal in Maryland. New runs are being added, such as an embryo 70-mile Laurel Highlands Trail run in Pennsylvania, the 100-mile Western States Trail in the Sierra Nevadas, and the 145-mile run across Death Valley and to the top of Mount Whitney, and it seems that there is something for everybody.

These runs range from hard-fought races to survival struggles where often the winner is also the only finisher. They range from events in which the chief enemy is boredom with many tens of miles on the track to those where extremes of hills, temperature, lack of water, and exposure play a significant part. It is a paradox that when runners are reaching for the marathon as an "ultimate goal" they are advised by a national running magazine to "choose an easy course"! Fortunately ultra-marathon runners have not yet tried to achieve their goals by lowering their targets.

Running an ultra-marathon is significantly different from running a marathon. For distances above 50 miles, it is probably not possible to pack sufficient glycogen into the body to avoid "hitting the wall," but long runs are advisable to train the body to use fat as its source of energy in the later stages of the run. Thus these long races have to be run in the recognition that the runner has to meet and penetrate the wall we have spoken about in earlier chapters. The runner goes through periods of intense depression and then a reawakening freshness, which require a good deal of mental toughness to withstand. Perhaps for this reason, ultra-marathoners tend to be older than marathoners, just as marathoners are older than short-distance runners. Eighteen of the top twenty-five performers over 100 kilometers in 1977 were over 30, and fifteen out of the top twenty performances ever over 100-mile races in the U.S. were placed on record by over-30-year-olds.

Besides considerable mental fortitude, these races occupy such lengths of time that pace and diet have to be differently arranged than in the shorter marathon events. Typically a 100-kilometer race may last 8–10 hours, while a 100-miler can last 13–20 hours. During this time a top ultra-marathoner, Tom Osler, recommends mixing short periods of walking (say 5 minutes) in with running (say every 20 minutes). In this way stiffness is warded off for great lengths of time, and Osler finds that he has completed ultras up to 100 miles in length in relative comfort. If he wants to *race* the distance without any short periods of walking, then the time is shorter but the price is much greater.

We cannot emphasize fluid replacement too strongly. To quote Nick Marshall: "Dehydration is life-threatening and in races of 6 hours and more dehydration hovers in the background even if the weather is cool." It is most important to drink plenty of liquids. Further, because of the length of these ultra-marathons, there is not only a need to drink considerable amounts of fluid, but it is possible to take solids and have the body use them within the time span of the race. Osler recommends drinks with sugar, large amounts of sugar, only for races and runs longer than the marathon. They sustain him, but wisely he realizes that one man's sugar is another man's doom, so he also recommends experimenting with sugar during training runs first to find out whether it helps and in what quantities it should be used. For the record, he uses 1½ pounds per gallon of fluid!

Other runners will eat solids in the form of cookies or small pieces of chocolate, all in fairly small amounts. Others swear by mixtures of juice and honey. It has to be a very personal choice of something that your body can assimilate and your mind can recognize as beneficial.

This book is not written for the ultra-marathoner, but for the marathon runner who may want to know what lies ahead. If you are seriously thinking about making the large step forward, then the very best thing you can do is to seek out an experienced *long*-distance runner and ask his advice.

Tom Osler offers excellent words of wisdom: "Remember that to be a distance runner is to first learn to listen to your body's message. Try different suggestions, have an open mind, but above all, use common sense. If something doesn't feel good, chances are it's no good for you. By all means, don't enter into ultra-marathoning like the Marines landing on Iwo Jima. This is a very difficult sport, with great potential for injury and illness. However, by simply stopping before you get too tired, you can enjoy it." Yet, even Osler is still learning.

## Little by little

An ounce of application is worth a ton of theory. Thus the first attempt at distance running beyond the marathon will dispel some of the uncertainties and doubts, and it will certainly provide meaningful experience.

After a couple of years of thinking about it, and prodded by the need to write this chapter, Graham took the big step of agreeing to run the Laurel Highlands Trail with three others, two of whom, Paul and Joe Butchko, are the only runners to have successfully completed the full 70 miles of rough footing in a single run. The trail runs from Ohiopyle to Johnstown in Pennsylvania along a mountain ridge at an average altitude of 2,800 feet. The starting climb to the ridge is 1,600 feet over the first 7 miles, with a corresponding drop at the end. The trail itself is administered by the state. It is roughly cleared and well marked at each mile. Creeks are bridged, but the path winds and rolls so that very little forward steady running is possible. Additionally the trail has an infinity of obstacles—rocks, stumps, steps, cross-trail logs, and stones—so much so that Graham now holds the fall record for the trail, 10 times in the first 20 miles.

Thus he learned a first lesson: Mountain trail running is significantly different from road running. Times are not comparable, since in trail running a considerable effort and concentration is needed just to maintain footing. Even at 8 minutes a mile there is only a second available to survey obstacles on the next 3 yards. There is a mental strain in never being able to look up from the trail, and the pace is automatically curtailed. If you run any faster than a certain comfortable rate, you tend to fall over. Be warned, if you choose to extend your distance running, then maybe a longer road race will be easier.

While running the longer distances, the scale of everything goes up. Whereas in a marathon one thinks in terms of 3 to 5 miles, the interval between aid stations, Graham found that in the Laurel Highlands Trail run he thought of 10-to-15-mile intervals. Times are likewise expanded in

Photo 19 (OPPOSITE)
Wraithlike on the trail! Graham is still fast enough at 31 miles into an ultra-marathon to beat the camera shutter. (*Photo by Mel Cowgill*)

scale: minutes expand to hours, especially at trail-running pace. Distance and time expansion is not difficult, because background long slow distance training had been at this level. He found himself treating the 33–35-mile point as the critical period rather than the 18–21-mile equivalent section of the marathon.

Water in road races is not necessarily a problem, because aid stations can be set up easily by supporters. On a trail run things are different. Access points are limited, and between access points the runner may have to rely on ground water, previously placed caches, and/or carried liquid. In this case, the runner carried two 8-ounce bottles in a waist bag constructed from sheet linen. The system worked without a hitch. He used a 3:1 (by volume) mixture of ERG and sugar, a mixture which had seemed optimum in training. It tasted sickly sweet to start with but on the run it was almost tart and very satisfying. This is a personal recipe, and any ultra-marathon aspirant should test his own needs and taste buds in long prior training runs.

Mileage before the run would have predicted no problem in running to 34 miles. Split times later showed that indeed the pace was very steady and better than previously planned throughout the first 35 miles. Thereafter the pace slowed.

While sugar helped over the whole run, it didn't seem to push out the glycogen exhaustion point. Also, there was no apparent comfortable period after the depression which more experienced ultra-marathoners have discovered. Park Barner, an ultra-marathoner par excellence, has said: "In the marathon I don't get that second wind as in my longer slower runs and so I don't feel like picking it up once I set my pace. The second wind I get is interesting in that the slower I start out (in the ultra-distances), the longer it takes for the good feeling to set in and once it does I can make it last longer by holding back my pace. Pace has everything to do with it. I guess switching to burning fat is what causes the feeling."

Nick Marshall, another premier long-distance runner, also refers to a turning point beyond which there is no further deterioration. In his 72-mile Tahoe race he found an "eerie state of uncomfortable equilibrium." Unfortunately this never happened to Graham, perhaps since it was masked by shoe difficulties, but it remains to be investigated further. In any case it is clear that mental states are crucial, and Marshall notes that the "equilibrium" may come only from the mental turning point when you conclude that finishing is a certainty.

The runners did follow Tom Osler's recommendation to mix walking with running to cover the distance without severe damage. Thus they took advantage of the many hills to drop to a fast walk. If it had been a strict race a shorter time could be achieved by always running, but a price would be paid in some muscle breakdown and a longer recovery. They paid strict attention to maintaining a fairly easy overall pace.

In the end, one runner, Jim Swigart, made 57 miles and the others stopped at 46 miles because it was clear that time was being lost and the last few miles would have had to be run in the dark—an insupportable idea after falling so much in the light. Graham learned another lesson: at mile 5 his right foot tore through the nylon side of his shoe, and the ensuing 5-inch rip allowed his foot to slip partially out of the shoe at every pace. Finally, 39 miles later (!), he was able to change shoes, but the damage to the race timing was done already, so stopping at 20 miles beyond the marathon distance was no difficulty. The shoes chosen for running rough trails must be strong not only for forward running but also for lateral twisting and turning. Shoes with any structural weakness should be rejected—30 to 40 miles can accentuate very slight defects.

Curiously, muscular strains after 46 miles on the trail were different from the usual marathon crop. Toes were completely undamaged except for those that protruded from the shoe! Hamstrings were unstressed but the inside quadriceps were sore to the touch. Other muscles in the bottom, the gluteus medius and the gluteus maximus, which when sore cause the runner to waddle like a duck, were presumably stressed by the constant twisting and turning. Falling, of course, provided its own special and distinct marks of experience. However, dancing, golf, and tennis with a little judicious running in the next three days provided for quick recovery from most of the discomfort.

The run dispelled many doubts for Graham. He is now confident that distances beyond the marathon are personally achievable, and a 50-mile road race may be the next small step. Clearly the 70-mile trail run will have to be completed next year—with good equipment and good confidence. It is revealing that his diary for the run showed a pre-run entry of "Feel OK, but butterflies!" while the evening entry showed "Butterflies dead!" Confidence grows with experience. If in doubt, try it—little by little.

## Postscript

No one can run exactly as you can. We agree with Marshall when he writes that the concept of an authority in running is "largely hocus-pocus." This is especially true in distances beyond the marathon, an area in which so few studies have been performed. What this chapter has presented is a reasoned extrapolation of what we know about the 26 mile 385 yard distance together with experience of a single occasion. If you want to explore your limits by running far, then remember that you are entering uncharted waters. Good luck!

# Appendix I
# Marathon Performances

It is tempting to title this appendix "Marathon Records," but this would be misleading, since it is extremely difficult to compare marathon times from one race to another, or from one day to another. In track races it is possible to establish rules for allowable wind speeds, or even altitude limits, but in a race which takes over 2 hours on varying qualities of open road during which time the weather conditions can change, attempts at standardization are doomed to failure. Thus there are really no records. At best there can only be the fastest time for a particular course. Times are only comparable in head-to-head competition.

Marathon times are a function of a number of variables. Competition is most important—the best bring out the best. Variables of the course itself—surface quality, distribution and severity of any hills, and whether it is out-and-back, a loop, or laps—all clearly affect times. Principally, however, the best times are recorded when the weather is right: temperatures in the low 50s, overcast skies and low humidity—running weather! Then when everything comes together *and* the runner is mentally and physically well prepared, the best times are recorded.

However, it is also important that the course be certified in distance, preferably according to the rules established by T. Corbitt of the Road Runners Clubs of America. The accuracy is very exacting, since, for example a 1 percent error in distance results in about 78 seconds in time on a very fast run. However, a 1 percent distance error can be obtained using a measuring wheel with less than 0.1 inch of dirt or mud on the wheel's rim!

### World times

The men's list is provided only to 2:12:20, since it very rapidly becomes unwieldingly large. Moreover, only a single best time is given for each runner, although they may have run several under the 2:13 limit. Rodgers, for example, ran 2:10:13 at Boston in 1978, although the list just shows his 1979 2:09:27, also at Boston.

The women's list is cut off at 2:45:00, since, as the dates show, it changes so rapidly.

167

# World times

| **MEN** | | | **WOMEN** | | |
|---|---|---|---|---|---|
| 2:08:34 | Derek Clayton (AUS) | 1969 | 2:27:33 | Grete Waitz (NOR) | 1979 |
| 2:09:06 | Shigeru So (JAP) | 1978 | 2:31:23 | Joan Benoit (USA) | |
| 2:09:12 | Ian Thompson (GBR) | 1974 | 2:34:26 | Jacqueline Gareau (CAN) | 1980 |
| 2:09:27 | Bill Rodgers (USA) | 1979 | 2:34:48 | C. Vahlensieck (GFR) | 1977 |
| 2:09:28 | Ron Hill (GBR) | 1970 | 2:35:08 | Patti Lyons (USA) | 1980 |
| 2:09:55 | W. Cierpinski (GDR) | 1976 | 2:35:16 | Chantal Langlace (FRA) | 1977 |
| 2:10:00 | Marc Smet (BEL) | 1979 | 2:36:12 | Gayle Olinek (CAN) | 1979 |
| 2:10:09 | Jerome Drayton (CAN) | 1975 | 2:36:24 | Julie Brown (USA) | 1978 |
| 2:10:12 | Toshihiko Seko (JAP) | 1978 | 2:36:27 | Joyce Smith (GBR) | 1979 |
| 2:10:15 | Jeff Wells (USA) | 1978 | 2:37:37 | Lorraine Moller (NZL) | 1979 |
| 2:10:20 | Dave Chettle (AUS) | 1975 | 2:37:57 | Kim Merritt (USA) | 1977 |
| 2:10:20 | Tony Sandoval (USA) | 1979 | 2:38:10 | M. Angenvoorth (GFR) | 1977 |
| 2:10:30 | Frank Shorter (USA) | 1972 | 2:38:19 | J. Hansen (USA) | 1975 |
| 2:10:38 | Akio Usami (JAP) | 1970 | 2:38:33 | Gill Adams (GBR) | 1979 |
| 2:10:40 | Takeshi So (JAP) | 1979 | 2:38:50 | Sue Krenn (USA) | 1979 |
| 2:10:48 | Bill Adcocks (GBR) | 1968 | 2:39:11 | Miki Gorman (USA) | 1976 |
| 2:10:51 | Bernie Ford (GBR) | 1979 | 2:39:22 | Laurie Binder (USA) | 1980 |
| 2:10:54 | John Lodwick (USA) | 1979 | 2:39:37 | S. Grottenberg (NOR) | 1979 |
| 2:11:05 | Hideki Kita (JAP) | 1978 | 2:39:48 | Elizabeth Hassall (AUS) | 1979 |
| 2:11:12 | Eamon O'Reilly (USA) | 1970 | 2:39:48 | Gail Volk (USA) | 1979 |
| 2:11:13 | John Farrington (AUS) | 1973 | 2:40:37 | Carol Gould (GBR) | 1979 |
| 2:11:13 | Karel Lismont (BEL) | 1976 | 2:41:14 | D. Rasmussen (DEN) | 1979 |
| 2:11:13 | Dick Quax (NZL) | 1979 | 2:41:48 | Celia Peterson (USA) | 1978 |
| 2:11:15 | Esa Tikkanen (FIN) | 1978 | 2:41:49 | Marty Cooksey (USA) | 1978 |
| 2:11:16 | Don Kardong (USA) | 1976 | 2:41:50 | Kathleen Samet (USA) | 1980 |
| 2:11:17 | Seiichiro Sasaki (JAP) | 1967 | 2:42:08 | Sue Kinsey (USA) | 1979 |
| 2:11:17 | Jack Fultz (USA) | 1978 | 2:42:23 | Ellison Goodall (USA) | 1980 |
| 2:11:19 | Jack Foster (NZL) | 1974 | 2:42:24 | Liane Winter (GFR) | 1975 |
| 2:11:25 | Randy Thomas (USA) | 1978 | 2:42:44 | Beth Guerin (USA) | 1979 |
| 2:11:30 | Veli Balli (TUR) | 1976 | 2:43:02 | Sue Peterson (USA) | 1979 |
| 2:11:32 | Vladimir Bugrov (SOV) | 1972 | 2:43:14 | Vreni Forster (SWI) | 1979 |
| 2:11:34 | Kazimierz Pawlik (POL) | 1979 | 2:43:38 | C. Dalrymple (USA) | 1979 |
| 2:11:34 | Jozef Stefanowski (POL) | 1979 | 2:43:51 | Jan Arenz (USA) | 1979 |
| 2:11:35 | Kebede Balcha (ETH) | 1979 | 2:43:51 | Jane Robinson (USA) | 1979 |
| 2:11:36 | Kenny Moore (USA) | 1970 | 2:44:11 | Gillian File (NZL) | 1978 |
| 2:11:40 | Chang Sop Choe (NKO) | 1979 | 2:44:29 | Karen Blackford (USA) | 1979 |
| 2:11:43 | Kevin Ryan (NZL) | 1978 | 2:44:33 | Dana Slater (USA) | 1979 |
| 2:11:45 | Giuseppe Cindolo (ITA) | 1975 | 2:44:40 | Toni Antoinette (USA) | 1980 |
| 2:11:50 | Kirk Pfeffer (USA) | 1979 | 2:44:52 | Gayle Barron (USA) | 1978 |
| 2:11:52 | Herm Atkins (USA) | 1979 | 2:44:53 | Gail MacKean (CAN) | 1979 |
| 2:11:53 | John Dimick (USA) | 1979 | 2:45:00 | Beverly Shingles (NZL) | 1978 |

**MEN**

| | | |
|---|---|---|
| 2:11:54 | Steve Hoag (USA) | 1975 |
| 2:11:55 | Bill Scott (AUS) | 1979 |
| 2:11:55 | Chris Wardlaw (AUS) | 1979 |
| 2:11:57 | Leonid Moiseyev (SOV) | 1977 |
| 2:11:59 | Nikolay Penzin (SOV) | 1978 |
| 2:12:00 | Shivnath Singh (IND) | 1978 |
| 2:12:00 | Morio Shigematsu (JAP) | 1965 |
| 2:12:03 | Eckhard Lesse (GDR) | 1974 |
| 2:12:04 | Hayami Tanimura (JAP) | 1969 |
| 2:12:04 | Jim Alder (GBR) | 1970 |
| 2:12:05 | Tom Fleming (USA) | 1975 |
| 2:12:11 | P. Paivarinta (FIN) | 1978 |
| 2:12:12 | A. Bikela (ETH) | 1964 |
| 2:12:12 | Y. Unetani (JAP) | 1970 |
| 2:12:19 | D. Faircloth (GB) | 1970 |
| 2:12:20 | G. Barrett (AUS) | 1978 |

[a] 2:11:05.6 is a pace of 5:00 minutes per mile over the 26 miles 385 yards. Nineteen runners have so far bettered this average pace.

[b] 2:37:18.8 is a pace of 6:00 minutes per mile. Only nine women have so far run at a faster overall rate.

### Age times

Since young children are not encouraged to run the marathon in Europe and in most cases are officially excluded from races, world age times are not available for the young and the following list only includes U.S. runners. Then there are the ladies, who are establishing better times in each race. Since women began to be accepted grudgingly into marathon races their times have rapidly decreased as better competition and targets became available.

## Age times

| | **MEN** | | **WOMEN** | |
|---|---|---|---|---|
| 4 | 6:03:35 | Brent Bogle | | None |
| 5 | 5:25:09 | Bucky Cox | | None |
| 6 | 5:08:00 | Andy Hill | 4:00:36 | Jennifer Amyx |
| 7 | 3:55:04 | Andy Hill | 4:40:04 | Laura L. Dodge |
| 8 | 3:15:42 | Kevin Strain | 3:51:09 | Amy Cartwright |

169

# Age Times (*cont.*)

| | MEN | | | WOMEN | |
|---|---|---|---|---|---|
| 9 | 2:55:59 | Wesley Paul | 3:11:01 | Julie Mullin | |
| 10 | 2:57:24 | Reggie Heywood | 2:58:01 | Julie Mullin | |
| 11 | 2:48:53 | Eric Davis | 3:02:47 | Julie Mullin | |
| 12 | 2:47:09 | Reggie Heywood | 3:04:38 | Debbie Koffel | |
| 13 | 2:43:02 | Tom Ansberry | 2:55:00 | Lora Cartwright | |
| 14 | 2:31:24 | Bob Planta | 2:50:21 | Diane Barrett | |
| 15 | 2:29:11 | Mitch Kingery | 2:46:23 | Diane Barrett | |
| 16 | 2:23:47 | Mitch Kingery | 2:51:38 | Marjorie Kaput | |
| 17 | 2:23:05 | Clancy Devery | 2:46:46 | Irene Griffith | |
| 18 | 2:17:44 | Kirk Pfeffer | 2:39:48 | Gail Volk | |
| 19 | 2:17:58 | Kirk Pfeffer | 2:42:44 | Beth Guerin | |
| 20 | 2:13:59 | Dave Segura | 2:44:33 | Dana Slater | |
| 21 | 2:14:45 | C. Hattersley | 2:35:15 | Joan Benoit | |
| 22 | 2:14:25 | Tom Fleming | 2:35:41 | Joan Benoit | |
| 23 | 2:10:15 | Jeff Wells | 2:36:24 | Julie Brown | |
| 24 | 2:11:25 | R. Thomas | 2:39:43 | Kim Merritt | |
| 25 | 2:10:20 | T. Sandoval | 2:41:32 | Patti Lyons | |
| 26 | 2:11:45 | Frank Shorter | 2:38:19 | Jacki Hansen | |
| 27 | 2:09:55 | Bill Rodgers | 2:47:19 | L. McBride | |
| 28 | 2:10:10 | Bill Rodgers | 2:45:36 | P. DeMoss | |
| 29 | 2:10:55 | Bill Rodgers | 2:38:50 | Sue Krenn | |
| 30 | 2:10:13 | Bill Rodgers | 2:43:38 | Kathy Smet | |
| 31 | 2:09:27 | Bill Rodgers | 2:43:38 | Kathy Smet | |
| 32 | 2:12:11 | Bill Rodgers | 2:43:43 | L. Binder | |
| 33 | 2:14:56 | Chris Stewart | 2:44:52 | Gayle Barron | |
| 34 | 2:18:01 | McAndrew | 2:43:02 | Sue Petersen | |
| 35 | 2:15:52 | Norman Higgins | 2:47:36 | Sue Petersen | |
| 36 | 2:17:43 | Herb Lorenz | 2:47:52 | C. Dalrymple | |
| 37 | 2:16:45 | Mike Manley | 2:43:38 | C. Dalrymple | |
| 38 | 2:20:20 | Ed Fry | 2:46:36 | Miki Gorman | |
| 39 | 2:21:01 | Bill Hall | 2:54:50 | Jean Ullyot | |
| 40 | 2:24:41 | Herb Lorenz | 2:47:45 | Miki Gorman | |
| 41 | 2:20:47 | Fritz Mueller | 2:39:11 | Miki Gorman | |
| 42 | 2:26:00 | Fritz Mueller | 2:43:10 | Miki Gorman | |
| 43 | 2:28:01 | John Brennand | 2:50:53 | E. Carlson | |
| 44 | 2:27:02 | Cahit Yeter | 2:54:09 | Miki Gorman | |
| 45 | 2:29:07 | James McDonagh | 2:57:41 | Nicki Hobson | |
| 46 | 2:28:49 | James McDonagh | 3:00:13 | Nicki Hobson | |
| 47 | 2:30:26 | Hal Higdon | 3:04:55 | Nicki Hobson | |
| 48 | 2:36:18 | U. Kaempf | 3:04:19 | Ruth Anderson | |
| 49 | 2:36:56 | T. Bailey | 2:58:11 | Toshiko D'Elia | |

| | MEN | | | WOMEN | |
|---|---|---|---|---|---|
| 50 | 2:36:49 | T. Bailey | 3:04:26 | C. Cartwright |
| 51 | 2:35:48 | Jim O'Neil | 3:18:48 | M. Miller |
| 52 | 2:36:47 | Alex Ratelle | 3:14:20 | M. Miller |
| 53 | 2:31:56 | Alex Ratelle | 3:05:02 | M. Miller |
| 54 | 2:32:34 | Alex Ratelle | 3:21:01 | Helen Dick |
| 55 | 2:36:04 | Alex Ratelle | 4:25:14 | Lynn Edwards |
| 56 | 2:39:42 | E. Almeida | 4:02:46 | Lynn Edwards |
| 57 | 2:48:32 | J. A. Kelley | 3:27:45 | Marcie Trent |
| 58 | 2:51:44 | William Andberg | 4:09:25 | Edith Dalton |
| 59 | 2:52:29 | Clive Davies | 3:34:22 | Marcie Trent |
| 60 | 2:47:46 | Clive Davies | 3:26:16 | Marcie Trent |
| 61 | 2:50:54 | Clive Davies | 3:42:42 | Marcie Trent |
| 62 | 2:49:17 | Clive Davies | 4:11:42 | Kay Alkinson |
| 63 | 2:48:04 | Clive Davies | 5:11:25 | Burnis Hicks |
| 64 | 2:42:44 | Clive Davies | 5:30:27 | Burnis Hicks |
| 65 | 2:53:03 | M. Montgomery | 5:15:55 | Burnis Hicks |
| 66 | 2:56:45 | M. Montgomery | | None |
| 67 | 3:20:39 | Norman Bright | | None |
| 68 | 2:54:49 | M. Montgomery | | None |
| 69 | 3:00:57 | M. Montgomery | | None |
| 70 | 3:15:45 | M. Montgomery | 4:45:02 | Mavis Lindgren |
| 71 | 3:07:03 | M. Montgomery | 4:38:46 | Mavis Lindgren |
| 72 | 3:14:48 | M. Montgomery | 4:37:35 | Mavis Lindgren |
| 73 | 3:26:05 | M. Montgomery | | None |
| 74 | 3:45:15 | Fred Grace | | None |
| 75 | 3:47:20 | Lou Gregory | | None |
| 76 | 3:53:29 | Lou Gregory | | None |
| 77 | 4:14:12 | Lou Gregory | | None |
| 78 | 4:06:20 | Paul Spangler | | None |
| 79 | 3:59:47 | Paul Spangler | | None |

Race records

Appendix II provides a listing of all the U.S. and Canadian marathons in 1978, and the current records for those marathons are given for men and women in the alphabetical list. These records give you some idea of whether the course is a relatively fast or slow one.

The premier race is naturally the Olympic event. Figure 1 showed how the winning times have lowered over the years from over 3 hours to the present record of 2:09:55 set at Montreal in 1976 by Waldemar Cierpinski of East Germany.

Here are the first six positions in all the modern Olympic marathons:

## Olympic records

| | | |
|---|---|---|
| **1896** ATHENS (40 km.) | 1. Spyridon Louis (GR) | 2:58:50 |
| | 2. Charilaos Vasilakos (GR) | 3:06:03 |
| | 3. Gyula Keliner (HUNG) | 3:06:35 |
| | 4. Ioannis Vretos (GR) | |
| | 5. Eleftherlos Papasimeon (GR) | |
| | 6. Dimitrios Deliyannis (GR) | |
| **1900** PARIS (40.260 km.) | 1. Michel Theato (FR) | 2:59:45 |
| | 2. Emile Champion (FR) | 3:04:17 |
| | 3. Eranst Fast (SWE) | 3:37:14 |
| | 4. E. Resse (FR) | |
| | 5. Arthur Newton (US) | |
| | 6. John Cregan (US) | |
| **1904** ST. LOUIS (40 km.) | 1. Thomas Hicks (US) | 3:28:53 |
| | 2. Albert Corey (US) | 3:34:52 |
| | 3. Arthur Newton (US) | 3:47:33 |
| | 4. Felix Carvajal (CUBA) | |
| | 5. Demeter Velouis (GR) | |
| | 6. D. J. Kneeland (US) | |
| **1908** LONDON (42.195 km.) | 1. Johnny Hayes (US) | 2:55:19 |
| | 2. Charles Hefferon (S. AF) | 2:56:06 |
| | 3. Joseph Foresaw (US) | 2:57:11 |
| | 4. Alton Welton (US) | 2:59:45 |
| | 5. William Wood (CAN) | 3:01:44 |
| | 6. Frederick Simpson (CAN) | 3:04:29 |
| **1912** STOCKHOLM (40.2 km.) | 1. Kenneth MacArthur (S. AF) | 2:36:55 |
| | 2. Christian Gitsham (S. AF) | 2:37:52 |
| | 3. Gaston Strobino (US) | 2:38:43 |
| | 4. Andrew Sockalexis (US) | 2:42:08 |
| | 5. James Duffy (CAN) | 2:42:19 |
| | 6. Sigge Jaconsson (SWE) | 2:43:25 |
| **1920** ANTWERP (42.75 km.) | 1. Hannes Kolehmainen (FIN) | 2:32:36 |
| | 2. Juri Lossman (EST) | 2:32:49 |
| | 3. Valerio Arri (IT) | 2:36:33 |
| | 4. Auguste Broos (BEL) | 2:39:26 |
| | 5. Jaako Tuomikoski (FIN) | 2:40:11 |
| | 6. Sofus Rose (DEN) | 2:41:18 |

| | | |
|---|---|---|
| **1924**  PARIS (42.195 km.) | 1. Albin Stenroos (FIN) | 2:41:23 |
| | 2. Romeo Bertini (IT) | 2:47:20 |
| | 3. Clarence DeMar (US) | 2:48:14 |
| | 4. Lauri Halonen (FIN) | 2:49:48 |
| | 5. Sam Ferris (GB) | 2:52:26 |
| | 6. Miguel Plaza (CHILE) | 2:52:54 |
| **1928**  AMSTERDAM* | 1. Mohamed El Quafi (FR) | 2:32:57 |
| | 2. Miguel Plaza (CHILE) | 2:33:23 |
| | 3. Martti Marttelin (FIN) | 2:35:02 |
| | 4. Kanematsu Yamada (JAP) | 2:35:29 |
| | 5. Joey Ray (US) | 2:36:04 |
| | 6. Seiichiro Tsuda (JAP) | 2:36:20 |
| **1932**  LOS ANGELES | 1. Juan Carlos Zabala (ARG) | 2:31:36 |
| | 2. Sam Ferris (GB) | 2:31:55 |
| | 3. Armas Toivonen (FIN) | 2:32:12 |
| | 4. Duncan Mc. Wright (GB) | 2:32:41 |
| | 5. Seiichiro Tsuda (JAP) | 2:35:42 |
| | 6. Onbai Kin (JAP) | 2:37:28 |
| **1936**  BERLIN | 1. Kitei Son (JAP) | 2:29:20 |
| | 2. Ernest Harper (GB) | 2:31:24 |
| | 3. Shoryu Nan (JAP) | 2:31:42 |
| | 4. Erkki Tamila (FIN) | 2:32:45 |
| | 5. Vaino Muinonen (FIN) | 2:33:46 |
| | 6. Johannes Coleman (S. AF) | 2:36:17 |
| **1948**  LONDON | 1. Delfo Cabrera (ARG) | 2:34:52 |
| | 2. Tom Richards (GB) | 2:35:08 |
| | 3. Etienne Gailly (BEL) | 2:35:34 |
| | 4. Johannes Coleman (S. AF) | 2:36:06 |
| | 5. Eusebio Guinez (ARG) | 2:36:36 |
| | 6. Thomas Sidney Luyt (S. AF) | 2:38:11 |
| **1952**  HELSINKI | 1. Emil Zatopek (CZECH) | 2:23:04 |
| | 2. Reinaldo Gorno (ARG) | 2:25:35 |
| | 3. Gustaf Jansson (SWE) | 2:26:07 |
| | 4. Yoon Chil Choi (KOR) | 2:26:36 |
| | 5. Veikko Karvonen (FIN) | 2:26:42 |
| | 6. Delfo Cabrera (ARG) | 2:26:43 |
| **1956**  MELBOURNE | 1. Alain Mimoun (FR) | 2:25:00 |
| | 2. Franjo Mihalic (YUG) | 2:26:32 |
| | 3. Veikko Karvonen (FIN) | 2:27:47 |

* The Olympic marathon distance was standardized in 1924 at 42.195 km. or 26 miles 385 yards.

173

**1956** MELBOURNE (*cont.*)

|  |  |
|---|---|
| 4. Chang-Hoon Lee (KOR) | 2:28:45 |
| 5. Yoshiaki Kawashima (JAP) | 2:29:19 |
| 6. Emil Zatopek (CZECH) | 2:29:34 |

**1960** ROME

|  |  |
|---|---|
| 1. Abebe Bikila (ETH) | 2:15:17 |
| 2. Rhadi Ben Abdesselem (MOR) | 2:15:42 |
| 3. Barry Magee (NZ) | 2:17:19 |
| 4. Konstantin Vorbiev (USSR) | 2:19:10 |
| 5. Sergey Popov (USSR) | 2:19:19 |
| 6. Thyge Torgersen (DEN) | 2:21:04 |

**1964** TOKYO

|  |  |
|---|---|
| 1. Abebe Bikila (ETH) | 2:12:12 |
| 2. Basil Heatley (GB) | 2:16:20 |
| 3. Kokichi Tsuburaya (JAP) | 2:16:23 |
| 4. Brian Kilby (GB) | 2:17:03 |
| 5. Jozsef Suto (HUNG) | 2:17:56 |
| 6. Buddy Edelen (US) | 2:18:13 |

**1968** MEXICO CITY

|  |  |
|---|---|
| 1. Mamo Wolde (ETH) | 2:20:27 |
| 2. Kenji Kimihara (JAP) | 2:23:31 |
| 3. Mike Ryan (NZ) | 2:23:45 |
| 4. Ismail Akcay (TUR) | 2:25:19 |
| 5. Bill Adcocks (GB) | 2:25:33 |
| 6. Merawi Gebru (ETH) | 2:27:17 |

**1972** MUNICH

|  |  |
|---|---|
| 1. Frank Shorter (US) | 2:12:20 |
| 2. Karel Lismont (BEL) | 2:14:32 |
| 3. Mamo Wolde (ETH) | 2:15:09 |
| 4. Kenny Moore (US) | 2:15:40 |
| 5. Kenji Kimihara (JAP) | 2:16:27 |
| 6. Ron Hill (GB) | 2:16:35 |

**1976** MONTREAL

|  |  |
|---|---|
| 1. Waldemar Cierpinski (GDR) | 2:09:55 |
| 2. Frank Shorter (US) | 2:10:46 |
| 3. Karel Lismont (BEL) | 2:11:13 |
| 4. Don Kardong (US) | 2:11:16 |
| 5. Lasse Viren (FIN) | 2:13:11 |
| 6. Jerome Drayton (CAN) | 2:13:30 |

**1980** MOSCOW

1.
2.
3.
4.
5.
6.

Apart from the Olympic event, the race to which most marathon runners can aspire if they can meet the qualifying standards is the Boston or B.A.A. Marathon held each Patriot's Day in Boston, Mass. Figure 2 showed how the winning times have lowered over the years to the present record of 2:09:55, which equals the Olympic record. It was set by Bill Rodgers in 1975.

Women have only recently managed to force themselves into the Boston Marathon (from 1972) and therefore their records are much more recent. The Boston event has always been closely controlled according to AAU rules and therefore has never been innovative. ("Tradition! Tradition!" was Tevye's excuse too.) Indeed, the rules up to 1969 included such archaic concepts as that women should not run *with* men, nor should run without a chaperone! Fortunately the AAU rules have never been sacrosanct, and now we can report how well the women are doing.

So much for other people's marathon times. However, the attraction of the marathon can be described in exactly the same way that Glenda Jackson describes acting as her life: "It provides the fulfillment of never being fulfilled. You're never as good as you'd like to be." What we are really concerned with is our own progress and our own best times. Thus pages 180–183 are provided for your own record. Each bettered time is a partial fulfillment!

**Photo 20**
There is satisfaction in your first marathon. Jeff Dorko encompasses his wife Cheryl after her first completion at the North Park Boston Qualifier, Pittsburgh, March 1978. (*Photo by John Graham*)

## MEN

| Year | | | | | | |
|---|---|---|---|---|---|---|
| 1897 | John McDermott | 2:55:10 | James Kiernan | 3:02:— | Edward Rhell | 3:02:— |
| 1898 | Ron McDonald | 2:42:00 | Hamilton Gray | 2:45:— | Robert McLennon | 2:48:02 |
| 1899 | Lawrence Brignolia | 2:54:38 | Dick Grant | 2:57:— | Bart Sullivan | 3:02:01 |
| 1900 | James Caffrey | 2:39:44 | Bill Sherring | 2:41:— | Dick Grant | |
| 1901 | James Caffrey | 2:29:23 | Bill Davis | 2:34:45 | Sammy Mellor | 2:44:34 |
| 1902 | Sammy Mellor | 2:43:12 | J. J. Kenney | 2:45:— | John Lorden | |
| 1903 | John Lorden | 2:41:29 | Sammy Mellor | 2:47:— | Mike Spring | 2:53:— |
| 1904 | Mike Spring | 2:38:04 | Tom Hicks | 2:39:34 | Tom Cook | |
| 1905 | Fred Lorz | 2:38:25 | Louis Marks | 2:39:50 | Bob Fowler | 2:42:35 |
| 1906 | Tim Ford | 2:45:45 | David Kneeland | 2:45:51 | Sammy Mellor | |
| 1907 | Tom Longboat | 2:24:24 | Bob Fowler | 2:27:— | John Hayes | 2:30:38 |
| 1908 | Tom Morrisey | 2:25:43 | John Hayes | 2:26:04 | Bob Fowler | |
| 1909 | Henri Renaud | 2:53:36 | Harry Jensen | 2:57:— | Patrick Grant | 2:58:— |
| 1910 | Fred Cameron | 2:28:52 | Clarence DeMar | 2:29:52 | James Cockery | 2:34:— |
| 1911 | Clarence DeMar | 2:21:39 | Festus Madden | | Alexis Ahlgren | |
| 1912 | Mike Ryan | 2:21:18 | Andrew Sockalexis | 2:21:52 | Festus Madden | |
| 1913 | Fritz Carlson | 2:25:14 | Andrew Sockalexis | 2:27:12 | Harry Smith | 2:28:24 |
| 1914 | James Duffy | 2:25:01 | Edouard Fabre | 2:25:— | Villar Kyronen | |
| 1915 | Edouard Fabre | 2:31:41 | Cliff Horne | 2:33:01 | Sidney Hatch | 2:35:47 |
| 1916 | Arthur Roth | 2:27:16 | Villar Kyronen | 2:27:58 | Sidney Hatch | |
| 1917 | Bill Kennedy | 2:28:37 | Sidney Hatch | 2:30:10 | Clarence DeMar | 2:31:05 |
| 1918 | Military Team Race | | | | | |
| 1919 | Carl Linder | 2:29:13 | Willie Wick | | Otto Laakso | |
| 1920 | Peter Trivoulidas | 2:29:31 | Arthur Roth | 2:30:31 | (?) | |

| Year | First | Time | Second | Time | Third | Time |
|------|-------|------|--------|------|-------|------|
| 1921 | Frank Zuna | 2:18:57 | Chuck Mellor | 2:22:12 | Peter Trivoulidas | 2:22:49 |
| 1922 | Clarence DeMar | 2:18:10 | Villa Ritola | 2:21:44 | Albert Smoke | |
| 1923 | Clarence DeMar | 2:23:37 | Frank Zuna | 2:25:20 | Willie Carlson | |
| 1924 | Clarence DeMar | 2:29:40 | Chuck Mellor | 2:35:04 | Frank Wendling | 2:37:40 |
| 1925 | Chuck Mellor | 2:33:00 | Clarence DeMar | 2:33:37 | Frank Zuna | 2:35:35 |
| 1926 | John Miles | 2:25:40 | Albin Stenroos | 2:29:40 | Clarence DeMar | 2:32:15 |
| 1927 | Clarence DeMar | 2:40:22 | Karl Koski | 2:44:41 | Bill Kennedy | |
| 1928 | Clarence DeMar | 2:37:07 | James Henigan | | Joey Ray | 2:41:56 |
| 1929 | John Miles | 2:33:08 | Karl Koski | 2:35:26 | Villar Kyronen | 2:35:44 |
| 1930 | Clarence DeMar | 2:34:48 | Villar Kyronen | 2:36:27 | Karl Koski | 2:38:— |
| 1931 | James Henigan | 2:46:45 | Fred Ward | 2:49:03 | Karl Koski | 2:53:27 |
| 1932 | Paul DeBruyn | 2:33:36 | James Henigan | 2:34:32 | John McLeod | |
| 1933 | Leslie Pawson | 2:31:01 | Dave Komonen | 2:36:— | (?) | |
| 1934 | Dave Komomen | 2:32:53 | John A. Kelley | 2:36:— | (?) | |
| 1935 | John A. Kelley | 2:32:07 | Pat Dengis | 2:34:11 | (?) | |
| 1936 | Ellison Brown | 2:33:40 | Billy McMahon | 2:35:27 | (?) | |
| 1937 | Walter Young | 2:33:20 | John A. Kelley | 2:39:— | Leslie Pawson | 2:41:46 |
| 1938 | Leslie Pawson | 2:35:34 | Pat Dengis | 2:36:40 | John A. Kelley | 2:37:34 |
| 1939 | Ellison Brown | 2:28:51 | Don Heinicke | 2:31:— | Walter Young | 2:31:— |
| 1940 | Gerard Cote | 2:28:28 | John A. Kelley | 2:32:03 | Don Heinicke | |
| 1941 | Leslie Pawson | 2:30:38 | John A. Kelley | 2:31:26 | Don Heinicke | 2:35:— |
| 1942 | Joe Smith | 2:26:51 | Lou Gregory | 2:28:03 | Carl Maroney | 2:36:13 |
| 1943 | Gerard Cote | 2:28:25 | John A. Kelley | 2:30:00 | Fred McGlone | 2:30:41 |
| 1944 | Gerard Cote | 2:31:50 | John A. Kelley | 2:31:— | Charles Robbins | 2:38:31 |
| 1945 | John A. Kelley | 2:30:40 | Lloyd Bairstow | 2:32:50 | (?) | |
| 1946 | Stylianos Kyriakides | 2:29:27 | John A. Kelley | 2:31:27 | Gerard Cote | 2:36:34 |
| 1947 | Yun Bok Suh | 2:25:39 | Mikko Heitanen | 2:29:— | Ted Vogel | 2:30:10 |
| 1948 | Gerard Cote | 2:31:02 | Ted Vogel | 2:31:46 | Jesse Van Zant | 2:36:— |

## MEN

| Year | | | | | |
|---|---|---|---|---|---|
| 1949 | Gosta Leandersson | 2:31:50 | Vic Durgall | 2:34:58 | Louis White |
| 1950 | Kee Yong Ham | 2:32:39 | Kil Yoon Song | 2:35:58 | Yoon Chil Choi |
| 1951 | Shigeki Tanaka | 2:27:45 | John Lafferty | 2:31:15 | Ath. Ragazos 2:35:27 |
| 1952 | Doroteo Flores | 2:31:53 | Vic Dyrgall | 2:36:41 | Luis Velasquez 2:40:08 |
| 1953 | Keizo Yamada | 2:18:51 | Veikko Karvonen | 2:19:19 | Gosta Leandersson 2:19:36 |
| 1954 | Veikko Karvonen | 2:20:39 | Jim Peters | 2:22:40 | Erkki Puolakka 2:24:25 |
| 1955 | Hideo Hamamura | 2:18:22 | Eino Pulkkinen | | Nick Costes |
| 1956 | Antti Viskari | 2:14:14 | John J. Kelley | 2:14:33 | Eino Oksanen 2:17:56 |
| 1957 | John J. Kelley | 2:20:05 | Veikko Karvonen | 2:23:54 | Chung Woo Lim 2:24:59 |
| 1958 | Franjo Mihalic | 2:25:54 | John J. Kelley | 2:30:51 | Eino Pulkkinen 2:37:04 |
| 1959 | Eino Oksanen | 2:22:42 | John J. Kelley | 2:23:43 | Gordon Dickson 2:24:04 |
| 1960 | Paavo Kotila | 2:20:54 | Gordon McKenzie | 2:22:18 | Jim Green 2:23:37 |
| 1961 | Eino Oksanen | 2:23:39 | John J. Kelley | 2:23:54 | Fred Norris 2:26:46 |
| 1962 | Eino Oksanen | 2:23:48 | Paavo Pystynen | 2:24:58 | Alex Breckenridge 2:27:17 |
| 1963 | A. Vandendriessche | 2:18:58 | John J. Kelley | 2:21:09 | Brian Kilby 2:21:43 |
| 1964 | A. Vandendriessche | 2:19:59 | Tenho Salakka | 2:20:48 | Ron Wallingford 2:20:51 |
| 1965 | Morio Shigematsu | 2:16:33 | Hideaki Shishido | 2:17:13 | Takayuke Nakao 2:17:31 |
| 1966 | Kenji Kimihara | 2:17:11 | Seiichiro Sasaki | 2:17:24 | Toru Terasawa 2:17:46 |
| 1967 | Dave McKenzie | 2:15:45 | Tom Laris | 2:16:48 | Yutaki Aoki 2:17:17 |
| 1968 | Amby Burfoot | 2:22:17 | Bill Clark | 2:22:49 | Alfredo Penaloza 2:25:06 |
| 1969 | Yoshiaki Unetani | 2:13:49 | Pablo Garrido | 2:17:30 | Alfredo Penaloza 2:19:56 |
| 1970 | Ron Hill | 2:11:30 | Eamon O'Reilley | 2:11:12 | Pat McMahon 2:14:53 |
| 1971 | Alvaro Mejia | 2:18:45 | Pat McMahon | 2:18:50 | John Halberstadt 2:22:23 |
| 1972 | Olavi Suomalainen | 2:15:39 | Victor Mora | 2:15:57 | Jacinto Sabinal 2:16:10 |

| Year | | | | | | |
|---|---|---|---|---|---|---|
| 1973 | Jon Anderson | 2:16:03 | | | Cliff Buchanan | 2:17:46 |
| 1974 | Neil Cusack | 2:13:39 | Tom Fleming | 2:14:25 | Jerome Drayton | 2:15:40 |
| 1975 | Bill Rodgers | 2:09:55 | Steve Hoag | 2:11:54 | Tom Fleming | 2:12:05 |
| 1976 | Jack Fultz | 2:20:19 | Mario Cuevas | 2:21:13 | Jose DeJesus | 2:22:10 |
| 1977 | Jerome Drayton | 2:14:46 | Veli Bally | 2:15:44 | Brian  Maxwell | 2:17:21 |
| 1978 | Bill Rodgers | 2:10:13 | Jeff Wells | 2:10:15 | Essa Tikkanen | 2:11:15 |
| 1979 | Bill Rodgers | 2:09:27 | Toshihiko Seko | 2:10:12 | Robert J. Hodge | 2:12:30 |
| 1980 | Bill Rodgers | 2:12:11 | Marco Marchei | 2:13:20 | Ron Tabb | 2:14:48 |
| 1981 | | | | | | |

## WOMEN

| Year | | | | | | |
|---|---|---|---|---|---|---|
| 1966* | Roberta Gibb Bingay | 3:21:40 | Katherine Switzer | 4:20:02 | Nina Kuscik | 3:46:— |
| 1967* | Roberta Gibb Bingay | 3:27:17 | Marjorie Fish | 4:45:— | S. Zerrangi | 3:30:— |
| 1968* | Roberta Gibb Bingay | 3:40:— | | | | |
| 1969* | Sara Mae Berman | 3:22:46 | Elaine Pederson | 3:43:— | Katherine  Switzer | 3:25:— |
| 1970* | Sara Mae Berman | 3:05:07 | Nina Kuscik | 3:12:16 | Katherine Switzer | 3:29:51 |
| 1971* | Sara Mae Berman | 3:08:30 | Nina Kuscik | 3:09:00 | Jenny Taylor | 3:16:30 |
| 1972 | Nina Kuscik | 3:10:26 | Elaine Pederson | 3:20:35 | Nina Kuscik | 2:55:12 |
| 1973 | Jacki Hansen | 3:05:59 | Nina Kuscik | 3:09:00 | Gayle Barron | 2:54:11 |
| 1974 | Miki Gorman | 2:47:11 | C. Kofferschlager (WG) | 2:53:— | D. B. Doolittle | 2:56:26 |
| 1975 | Liane Winter (WG) | 2:42:33 | Katherine Switzer | 2:51:37 | Lisa Lorrain | 2:56:04 |
| 1976 | Kim Merritt | 2:47:10 | Miki Gorman | 2:52:27 | Jane Killion | 2:47:22 |
| 1977 | Miki Gorman | 2:48:33 | Marilyn Bevans | 2:51:12 | Susan C. Krenn | 2:38:50 |
| 1978 | Gayle Barron | 2:44:52 | Penny DeMoss | 2:45:34 | Gilliam Adams | 2:39:17 |
| 1979 | Joan Benoit | 2:35:15 | Patti Lyons | 2:38:22 | | |
| 1980 | Jacqueline Gareau | 2:34:26 | Patti Lyons | 2:35:08 | | |
| 1981 | | | | | | |

\* Unofficial times.

Personal marathon performances

| NO. | DATE | MARATHON | TIME | RATE (Min./Mile) | PLACE | | NOTES |
|-----|------|----------|------|-----------------|-------|------|-------|
|     |      |          |      |                 | Open | Age group | |

Personal marathon performances (*cont.*)

| NO. | DATE | MARATHON | TIME | RATE (Min./Mile) | PLACE | | NOTES |
|-----|------|----------|------|------------------|-------|------|-------|
|     |      |          |      |                  | Open | Age group |     |

# Appendix II
# Marathon Listings

The number of marathons has grown steadily in recent years: 1968, 38 marathons; 1969, 44; 1970, 73; 1971, 102; 1972, 124; 1973, 127; 1974, 135; 1975, 144; 1976, 150; 1977, 180; 1978, over 240 in the U.S.A. Numbers have now grown uncertain simply because almost every running club has found that runners want a marathon of their own, almost as much as the 1-mile fun run.

Nevertheless, numbers of marathon races seem to have leveled off, while the number of marathoners in each is still rising, and of course the problems of organizing a large race (large in terms of numbers of entrants) are being forced upon races which were essentially small to start with. The following list is of 290 marathons, provided to enable you to choose your races. Only essential information is provided, although in each case the contact will be able to provide more.

The relevant information which you need includes the date and time, the starting and registration locations, details about the course, and what aid and what time information (splits) will be given. You need to know how to enter and what the cost is and whether there are any terms or qualifications regarding age or membership (some national organizations exact a feudal toll from both race organizers and runners), and the time limit for entries. The race organizer also ought to be able to tell you something about local lodgings and facilities for changing and showering if you come from some distance, and he may or may not be prepared to tell you about local attractions to keep friends and family happy while you run. Finally, you may like to know about the competition, what the winners' times were last year, what the course records are, and of course whether there are any awards for the coming race. The director may also tell you how results will be given to you, whether through the mail or by posting immediately after the race. Generally you can get most of this information at the cost of an inquiry and a stamped self-addressed return envelope.

The following list doesn't attempt to provide this information, because it would be out of date almost immediately. What we have tried to provide is the following:

- the location of the race
- the month in which it is held
- the name and address of the contact

- a basic description of the course
- the record time for the course
- some indication of the size of the field
- whether the course is certified (in case you are seeking to qualify for Boston on a certified-distance course)

A race can have several forms: from A to B with a different ending point from the start; an out-and-back over the same half-marathon route; a loop course; or a multiple-loop course, some with as many as eight loops. The forms are in order of increasing ease of organization but also in order of difficulty to the runners. It is much easier to quit on a multiple-loop course, where you have to convince yourself to go another lap past the home base when everything is hurting. The list gives you this basic route configuration.

A complete course description should also tell you whether it has hills, and whether these are at significant points, or whether the terrain is rolling. The Maryland Marathon has a significant hill at 18 miles, whereas the Fiesta Bowl is gradually downhill after mile 6. Boston is basically downhill overall but has four short rises at 16 to 19 miles which can be difficult if you have expended too much energy earlier on. Some race directors will even provide profiles of their courses so that you can plan ahead. Furthermore it is nice to know the surface: asphalt, dirt trails, concrete, any grass. Is there protection from cars, or is the race through residential or business districts? Finally, a good race director will give the entrant some indication of the usual weather to be expected.

Table 16, the cross-table preceding the list, will simplify selecting a race at the time and place you prefer. Under the state and month subdivisions we've noted by number the marathon in the following alphabetical listing that will take place in the state during that month. The listing is as complete as we can manage at the final drafting of this book, but since the field is expanding so rapidly it is inevitable that there will be some additions and, just as inevitably, some of the poorer-organized races will disappear from the list.

From the cross-table you will notice that marathons are grouped into a spring and fall season, although there is a reduction in the number during April as the faithful make their annual pilgrimage to Boston. No other marathon makes that sort of dent in the annual listing.

Foreign races are treated at the end of the alphabetical listing, and they are few enough not to need a similar cross-table.

Two planned marathons (Nos. 93 and 143) are not established in date in Kentucky and Texas and are therefore not included in the cross-table. (Note also that No. 34 has been withdrawn from the listing.)

Marathons numbered 228 and above are also included in the table, but they are not in alphabetical order because of their late addition to the listing.

185

# Table 16
## Where and when in the U.S.

| State | Jan. | Feb. | Mar. | Apr. | May | Jun. | Jul. | Aug. | Sep. | Oct. | Nov. | Dec. | Total |
|---|---|---|---|---|---|---|---|---|---|---|---|---|---|
| ALABAMA | | | | | | | 173 | | | | | 96 | 1 |
| ALASKA | | | 6 | | 26 66 243 | 121 202 | | | 50 | | | | 7 |
| ARIZONA | | 5 | | | | | | | 56 | 37 | | 52 | 4 |
| ARKANSAS | | 77 | | 86 | | | | | | | | | 3 |
| CALIFORNIA (NORTHERN) | 157 | 220 | 13 | 33 | 9 153 | | 186 | | | 184 194 | | 109 113 | 11 |
| CALIFORNIA (SOUTHERN) | 125 226 | 12 84 167 | 111 112 | 130 139 150 151 | 144 189 | 155 213 239 | 136 | 51 241 | | 82 187 244 | 183 | 221 | 24 |
| COLORADO | | | | | 209 | | | 162 201 | | 45 | | 171 | 5 |
| CONNECTICUT | | | 98 | | | | | | | | | 181 | 2 |
| DELAWARE | | | 44 | | | | | | | | | | 1 |
| FLORIDA | | 75 124 212 | 57 58 | | | | | | | | 196 | 149 | 7 |
| GEORGIA | 7 158 | 161 | 10 | | | | 14 | | | | 23 | | 5 |
| HAWAII | | | 119 | | | | | | | 63 | | 88 | 4 |
| IDAHO | | | | | 36 | | | | | | 106 | | 2 |

| State | References |
|---|---|
| ILLINOIS | 17, 43, 49, 195, 8, 178, 206, 219, 40, 25, 120, 60, 85, 10 |
| INDIANA | 223, 115, 165, 6 |
| IOWA | 47, 210, 41, 242, 38, 90, 6 |
| KANSAS | 99, 211, 203, 122, 4 |
| KENTUCKY | 100, 16, 2 |
| LOUISIANA | 117, 92, 31, 3 |
| MAINE | 156, 230, 2 |
| MARYLAND | 216, 104, 107, 237, 118, 5 |
| MASSACHUSETTS | 21, 190, 214, 11, 163, 172, 6 |
| MICHIGAN | 218, 185, 132, 20, 147, 236, 129, 238, 8 |
| MINNESOTA | 72, 199, 198, 32, 4 |
| MISSISSIPPI | 126, 1 |
| MISSOURI | 59, 205, 22, 81, 4 |
| MONTANA | 70, 94, 2 |
| NEBRASKA | 108, 133, 148, 208, 4 |
| NEVADA | 105, 102, 3 |
| NEW HAMPSHIRE | 42, 191, 232, 3 |
| NEW JERSEY | 127, 95, 231, 233, 3 |

Where and when in the U.S. (*cont.*)

| State | Jan. | Feb. | Mar. | Apr. | May | Jun. | Jul. | Aug | Sep. | Oct. | Nov. | Dec. | Total |
|---|---|---|---|---|---|---|---|---|---|---|---|---|---|
| NEW MEXICO | | | | | | | | | | 1<br>35 | | | 2 |
| NEW YORK | | | 18<br>48<br>89<br>179 | 131<br>135 | 27<br>55<br>227 | | | | 101<br>182 | 53<br>134<br>192 | | | 14 |
| NORTH CAROLINA | 140 | | | | 91 | | 71 | | | 74<br>234 | 2 | 28 | 7 |
| NORTH DAKOTA | | | | | | 141 | | | | | | | 1 |
| OHIO | | | 4<br>83 | | 65<br>174<br>240 | 67 | | | | | 128 | | 7 |
| OKLAHOMA | | | 146 | | 177 | | | | | | | | 2 |
| OREGON | | 207 | | | | 245 | | 39 | 138 | | 166 | | 5 |
| PENNSYLVANIA | | 19<br>137 | 79<br>168<br>176 | 159 | 142 | 68 | | | 169<br>235<br>248 | 97<br>170<br>229 | 80<br>160 | | 16 |
| RHODE ISLAND | | | | | | | | | | 145 | | | 1 |
| SOUTH CAROLINA | | 24 | | | | | | | | | | | 1 |
| SOUTH DAKOTA | | | | | | | | | | | 110 | | 1 |
| TENNESSEE | | 123<br>193 | | | | | | | 3 | | 54 | | 4 |

| | | | | | | | | | | | | | |
|---|---|---|---|---|---|---|---|---|---|---|---|---|---|
| TEXAS | 87 154 | | 62 64 | 204 | 61 103 | | | | 228 | | | 225 | 9 |
| UTAH | | | | | 69 | | 46 | 76 | | 164 | | | 3 |
| VERMONT | | | 180 | | | | | | | | | | 1 |
| VIRGINIA | | | | | | | | | | 175 217 | | | 3 |
| WASHINGTON | | | | 15 215 | | 246 | | | 197 | 29 188 | | | 6 |
| WEST VIRGINIA | | | 78 | | | | | | | | | | 1 |
| WISCONSIN | | | | 222 | 73 224 | 114 | | 152 | 247 | 200 | | | 7 |
| WYOMING | | | | | | | 30 | | | | | | 1 |
| DISTRICT OF COLUMBIA | | | | | | | | | | | 116 | | 1 |
| TOTALS | 9 | 22 | 30 | 20 | 28 | 22 | 15 | 10 | 22 | 32 | 18 | 17 | 245 |

U.S. marathons

| | Race | Mo. | Place | Contact | Conditions | Finished | Records | |
|---|---|---|---|---|---|---|---|---|
| 1 | ALBUQUERQUE | Oct. | Kit Carson Park Albuquerque, N.M. | Gil Duran Box 4071 New Mexico TC Albuquerque, N.M. 87106 | Two laps, out and back | 86 (1977) | 2:32:45 4:36:28 | Emmett Hunt Barrett Salazar |
| 2 | ALL AMERICAN | Nov. | Fort Bragg, N.C. | Recreation Services Officer 82nd Airborne Division Fort Bragg, N.C. 28307 | Point to point, hilly | 134 (1977) | 2:32:48 3:22:22 | Bill Hall Martha Klopfer |
| 3 | ANDREW JACKSON | Sep. | Union University Jackson, Tenn. | Jackson Rec. and Parks Dept. 619 W. Forest Jackson, Tenn. 38301 | Two loops, certified | 87 (1977) | 2:29:30 3:04:46 | David Collins Cathy Sigler |
| 4 | ATHENS | Mar. | Peden Stadium Athens, Ohio | Ellsworth J. Holden, Jr. 26 Northwood Athens, Ohio 45701 | Out and back, mostly flat on rural roads | 123 (1978) | 2:20:41 3:37:48 | Carl Hatfield Maureen Keller |
| 5 | ARIZONA ADMISSIONS DAY | Feb. | Marriott Hotel Tucson, Ariz. | J. McGee Evans 400 N. 2nd Ave. Tucson, Ariz. 85705 | One loop flat, certified | 157 (1977) | 2:20:03 3:25:04 | Blair Johnson Margie Lopez |
| 6 | ARKANSAS | Mar. | Booneville, Ark. | Robert Wald 118 East Main Booneville, Ark. | Mostly flat | | 2:30:36 3:27:49 | James Gudgel Pat Wyatt |

| # | Name | Month | Location | Contact | Course | Entrants | Times | Winners |
|---|------|-------|----------|---------|--------|----------|-------|---------|
| 7 | ATLANTA | Jan. | Westminster School Track Atlanta, Ga. | Jeff Galloway c/o Phidippides 1544 Piedmont Rd. NE Atlanta, Ga. 30324 | Two loops, hilly residential streets; elevation change 270' max. | 158 (1978) | 2:21:27 2:57:11 | Lee Fidler Gayle Barron |
| 8 | AURORA | Jul. | Aurora YMCA Aurora, Ill. | Mark Harrington Aurora Marathon 460 Garfield Ave. Aurora, Ill. 60506 | Out and back, two loops, completely flat | [Over 450 started in 1978.] | 2:32:48 3:31:36 | Tom Antzcak Laurie Rossi |
| 9 | AVENUE OF THE GIANTS | May | Redwoods State Park Weott, Calif. | Dick Meyer Rt. 1, Box 153-A Eureka, Calif. 95501 | Two laps, flat through redwoods; certified | 1,553 (1978) | 2:17:43 2:50:18 | Bill Scobey Jacqueline Hansen |
| 10 | AVON | Mar. | Avon Building Cotillion Rd. Atlanta, Ga. | Bill Neace Avon International Marathon Box 13885 Atlanta, Ga. 30324 | Two loops slightly rolling residential | 135 (1978) | 2:46:16 | Marty Cooksey [Restricted to women.] |
| 11 | B.A.A. | Apr. | Hopkinton, Mass. | Will Cloney Boston A.A. 150 Causeway St. Boston, Mass. 02114 | Point to point, certified Overall downhill but hills at 16–19 miles; good spectator support | 3,826 under 4:00 (1978) | 2:09:55 2:42:33 | Bill Rodgers Liane Winter |
| 12 | BAKERSFIELD | Feb. | West High School Track Bakersfield, Calif. | Bakersfield TC Box 9391 Bakersfield, Calif. 93309 | Two laps, no hills; certified | 60 (1978) | 2:24:13 3:09:24 | Paul Cook Marie Albert |
| 13 | BIDWELL CLASSIC | Mar. | Bidwell Park Chico, Calif. | Walt Schafer 1413 Salem St. Chico, Calif. 95926 | Two loops and flat | 219 (1978) | 2:30:27 3:01:38 | James Barker Merrill Cray |

U.S. marathons *(cont.)*

| | Race | Mo. | Place | Contact | Conditions | Finished | Records | |
|---|---|---|---|---|---|---|---|---|
| 14 | BIG ISLAND | Jul. | Hilo Hawaiian Hotel Hilo, Hawaii | Big Island Marathon Box 1381 Hilo, Hawaii 96720 | Two laps with some hills; certified | 274 (1977) | 2:28:06 3:07:47 | James Barker Cindy Dalrymple |
| 15 | BIRCH BAY | Apr. | Birch Bay State Park Blaine, Wash. | James Pearson 2509 Chuckanut Dr. Bellingham, Wash. 98225 | Two laps; certified | 145 (1978) | 2:26:17 3:19:06 | Matt Yeo Janet Heinonen |
| 16 | BLUEGRASS | Dec. | Frankfort, Ky. | Jerry Stone 15 Merlin Dr. Georgetown, Ky. 40324 | Laps | 8 (1977) | 2:27:13 | David Collins |
| 17 | BOSTON QUALIFIER | Feb. | Champaign, Ill. | Illinois Track Club Box 2976 Station A Champaign, Ill. 61820 | Very flat low-key race | | | |
| 18 | BOSTON QUALIFIER | Mar. | Barton Hall Cornell University Ithaca, N.Y. | James Hartshorne 108 Key St. Ithaca, N.Y. 14850 | One rural rolling loop, 800 feet climbing | 56 (1978) | 2:33:30 3:26:09 | Jim Andrews Margaret Weaver |
| 19 | BOSTON QUALIFIER | Feb. | North Park Pittsburgh, Pa. | Harvey D. Kucherer 1321 Foxwood Dr. Monroeville, Pa. 15146 | Five loops flat around lake; certified | 86 (1978) | 2:29:20 3:18:35 | Max Barr Susan Hollick |
| 20 | BRECKENRIDGE | Jul. | Breckenridge High School Mich. | Breckenridge Track Club 8532 McClelland Rd., Breckenridge, Mich. 48615 | Out and back, mostly flat; certified | 131 (1978) | 2:26:30 3:22:15 | Jacque Varty Anne Luce |

| # | Name | Month | Location | Race Director / Address | Course | Number (Year) | Times | Winners |
|---|---|---|---|---|---|---|---|---|
| 21 | BROCKTON | Feb. | D. W. Field Park Brockton, Mass. | Joe Tomaselli Greater Brockton Striders 68 Malvern Rd. Brockton, Mass. 02401 | Certified | | | Kenn Winn |
| 22 | BUSHWACKER | Jun. | Lyons Park Nevada, Mo. | M. Ted Moore 1008 N. Washington Nevada, Mo. 64772 | | 12 (1978) | 2:42:49 | Steve Nigh |
| 23 | CALLAWAY GARDENS | Nov. | Pine Mountain (Overlook Pavilion) Ga. | Steve McWilliams 1325 N. Highland Ave., Atlanta, Ga. 30306 | Three loops around lake; certified | 200+ (1977) | 2:30:13 3:14:28 | Kenn Winn Nancy Parker |
| 24 | CAROLINA | Feb. | Physical Education Center University of S. C. | Governor's Council on Physical Fitness 2600 Bull St. Columbia, S.C. 29201 | Out and back with two loops, rolling | 180 (1977) | 2:19:03 2:51:13 | Benji Durden Lisa Lorrain |
| 25 | CCAP SOUTHERN ILLINOIS | Sep. | Library Park Flora, Ill. | Mrs. Rose Gill Clay County Advocate Press Box 160 Flora, Ill. 62839 | Out and back | 64 (1977) | 2:34:45 3:28:16 | Paul Kish Karen Kokesh |
| 26 | CHAD OGDEN MEMORIAL | May | Kodiak, Alaska | Kodiak Chamber of Commerce Box 1485 Kodiak, Alaska 99615 | | | | |
| 27 | CHAMPLAIN VALLEY YMCA | May | International Border Rouses Point, N.Y. | Race Director, YMCA, 13 Oak St. Plattsburgh, N.Y. 12901 | Point to point, flat, some dirt and grass | 277 (1978) | 2:27:40 3:14:00 | Ralph Thomas Ellen Turkel |

U.S. marathons (*cont.*)

| | Race | Mo. | Place | Contact | Conditions | Finished | Records | |
|---|---|---|---|---|---|---|---|---|
| 28 | CHARLOTTE OBSERVER | Dec. | Observer Building Charlotte, N.C. | Phidippides Athletes Foot Wear 4400 Sharon Rd. Charlotte, N.C. 28211 | Out and back; certified | 349 (1977) | 2:19:04 3:18:14 | Lee Fidler Marge Loewer |
| 29 | CHENEY | Nov. | Moos Field Cheney, Wash. | Ruth VanKuren 418 Cocolalla Cheney, Wash. 99004 | One loop with some hills; certified | 77 (1977) | 2:23:00 3:25:12 | Terry Heath Rebecca Herzberg |
| 30 | CHEYENNE FRONTIER DAYS | Jul. | Laramie County Community College Cheyenne, Wyo. | Cheyenne Track Club, Box 10154 Cheyenne, Wyo. 82001 | Loops with out and back, some hills; certified | 115 (1977) | 2:35:54 3:16:48 | Richard Bishop Mary L. Matson |
| 31 | CHRISTMAS FESTIVAL | Dec. | Natchitoches, La. | Jerry Dyes Athletic Dept. Northwestern State University Natchitoches, La. 71457 | One loop, flat | 12 (1977) | 2:45:34 | Windell Bonner |
| 32 | CITY OF LAKES | Oct. | Lake Harriet Minneapolis, Minn. | Jeff Winter c/o MDRA 1400 Park Ave. Minneapolis, Minn. 55404 | Four flat laps; certified | 371 (1977) | 2:21:02 3:03:10 | Barney Klacker Jan Arenz |
| 33 | CLEAR LAKE | Apr. | Clear Lake Lakeport, Calif. | Lake County Chamber of Commerce Box 517 Lakeport, Calif. | Rolling hills on lake shoreline | 105 (1978) | 2:39:28 3:28:55 | Noel Lincicome Daphne Dunn |

| | | | | | | | | |
|---|---|---|---|---|---|---|---|---|
| 35 | CLOVIS | Oct. | Cannon Air Force Base Clovis, N.M. | Bill Gaedke 1720 Avondale Clovis, N.M. 88101 | One loop | 157 (1977) | 2:37:55 4:05:13 | Bill Welsh Valerie Plettenberg |
| 36 | COEUR D'ALENE | May | Coeur D'Alene, Idaho | North Idaho Road Runners, Route 2, Box 378 A Coeur D'Alene, Idaho 83814 | | 267 (1978) | 2:27:35 3:13:19 | Don Kardong Judy Groombridge |
| 37 | COPPER VALLEY | Oct. | San Carlos Reservation Globe, Ariz. | Globe Chamber of Commerce Attn: Tom E. Anderson, Box 2539 Globe, Ariz. 85501 | Point to point, gradual climb | 66 (1977) | 2:41:28 5:00:10 | Tom Rotkis Renee Calvert |
| 38 | COVERED BRIDGE | Oct. | Winterset, Iowa | Jerrold Oliver F&M Bank Building Winterset, Iowa 50273 | Out and back and hilly | 72 (1977) | | [New course in 1978.] |
| 39 | CRATER LAKE | Aug. | Watchman Overlook Crater Lake, Oregon | Crater Lake Rim Run c/o Frank Shields Crater Lake, Ore. 97604 | One loop and hilly | 25 (1977) | 2:52:18 3:36:00 | Jeff Barrie Susan Thomas |
| 40 | CRAWFORDSVILLE JAYCEE | Aug. | Crawfordsville, Ind. | Henri Chase 32 Parliament Place, LH Crawfordsville, Ind. 47933 | City streets, state and county roads | | | [New race in 1978.] |
| 41 | CYCLONE COUNTRY | Jun. | Iowa State University Ames, Iowa | Dick Seagrave 2500 Kellogg Ames, Iowa 50010 | Double loop; certified | 13 (1977) | 2:29:16 | Wes Christ |
| 42 | DARTMOUTH MEDICAL SCHOOL | Oct. | Hanover, N.H. | Marathon Dartmouth Medical School Hanover, N.H. 03755 | One loop | 104 (1977) | 2:30:41 3:06:50 | Robert Duncan Carol Geig |

## U.S. marathons *(cont.)*

| | Race | Mo. | Place | Contact | Conditions | Finished | Records | |
|---|---|---|---|---|---|---|---|---|
| 43 | DEKALB | Apr. | Dekalb, Ill. | Roy Carlson 830 Edgebrook No. 229 Dekalb, Ill. 60115 | County highways | 152 (1978) | 2:32:59 | Jesse Garcia |
| 44 | DELAWARE NATIONAL GUARD | Mar. | Wilmington, Del. | Delaware National Guard Marathon Commission 1401 Newport Gap Pike Wilmington, Del. 19804 | Flat, out and back; to be certified | 178 (1978) | 2:30:02 3:17:47 | Dan Rincon Debbie Parks |
| 45 | DENVER YMCA | Oct. | Sloan's Lake Denver, Colo. | Phil Guries, YMCA 25 E. 16th Ave. Denver, Colo. 80202 | Laps, no hills | 128 (1977) | 2:28:48 3:17:47 | Dan Maynihan Donna Messenger |
| 46 | DESERET NEWS | Jul. | Big Mountain Salt Lake City, Utah | Deseret News Marathon Box 1257 Salt Lake City, Utah 84110 | Point to point, hilly | 309 (1977) | 2:20:24 3:13:40 | Scott Bringhurst Barbara Anton |
| 47 | DRAKE RELAYS | Apr. | Capitol Building Des Moines, Iowa | Robert Ehrhart Drake University Des Moines, Iowa 50311 | Point to point; certified; must be aged 19 or over to run | 805 (1978) | 2:15:19 2:47:46 | Charlie McMullen Janice Arenz |
| 48 | EARTH DAY | Mar. | Westbury, N.Y. | Sports Unit Eisenhower Park East Meadow, N.Y. 11443 | Five laps | 523 (1977) | 2:21:49 2:59:43 | Paul Fetscher Nina Kuscsik |

| # | Name | Month | Location | Contact | Course | Field (Year) | Times | Winners |
|---|---|---|---|---|---|---|---|---|
| 49 | EDWARDSVILLE | Jun. | Southern Illinois Campus Edwardsville, Ill. | Robert Burker Southern Illinois University Edwardsville, Ill. 62026 | Out and back and hilly | 130 (1977) | 2:53:59 3:51:59 | Ole Kristensen Mel Landgon |
| 50 | EQUINOX | Sep. | University of Alaska Fairbanks, Alaska | William L. Smith Athletic Dept. University of Alaska Fairbanks, Alaska 99701 | | | | |
| 51 | EXECUTIVE SHARE HEALTH | Aug. | Irvine, Calif. | Mark Turin 4000 Park Newport Suite 408 Newport Beach, Calif. 92660 | | 13 (1978) | 2:36:54 4:00:00 | Michael Sayward Francine Solomon |
| 52 | FIESTA BOWL | Dec. | Carefree School Scottsdale, Ariz. | Race Director Fiesta Bowl Marathon 3410 E. Van Buren Phoenix, Ariz. 85008 | Point to point, gently downhill after 6 miles | 1,000 (1977) | 2:14:13 2:46:32 | Ed Mendoza Adrian Beames |
| 53 | FINGER LAKES | Oct. | Ithaca, N.Y. | James Hartshorne 108 Kay St., Ithaca, N.Y. 14850 | Point to point; certified | 55 (1977) | 2:30:09 3:21:29 | Peter Jeffers Melissa Behr |
| 54 | FIRST TENNESSEE BANK | Nov. | Snow Hill Community Chattanooga, Tenn. | Earl A. Marler, Jr. First Tennessee Bank 701 Market St. Chattanooga, Tenn. 37402 | Two laps with hills; certified | 80 (1977) | 2:34:08 3:17:09 | Kevin Harper Jill Hall |
| 55 | FIRST TRUST—NORTH AREA YMCA* | May | Griffin Field Liverpool, N.Y. | Marathon Secretary 406 Ruth Rd. North Syracuse, N.Y. 13212 | Out and back, rolling; certified | 275 (1978) | 2:24:42 3:07:01 | Ed Norris Susan Kahler |

* Now called Burger King—North Area YMCA Marathon.

U.S. marathons (*cont.*)

| | Race | Mo. | Place | Contact | Conditions | Finished | Records | |
|---|---|---|---|---|---|---|---|---|
| 56 | FLAGSTAFF | Sep. | Fort Tuthill Flagstaff, Ariz. | Flagstaff Marathon Big Brothers of Flagstaff Box 1701 Flagstaff, Ariz. 86001 | One loop out and back at 7,000 feet | | [New race in 1978.] | |
| 57 | FLORIDA | Mar. | Cape Coral Bridge Ft. Myers, Fla. | Lou Cappi Ft. Myers–Lee County YMCA Box 6488 Ft. Myers, Fla. 33901 | Out and back | | 2:39:08 3:18:30 | Brad Blain Sue Olivik |
| 58 | FLORIDA RELAYS | Mar. | University of Florida Gainesville, Fla. | Paul E. Segersten Track Office University Athletic Association Box 14485 Gainesville, Fla. 32604 | Out and back, some hills; certified | 183 (1978) | 2:17:23 3:09:05 | Brian Quinn Carole McArthur |
| 59 | FORT WOOD OZARK | Feb. | Fort Leonard Wood, Mo. | | | | 2:52:15 3:18:32 | Dean Neal Amy Jones |
| 60 | FREEDOM | Oct. | Allerton Park Monticello, Ill. | Illinois Track Club Box 2976, Station A Champaign, Ill. 61820 | Three laps, flat; certified | 144 (1977) | 2:23:51 3:24:03 | Dike Stirrett Marianne Colter |
| 61 | FUNFEST | May | Medical Center Amarillo, Texas | Richard Taylor 4514 Cornell Amarillo, Texas 79109 | One loop, flat to rolling for last 7½ miles; certified | 102 (1978) | 2:27:08 3:49:— | Hector Ortiz Jill Sawyer |

| # | Name | Month | Location | Organizer/Address | Course | Finishers (Year) | Times | Winners |
|---|------|-------|----------|-------------------|--------|------------------|-------|---------|
| 62 | GALVESTON YMCA | Mar. | Galveston, Texas | Marathon organizer YMCA Galveston, Texas | | 222 (1978) | 2:29:51 3:23:— | Clent Mericle Vanessa Vajpos |
| 63 | GARDEN ISLE | Oct. | Vidinha Stadium Kauai, Hawaii | Greg Ogin c/o Kauai Stores, Box 711 Lihue, Kauai, Hawaii 96766 | One hilly loop; certified | | | [New race in 1978.] |
| 64 | GENE VANN BI-STATE | Mar. | Texarkana, Texas | Gene Vann Bi-State Marathon 3939 Summerhill Rd. Texarkana, Texas 75501 | Loop | 21 (1978) | 2:50:13 4:18:14 | John Stowers Deb Sullivan |
| 65 | GILBOA–PUTNAM COUNTY | May | Middle School Gilboa, Ohio | Sy Mah Box 52 Gilboa, Ohio 45847 | Out and back | 53 (1978) | 2:45:28 3:44:54 | Mark Lisak Melanie Newcombe |
| 66 | GLACIER | May | Girdwood, Alaska | Dr. George McCoy Box 318 Girdwood, Alaska 99587 | | 52 (1978) | 2:43:38 3:31:30 | Eric Skidmore Marcie Trent |
| 67 | GLASS CITY | Jun. | University of Toledo Track Toledo, Ohio | Arthur S. Johnson 2520 Aldringham Toledo, Ohio 43606 | Out and back, flat; certified | 369 (1977) | 2:26:44 3:01:56 | Donald Slusser Alexa Kraft |
| 68 | GOD'S COUNTRY | Jun. | Galeton High School Galeton, Pa. | Ralph J. Wentz c/o Nine Mile Motel Box 117 Ulysses, Pa. 16948 | Point to point on U.S. 6 over one big mountain, climbing 900 feet and dropping 500 feet | 327 (1978) | 2:26:42 3:11:31 | Terry Stanley Emily Trejbal |
| 69 | GOLDEN SPIKE | May | Promotary, Utah | John Ensign Box 338 Brigham City, Utah 84302 | Point to point; certified | 300 (1978) | 2:35:42 3:41:25 | Steve Naylor Shauna Heiser |

## U.S. marathons (cont.)

| | Race | Mo. | Place | Contact | Conditions | Finished | Records | |
|---|---|---|---|---|---|---|---|---|
| 70 | GOVERNOR'S CUP | Jun. | Vigilante Campground York, Mont. | Mayo Ashley 1530 Jerome Pl. Helena, Mont. 59601 | Point to point | 80 (1977) | 2:34:27 3:34:00 | Orville Hess Yvonne Reiman |
| 71 | GRANDFATHER MOUNTAIN | Jul. | Appalachian State University Boone, N.C. | Marathon Coordinator Appalachian State University Boone, N.C. 28608 | Climbs 1,300 feet; certified | 58 (1977) | 2:45:42 | Gareth Hayes |
| 72 | GRANDMA'S | Jun. | Two Harbors, Minn. | Scott Keenan 1533 W. Arrowhead Rd., Duluth, Minn. 55811 | Flat point to point; certified | 116 (1977) | 2:21:54 3:23:39 | Garry Bjorklund Wendy Hovland |
| 73 | GREEN BAY "BAREFOOT" | May | Green Bay, Wisc. | Barefoot Sports C-1306 Port Plaza Mall, Green Bay, Wisc. 54301 | | 16 (1978) | 2:36:44 | Jeff Pullen |
| 74 | GREENSBORO | Oct. | Greensboro, N.C. | Dave MacKenzie 1000 Fairmont Greensboro, N.C. 27401 | Two laps; certified | 63 (1977) | 2:20:28 3:15:17 | Scott Eden Kim Fisher |
| 75 | GREATER MIAMI | Feb. | Palmetto Senior High School Miami, Fla. | Eli Gagich 10852 North Kendall Dr., No. 212 Miami, Fla. 33176 | Flat, out and back; certified; must wear shirt to run | 92 (1977) | 2:27:46 | Chris Quimby |
| 76 | GREEN MOUNTAIN | Aug. | Allenholm Farms South Hero, Vt. | Leighton Walker 2 Redwood Terr. Essex Junction, Vt. 05452 | One flat loop; certified | 30 (1977) | | [New course in 1978.] |

| # | Name | Month | Location | Contact | Course | No. (Year) | Times | Winners |
|---|------|-------|----------|---------|--------|-----------|-------|---------|
| 77 | GROUND HOG DAY | Jan./Feb. | Petit Jean State Park Little Rock, Ark. | Ted Mathews 2200 Worthen Bank Building Little Rock, Ark. 72201 | Two laps; certified | | 2:21:55 3:33:05 | Terry Zeigler Donna Riley |
| 78 | HALL OF FAME | Mar. | Marshall University Huntington, W.Va. | Edward Canterbury 714 Mary St. Huntington, W.Va. 25704 | Out and back | 45 (1977) | 2:19:00 3:30:32 | Carl Hatfield Lind McFessel |
| 79 | HARRC-NAVY DEPOT | Mar. | Mechanicsburg, Pa. | Nick Marshall 211 N. 17th St. Camp Hill, Pa. 17011 | Flat laps | 69 (1977) | | [No race planned for 1978.] |
| 80 | HARRISBURG NATIONAL | Nov. | Capitol Building Harrisburg, Pa. | Park Barner/James Kuntz, YMCA Front and North Sts. Harrisburg, Pa. 17101 | Out and back; some hills; certified | 343 (1977) | 2:22:07 3:14:07 | Jeff Bradley Anne Blasco |
| 81 | HEART OF AMERICA | Sep. | Columbia, Mo. | Joe Duncan 4004 Defoe Dr. Columbia, Mo. 65201 | Loop with out and back, some hills | 129 (1977) | 2:29:15 3:09:21 | Dennis Hinkamp Joan Hirt |
| 82 | HEART OF SAN DIEGO | Oct. | Coronado San Diego, Calif. | c/o Race Director San Diego County Heart Association 3640 5th Ave. P.O. Box 3625 San Diego, Calif. 92103 | Flat point to point over the Coronado Bridge | | | [New race in 1978.] |
| 83 | HEARTWATCHERS | Mar. | Bowling Green University Toledo, Ohio | Fred Fineske 1707 Eastfield Maumee, Ohio 43537 | Point to point | 113 (1978) | 2:30:41 3:21:09 | Ed Steingraber, Max Barr Phyllis Braun |

# U.S. marathons (cont.)

| | Race | Mo. | Place | Contact | Conditions | Finished | Records | |
|---|---|---|---|---|---|---|---|---|
| 84 | HIDDEN VALLEY | Feb. | Newbury Park Academy Calif. | Marathon 180 Academy Dr. Newbury Park, Calif. 91320 | Out and back, some hills | 194 (1978) | 2:28:59 3:03:39 | Bruce Dewsberry Sue Petersen |
| 85 | HINSDALE | Nov. | Central High School Hinsdale, Ill. | Jim Hagel 102 N. Quincy Hinsdale, Ill. 60521 | One loop, flat; certified | 112 (1977) | 2:26:15 3:25:50 | Erma Tranter |
| 86 | HOGEYE | Apr. | Fayetteville, Ark. | Barry S. Brown University of Arkansas Fayetteville, Ark. 72701 | Out and back; certified | 42 (1978) | 2:47:06 3:46:02 | John Gaston Kathy Royce |
| 87 | HOUSTON | Jan. | Memorial Park Houston, Texas | George Kleeman 227 Faust Lane Houston, Texas 77024 | Laps with a few hills; certified | 572 (1978) | 2:17:11 3:00:34 | Ron Tabb Dorothy Doolittle |
| 88 | HONOLULU | Dec. | Aloha Tower Honolulu, Hawaii | Honolulu Marathon Association Box 27244 Chinatown Station Honolulu, Hawaii 96827 | Out and back, flat; certified | 2,899 (1977) | 2:17:24 2:44:44 | Jack Foster Kim Merritt |
| 89 | HUDSON–MOHAWK | Mar. | Physical Education Building Albany State College, N.Y. | Burke Adams 21 Chestnut Ct. Rensselaer, N.Y. 12144 | Four loops on flat concrete | 73 (1978) | 2:28:04 3:41:52 | Jack Callaci Jan Helker |
| 90 | IOWA CITY | Nov. | Iowa City, Iowa | Mike Kendall Iowa City Running Club, Box 1925 Iowa City, Iowa 52240 | Out and back, flat; certified | 90 (1977) | 2:28:55 3:02:47 | Raymond Hayes Mary Burns |

| | | | | | | | | |
|---|---|---|---|---|---|---|---|---|
| 91 | INTERNATIONAL MASTERS | May | North Carolina State University Raleigh, N.C. | Raiford Fulghum Box 590 Raleigh Parks and Recreation Raleigh, N.C. 27602 | Two laps with some hills | 13 (1977) | 2:44:55 | William King |
| 92 | INTERNATIONAL RICE FESTIVAL | Oct. | Crowley, La. | Dr. Charles Atwood 621 N. Ave. K Crowley, La. 70526 | Point to point; certified | 573 (1977) | 2:14:27 2:51:22 | Neil Cusack Dorothy Doolittle |
| 93 | JEFFERSON COUNTY METRO | | Louisville, Ky. | | | 263 (1977) | 2:26:55 3:13:02 | Brad Ferguson Cathy Fox |
| 94 | JERRY ANDERSON | Oct. | Kalispell Junior High Kalispell, Mont. | Mike Lyngstad 723 5th Ave. E. Kalispell, Mont. 59901 | Out and back, some hills; certified | 21 (1977) | 2:42:29 3:27:27 | John Wesley Judy Groombridge |
| 95 | JERSEY SHORE | Dec. | Asbury Park, N.J. | Convention Hall Jersey Shore Marathon Asbury Park, N.J. 07712 | Out and back, flat along shore roads; certified | 1,400 (1977) | 2:18:04 3:01:45 | Bill Sieben Jean Chodnicki |
| 96 | JOE STEELE ROCKET CITY | Dec. | Monte Sano Mountain Huntsville, Ala. | Harold Tinsley 8811 Edgehill Dr. Huntsville, Ala. 35802 | Point to point with some hills; certified | 323 (1977) | 2:17:35 2:52:37 | Steve Bolt Phyllis Hines |
| 97 | JOHNSTOWN | Oct. | Top of the Incline Johnstown, Pa. | Thomas Loughrin YMCA Market and Vine St. Johnstown, Pa. 15901 | One loop decline with drop in first half | 97 (1977) | 2:23:09 3:08:33 | Steve Molnar Lisa Matovcik |
| 98 | JOHN W. ENGLISH | Mar. | Wesleyan College Middletown, Conn. | Parks and Recreation Dept, City of Middletown Box 141 Middletown, Conn. 06457 | Two laps | 116 (1978) | 2:27:16 3:10:36 | George Pfeiffer Karen Saunders |

U.S. marathons (*cont.*)

| | Race | Mo. | Place | Contact | Conditions | Finished | Records | |
|---|---|---|---|---|---|---|---|---|
| 99 | KANSAS | Apr. | Memorial Stadium Lawrence, Kan. | Dr. Ed Elbel KU Relays Manager Allen Fieldhouse University of Kansas Lawrence, Kan. 66045 | Mostly flat out and back; certified | 232 (1978) | 2:20:01 3:09:10 | Bob Busby Karen Kokesh |
| 100 | KENTUCKY RELAYS | Apr. | University of Kentucky Lexington, Ky. | Kentucky Relays Marathon Jerry Stone, Chairman, Track Office, Memorial Coliseum University of Kentucky, Lexington, Ky. 40506 | | 79 (1978) | 2:26:16 3:31:50 | James Buell Cathy Fox |
| 101 | LAKE PLACID | Sep. | Paul Smith's College Lake Placid, N.Y. | R. A. Lopez Lake Placid Sports Council Lake Placid, N.Y. 12946 | Point to point; hilly | 30 (1977) | 2:30:— 2:59:— | Chas Duggan Nancy Dragoo |
| 102 | LAKE TAHOE | Jun. | Community Building Incline Village, Nev. | Lake Tahoe Track Club, Box 5983 Incline Village, Nev. 89450 | Out and back, hilly; certified | 91 (1977) | 2:38:04 3:41:51 | John Paulson Yevette Cotte |
| 103 | LAS COLONIAS | May | Pablos Grove Park San Antonio, Texas | Diego M. Vacca Central YMCA 903 N St. Mary's St. San Antonio, Texas 78215 | Out and back | 129 (1977) | 2:29:57 3:30:36 | Clint Mericle Sally Jurgensen |

| # | Name | Month | Location | Contact | Course | Finishers | Times | Winners |
|---|------|-------|----------|---------|--------|-----------|-------|---------|
| 104 | LAST TRAIN TO BOSTON | Mar. | Edgewood Area Aberdeen Proving Ground, Md. | Harry Piotrowski 4024 Old Federal Hill Rd. Jarretsville, Md. 21084 | Flat; certified | [54 started in 1978.] | 2:32:27 2:57:27 | Donald Ocana Sue Petersen |
| 105 | LAS VEGAS | Feb. | University of Nevada Las Vegas, Nev. | Tommy Hodges 6245 Hobart Las Vegas, Nev. 89107 | Point to point, flat; certified | 83 (1977) | | [New course in 1978.] |
| 106 | LES BOIS | Nov. | Barber Park Boise, Idaho | Basil Dahlstrom Box 9281 Boise, Idaho 83707 | Some hills, three laps | 79 (1977) | 2:27:04 3:32:27 | Denis O'Halloran Linda Leonard |
| 107 | LIFE AND HEALTH | Apr. | Frederick, Md. | Gary Wedemeyer 6856 Eastern Ave. N.W., Washington, D.C. 20012 | Out and back with a small loop | 388 (1978) | 2:31:05 | Bruce Dewsberry |
| 108 | LINCOLN | May | University of Nebraska Lincoln, Neb. | Race Director 2818 Cedar Ave. Lincoln, Neb. 68502 | Out and back; certified | 339 (1978) | 2:19:43 3:23:37 | Cliff Karthauser JoAnne Owens |
| 109 | LIVERMORE | Dec. | Livermore, Calif. | Livermore Jaycees Box 524 Livermore, Calif. 94450 | One loop; certified | 379 (1977) | 2:21:00 2:53:14 | Fritz Watson Vicky Bray |
| 110 | LONGEST DAY | Nov. | South Dakota State University Brookings, S.D. | Track Coach South Dakota State University Brookings, S.D. 57006 | One loop, no hills; certified | 83 (1977) | 2:25:42 3:04:43 | Mike Seaman Lynae Larson |
| 111 | LOS ALAMITOS | Mar. | Oak Junior High School Los Alamitos, Calif. | Mitch 10911 Oak St. Los Alamitos, Calif. 90720 | Loop, flat; certified | 254 (1978) | 2:31:39 2:47:07 | Frank Duarte Celia Peterson |

U.S. marathons (*cont.*)

| | Race | Mo. | Place | Contact | Conditions | Finished | Records | |
|---|---|---|---|---|---|---|---|---|
| 112 | LOS ANGELES | Mar. | L.A. Police Academy Los Angeles, Calif. | Fred Honda Municipal Sports Office 3900 Chevy Chase Dr., Los Angeles, Calif. 90039 | Out and back | 247 (1977) | 2:24:19 3:02:34 | Bill Scobey Judy Milkie |
| 113 | MADERA | Dec. | Madera High School Madera, Calif. | Coach Dee Dewitt 200 South L Madera, Calif. 93637 | Two flat laps; certified | 40 (1977) | 2:26:11 3:26:44 | Skip Houk Lucy Bunz |
| 114 | MADISON | Jun. | Capitol Square Madison, Wis. | Dale Roe 1517 Waunona Way Madison, Wis. 53713 | Rolling, point to point through city parks; certified; National Junior USTFF Champ | 246 (1977) | 2:26:03 2:57:43 | Kevin McDonald Patty Melby |
| 115 | MARATHON | Jun. | Dragway Vigo Co. Fair Grounds Terre Haute, Ind. | Dave Phegley Director, Indiana State University Terre Haute, Ind. 47809 | Out and back, gentle rolling through farmland; certified | 391 (1977) | 2:20:52 2:55:00 | Kirk Pfeffer Lora Cartwright |
| 116 | MARINE CORPS RESERVE | Nov. | Iwo Jima Monument Washington, D.C. | Col. James L. Fowler USMCR Headquarters Marine Corps (Code RESP) Washington, D.C. 20380 | Multiple but different loops, flat; certified | 5,833 (1978) | 2:19:36 2:54:12 | Kevin McDonald Sue Mallery |

| No. | Name | Month | Location | Address | Course | Entrants (year) | Times | Winners |
|---|---|---|---|---|---|---|---|---|
| 117 | MARDI GRAS | Jan. | Gernon Brown Gym New Orleans, La. | New Orleans Track Club, Inc. Box 30491 New Orleans, La. 70190 | Out and back, flat; certified | 357 (1978) | 2:20:22 2:59:55 | Ambrose Burfoot Doome Riley |
| 118 | MARYLAND | Dec. | Memorial Stadium Baltimore, Md. | Maryland Marathon Commission Box 11394 Baltimore, Md. 21239 | Out and back, rolling with one long hill at 17½ through 19 miles; certified | 1,545 (1977) | 2:13:46 2:51:18 | Gary Bjorkland Marilyn Bevans |
| 119 | MAUI | Mar. | Kahului War Memorial Gym Maui, Hawaii | Dave Wissmar c/o Wailea Box 888 Kihei, Maui, Hawaii 96753 | Point to point; certified | 373 (1978) | 2:24:31 3:02:42 | Duncan Macdonald Cindy Dalrymple |
| 120 | MAYOR DALEY | Sep. | Daley Plaza Chicago, Ill. | Miss Ruth Ratney 900 N. Michigan Ave., Chicago, Ill. 60611 | Point to point, very flat | 2,131 (1977) | 2:17:52 2:54:56 | Jim Cloeter Marilyn Bevans |
| 121 | MAYOR'S MIDNIGHT SUN | Jun. | Bartlett High School Anchorage, Alaska | Terry Martin 3960 Reka Dr., B-6 Anchorage, Alaska 99504 | Point to point with some hills; certified | 255 (1978) | 2:28:26 3:04:21 | Vernon Campbell Marion May |
| 122 | MEL VOSS MEMORIAL | Dec. | Lake Shawnee Topeka, Kan. | Gene Johnson 4330 Windsor Ct. Topeka, Kan. 66604 | Four laps | 33 (1976) | 2:29:20 2:55:45 | Mike Dunlap, Randy Fischer Terri Anderson |
| 123 | MEMPHIS | Feb. | Memphis, Tenn. | Bud Joyner 1676 Lawrence Ave. Memphis, Tenn. 38112 | | 50 (1978) | 2:24:15 3:21:51 | Terry Gallagher Wendy Truska |
| 124 | MIAMI (GREATER) | Feb. | Miami, Fla. | George Zell Box 557962 Miami, Fla. 33155 | Flat | 121 (1978) | 2:31:23 | Pat Chmiel |

U.S. marathons (*cont.*)

| | Race | Mo. | Place | Contact | Conditions | Finished | Records | |
|---|---|---|---|---|---|---|---|---|
| 125 | MISSION BAY | Jan. | Mission Bay<br>San Diego, Calif. | Mission Bay<br>Marathon<br>2691 Palace Dr.<br>San Diego, Calif.<br>92123 | Loops and<br>flat; certified | 1,777 (1978) | 2:16:03<br>2:54:06 | Kirk Pfeffer<br>Martha Cooksey |
| 126 | MISSISSIPPI | Dec. | Natchez Trace<br>Clinton, Miss. | Walter G. Howell<br>Box 4006<br>Clinton, Miss.<br>39058 | Point to point,<br>mostly flat | 97 (1977) | 2:41:57<br>5:02:14 | Joel Longerin<br>Nancy Alexander |
| 127 | MONMOUTH | Mar. | Monmouth, N.J. | Marathon<br>Monmouth County<br>Park System<br>P.O. Box 326<br>Lincroft, N.J. 07738 | | 51 (1978) | 2:35:17<br>4:23:33 | Dave Burgess<br>Francine Rabinowitz |
| 128 | MONROE | Nov. | Congress Inn<br>Hotel<br>Monroe, Ohio | Felix LeBlanc<br>1013 Tralee Trail<br>Dayton, Ohio 45430 | Out and back,<br>twice;<br>certified | 49 (1977) | 2:30:20<br>3:01:03 | Dave Erler<br>Sue Mallery |
| 129 | MOTOR CITY | Oct. | Belle Isle Park<br>Detroit, Mich. | Detroit Free Press,<br>Race<br>321 W. Lafayette<br>Blvd., Detroit, Mich.<br>48231 | One lap in<br>USA and<br>Canada | 328 (1977) | 2:12:00<br>2:55:59 | Jerome Drayton<br>Ann Forshee |
| 130 | MT. SAC RELAYS | Apr. | Mt. Sac College<br>Walnut, Calif. | Ponoma Jaycees<br>P.O. Box 285<br>Pomona, Calif.<br>91766 | Bad hills | 100+ (1978) | 2:26:52<br>3:35:— | Walt Waltmire<br>Marie Albert |

| | | | | | | | |
|---|---|---|---|---|---|---|---|
| **131** NASSAU COUNTY | Apr. | Long Island, N.Y. | Marathon Director Sports Unit Nassau County Dept. of Recreation and Parks Eisenhower Park East Meadow, N.Y. 11554 | | [800 started in 1977.] | | [New course in 1978.] |
| **132** NATIONAL JUNIOR COLLEGE | Jun. | Southwestern Michigan College Dowagiac, Mich. | Ronald Gunn Southwestern Michigan College Dowagiac, Mich. 49047 | Flat to rolling asphalt, one large loop | 56 (1978) | 2:23:56 3:08:10 | Tim Frye, Robin Holland Nina Crampe |
| **133** NEBRASKA PANHANDLE | Jun. | Scottsbluff, Neb. | Dan Wilder 1215 4th Ave. Scottsbluff, Neb. 69361 | Point to point at 3,800 feet | 52 (1978) | 2:31:19 3:30:10 | Rusty Molstad JoAnne Owens |
| **134** NEW YORK CITY | Oct. | Staten Island, N.Y. | Road Runners Club Box 881 FDR Station New York, N.Y. 10022 | Winding course on city streets through five boroughs | 8,000+ (1978) | 2:10:09 2:32:30 | Bill Rodgers Grete Waitz |
| **135** NEWSDAY | Apr. | East Meadow, Long Island, N.Y. | Road Runners Club Box 881 FDR Station New York, N.Y. 10022 | | 1,085 (1978) | 2:29:45 3:09:30 | Peter Squires Emily Trejbal |
| **136** NEWPORT BEACH | Jul. | Newport Beach, Calif. | Bob Gogne 1710 Santiago Dr. Newport Beach, Calif. 92660 | | | | [New race in 1978.] |

209

U.S. marathons (*cont.*)

| | Race | Mo. | Place | Contact | Conditions | Finished | Records | |
|---|---|---|---|---|---|---|---|---|
| 137 | NITTANY VALLEY | Feb. | Science Park Rd. State College, Pa. | Harry Groves Track Coach, Penn State University 263 Recreation Hall University Park, Pa. 16802 | Out and back with loop, rolling; certified | 51 (1978) | 2:27:47 3:05:54 | Dave Felice Liz Cunningham |
| 138 | NIKE–OTC | Sep. | Hayward Field Eugene, Ore. | Nike–OTC Marathon Athletic Department 99 W. 10th, Suite 105 Eugene, Ore. 07401 | Two flat laps, fast; certified | 251 (1977) | 2:13:15 2:37:57 | Jeff Wells Kim Merritt |
| 139 | NIKE–CATALINA | Apr. | Catalina Island, Calif. | | | 40 (1978) | 2:52:32 3:54:25 | Frank Bozanich Paulette Haltell |
| 140 | NORTH CAROLINA | Jan. | Bethel, N.C. | Clem Williams, Box 701 Bethel, N.C. 27812 | Out and back, flat; certified | 54 (1978) | 2:25:23 3:11:00 | Jack Fultz Henley Roughton |
| 141 | NORTH DAKOTA | Jun. | Fisher's Landing Grand Forks, N.D. | Dave Nieman Grand Forks YMCA Box 1317 Grand Forks, N.D. 58201 | Point to point, flat | 78 (1977) | 2:34:24 3:19:00 | Jim Miller Jan Arenz |
| 142 | NORTH PENN BOYS' CLUB | May | Memorial Park Lansdale, Pa. | George Groseibl Box 103 Lansdale, Pa. 19446 | Out and back, some hills; certified | 28 (1978) | 3:06:07 4:30:05 | Bill Donini Lisa Freundlich |
| 143 | NORTH TEXAS | | Denton, Texas | | | 22 (1978) | | |
| 144 | OCEANSIDE FEDERAL MEMORIAL DAY | May | Municipal Pier and Beach Stadium Oceanside, Calif. | Marathon 220 N. Tremont Oceanside, Calif. 92054 | Paved rolling hills, out and back | 141 (1978) | 2:33:36 3:24:31 | Donald Ocana Norma Miller |

| # | Name | Month | Location | Director/Address | Course | Entrants (year) | Times | Winners |
|---|------|-------|----------|------------------|--------|-----------------|-------|---------|
| 145 | OCEAN STATE | Oct. | Newport, R.I. | George Schobel 61 Crowfield Dr. Warwick, R.I. 02888 | | 964 (1977) | 2:18:37 2:47:20 | Bob Doyle Patricia Latora |
| 146 | OIL CAPITAL | Mar. | Mohawk Park Tulsa, Okla. | Larry Aduddell 6200 S. 221st E. Ave. Broken Arrow, Okla. 74012 | Laps, flat; certified | 117 (1978) | 2:18:00 3:14:54 | Terry Zeigler Marianne Pugh |
| 147 | OLIVER SCOTT HANSON | Sep. | McMorran Auditorium Port Huron, Mich. | John N. Hanchon 2922 Pine Grove Ave., Port Huron, Mich. 48060 | Out and back, no hills; certified | 32 (1977) | 2:31:52 3:22:42 | Ron Falck Marja Wright |
| 148 | OMAHA | Aug. | Omaha, Neb. | Sarah Carlos 1620 Dodge Omaha, Neb. 68102 | Out and back, flat; certified | [400+ entrants in 1977.] | 2:26:48 3:15:55 | Bob Busby Kelly Hiatt |
| 149 | ORANGE BOWL | Dec. | S.E. 2nd and Biscayne Blvd. Miami, Fla. | Marathon Coordinator, Physical Therapy Education Program Florida International University Tamiami Trail Miami, Fla. 33199 | Out and back; certified | 433 (1977) | 2:24:10 2:54:13 | Pat Chmiel Jane Killion |
| 150 | ORANGE COUNTY | Apr. | Featherley Park Orange County, Calif. | Pete Dowry 9593 Pettswood Dr. Huntington Beach, Calif. 92646 | Point to point, flat | 621 (1978) | 2:29:03 3:01:45 | Jeff Dettmer Sandra Kiddy |
| 151 | ORANGE GROVE | Apr. | Gentry Gym Loma Linda, Calif. | Loma Linda Lopers Box 495 Loma Linda, Calif. 92345 | Out and back | | [New race in 1978.] | |
| 152 | PAAVO NURMI | Aug. | Upson, Wis. to Hurley, Wis. | Hurley Chamber of Commerce 10th Ave. N. Hurley, Wis. 54534 | Point to point with some hills; certified | 708 (1977) | 2:20:18 2:55:12 | Tom Antczak Anita Ayers |

211

U.S. marathons *(cont.)*

| | Race | Mo. | Place | Contact | Conditions | Finished | Records | |
|---|---|---|---|---|---|---|---|---|
| 153 | PACIFIC SUN | May | College of Marin Mill Valley, Calif. | Marathon, Box 553 Mill Valley, Calif. 94941 | Out and back | 398 (1978) | 2:34:41 3:06:40 | Ron Nabors Elai Ivaldy-Miller |
| 154 | PALO DURO CANYON | Jan. | Palo Duro Canyon Canyon, Texas | Bob Dunbar 6526 Fulton Amarillo, Texas 79109 | Certified | 32 (1978) | 2:42:06 3:48:47 | Michael Jenkins Isabel Navarro |
| 155 | PALOS VERDES | Jun. | Peninsula Center Palos Verdes Peninsula, Calif. | Kiwanis Club of Palos Verdes Box 153 Palos Verdes Estates, Calif. 90274 | Point to point; certified | 2,371 (1978) | 2:20:04 2:57:55 | Ed Chaidaz Susan Petersen |
| 156 | PAUL BUNYAN | Jul. | University of Maine Bangor, Maine | Dick McGrath c/o Bangor Daily News, 491 Main St. Bangor, Maine 04401 | Out and back, one loop on asphalt | 313 (1978) | 2:28:19 3:03:15 | Keith Brown Maryann Gelermann |
| 157 | PAUL MASSON CHAMPAGNE | Jan. | Paul Masson Winery Saratoga, Calif. | Dan O'Keefe 20032 Rodriques Ave., Cupertino, Calif. 95041 | Three loops with a hill (230 feet) in each; certified | 672 (1978) | 2:20:06 2:59:14 | Brian Maxwell Penny DeMoss |
| 158 | PEACH BOWL | Jan. | Westminster School Atlanta, Ga. | Atlanta Track Club Box 11556 Atlanta, Ga. 30355 | Two laps; certified | | 2:16:18 2:51:30 | Neil Cusack Lisa Lorrain |
| 159 | PENN RELAYS | Apr. | Plaisted Hall No. 1 Boathouse Row Philadelphia, Pa. | Michael Costello Weightman Hall University of Pennsylvania Philadelphia, Pa. 19104 | Three laps on sidewalks in Fairmont Park; certified | 240 (1978) | 2:21:13 3:10:07 | Mark Stevenson Jill Adams |

| # | Race | Month | Location | Contact | Description | Entries (Year) | Times | Winners |
|---|------|-------|----------|---------|-------------|------|-------|---------|
| 160 | PHILADELPHIA | Nov. | Fairmont Park Philadelphia, Pa. | Tom Sander 515 W. Godfrey Ave. Philadelphia, Pa. 19126 | Three laps on sidewalks; certified | 240 (1978) | 2:21:57 2:55:46 | Bill Rodgers Cary Sundem |
| 161 | PHIDIPPIDES DISTANCE DAY | Feb. | Atlanta, Ga. | Wayne Roach 1736 N. Cliff Valley Way, Apt. J-1 Atlanta, Ga. 30307 | Five laps of Stone Mountain | 28 (1977) | 2:47:20 3:34:22 | Adrian Craven Marcie Trent |
| 162 | PIKES PEAK | Aug. | Manitou Springs, Colo. | Rudy Fahl 559 B Castle Rd. Colorado Springs, Colo. 80904 | Out and back, climbs from 7,000 to 14,000 feet on mountain trails; 28+ miles in length | 202 (1977) | 3:31:05 5:09:47 | Rick Trujillo Ruth Anderson |
| 163 | PITTSFIELD | May | Pittsfield, Mass. | Bob Lutz Physical Education Director Pittsfield YMCA 292 North St. Pittsfield, Mass. 01201 | | | | [New race in 1978.] |
| 164 | PIONEER | Oct. | Pine Valley Mountains St. George, Utah | Sherman C. Miller St. George Parks and Recreation Dept. 340 E. 200, So. St. George, Utah 84770 | Point to point from 5,600 to 2,754 feet | 38 (1977) | 2:27:17 3:09:13 | Steve Naylor Barbara Paterson |
| 165 | PIZZA HUT | Nov. | Indiana University Bloomington, Ind. | Ray Vandersteen Monroe County YMCA 817 W. 17th St. Bloomington, Ind. 47401 | Four rolling loops; certified | 224 (1977) | 2:25:44 3:19:15 | Nestor Moreno Charlene Soby |

U.S. marathons (*cont.*)

| | Race | Mo. | Place | Contact | Conditions | Finished | Records | |
|---|------|-----|-------|---------|-----------|----------|---------|---|
| 166 | PORTLAND | Nov. | University Portland, Ore. | Portland Marathon Portland Jaycees 824 S.W. 5th Ave. Portland, Ore. 97204 | One loop, flat | 741 (1977) | 2:23:07 3:07:27 | Robert Ladum Robin Bondy |
| 167 | PORTERVILLE, CENTRAL CALIFORNIA | Feb. | Porterville, Calif. | | | 16 (1978) | 2:39:17 | Dennis Stansauk |
| 168 | PREVENTION | Mar. | Velodrome Trexlertown, Pa. | John Wachter Race Director 1113 Broadway Bethlehem, Pa. 18015 | Three rural slightly rolling loops; certified | 204 (1978) | 2:33:06 | Paul Fetscher Cynthia Kimbleton |
| 169 | PRESQUE ISLE | Sep. | Presque Isle Park Erie, Pa. | Ed Whitman 451 W. 9th St. Erie, Pa. 16502 | Two flat loops of the park | 391 (1978) | 2:19:27 3:15:10 | Terrance Stanley Sarah Applegate |
| 170 | PROVIDENT–BULLETIN | Oct. | Memorial Hall Philadelphia, Pa. | Chris Tatreau Memorial Hall, West Park Philadelphia, Pa. 19131 | Three loops, flat; certified | 278 (1977) | 2:20:18 2:57:02 | Julio Piazza Nancy Kent |
| 171 | PUEBLO HOLIDAY | Dec. | Pueblo County High School Pueblo, Colo. | Jeff Arnold 230 Dittmer Ave. Pueblo, Colo. 81004 | Out and back | 33 (1977) | 2:31:51 | Ron Nabers |
| 172 | RACE OF CHAMPIONS | May | Holyoke, Mass. | Walter Childs Box 1484 Springfield, Mass. 01103 | Certified | | | |

| # | Name | Month | Location | Contact | Course | Entrants | Times | Winners |
|---|------|-------|----------|---------|--------|----------|-------|---------|
| 173 | RESURRECTION PASS | Jul. | Hope, Alaska | L. E. Haines Director of Student Services, University of Alaska 3221 Providence Dr. Anchorage, Alaska 99504 | Out and back, hilly | | 2:41:59 3:25:16 | Chris Haines Marian May |
| 174 | REVCO—WESTERN RESERVE | May | Hudson to Cleveland, Ohio | John O'Neil 116 Baker Building Case Western Reserve University Cleveland, Ohio 44106 | Point to point, fast; certified | [1,100 entrants in 1978.] | 2:15:02 2:47:01 | Tom Fleming Jacqueline Hansen |
| 175 | RICHMOND NEWSPAPERS | Oct. | Richmond, Va. | Race Director Richmond Newspapers Marathon 333 E. Grace St. Richmond, Va. 23219 | Out and back; certified | | | [New race in 1978.] |
| 176 | ROAD RUNNERS | Mar. | Plaisted Hall East River Dr. Philadelphia, Pa. | Joe McIlhinney 908 Cottman St. Philadelphia, Pa. 19111 | Three loops; certified | [56 started in 1977.] | 2:29:59 | Mike Butynes |
| 177 | ROADRUNNER | May | Gage, Okla. | Peggy Ford Box 428 Gage, Okla. 73843 | Out and back, flat; certified | 32 (1977) | 2:29:29 4:37:50 | Terry Zeigler Nancy Adams |
| 178 | ROCKFORD FOURTH OF JULY | Jul. | Welch School Rockford, Ill. | Marathon Rockford YMCA Y Blvd. Rockford, Ill. 61104 | One loop | | | [New race in 1978.] |
| 179 | ROMAN BOSTON QUALIFIER | Mar. | Rome, N.Y. | Carl Eilenberg WRNY Radio Box 67 Rome, N.Y. 13440 | One flat loop on asphalt; certified | 17 (1977) | 2:30:— | Larry Frederick, Ron Fillhart |

U.S. marathons (*cont.*)

| | Race | Mo. | Place | Conditions | Finished | Records | |
|---|---|---|---|---|---|---|---|
| 180 | ROTARY SHAMROCK | Mar. | Boardwalk Virginia Beach, Va. | Point to point, flat; certified | 456 (1978) | 2:24:15 3:20:48 | Jeff Galloway Jennifer Rood |
| 181 | RIDGEFIELD | Dec. | Ridgefield, Conn. | One loop | 80 (1977) | 2:26:14 3:17:26 | Robert Hirst Jean Schwab |
| 182 | ROCHESTER | Sep. | Liberty Pole Rochester, N.Y. | Out and back with some hills; certified | 147 (1977) | 2:25:39 3:50:54 | Dick Beurkle Susan Rowley |
| 183 | ROSE BOWL | Nov. | San Pedro, Calif. | Out and back | 453 (1977) | 2:28:20 2:59:48 | Don Moses Sue Petersen |
| 184 | SACRAMENTO | Oct. | William Land Park Sacramento, Calif. | Laps, flat; certified | 305 (1977) | 2:25:49 3:03:33 | Wayne Badgley Sally Edwards |
| 185 | SAGINAW–BAY | May | Delta College Saginaw, Mich. | One loop; certified | | 2:24:03 3:20:56 | Bill Stewart Sandra Ruohoniemi |

Contact column:

180: Jerry Bocrie 609 Hassell Dr. Chesapeake, Va. 23320

181: Ridgefield Marathon Ridgefield Boys Club Ridgefield, Conn. 06877

182: Eugene Osburn 561 Van Voorhis Ave., Rochester, N.Y. 14617

183: Rose Bowl Marathon Pasadena YMCA 235 Holly St. Pasadena, Calif. 91101

184: John McIntosh 4120 El Camino Ave. Sacramento, Calif. 95821

185: Marathon, Forddy Kennedy c/o Physical Education Dept. Delta College University Center, Mich. 48710

| # | Name | Month | Location | Contact | Entries (Year) | Time | Winners |
|---|------|-------|----------|---------|----------------|------|---------|
| 186 | SAN FRANCISCO | Jul. | Golden Gate Park San Francisco, Calif. | Jim Scannell 342—24th Ave. No. 202 San Francisco, Calif. 94121 | Out and back, mainly flat | 841(1977) | 2:24:59 2:53:20 | Athol Barton Tena Alex |
| 187 | SANTA BARBARA | Oct. | La Plaza Stadium Santa Barbara, Calif. | John Brennand 4476 Meadowlark Lane, Santa Barbara, Calif. 93105 | Out and back; certified | | 2:25:03 2:56:07 | Fritz Watson Sue Petersen |
| 188 | SEATTLE | Nov. | Seward Park Seattle, Wash. | Evan Shull, c/o Dr. Dean Ingram 507 Cobb Medical Center, Seattle, Wash. 98101 | Twice out and back | 762 (1977) | 2:18:28 2:57:23 | Bill Glad Gabriele Anderson |
| 189 | SENIOR OLYMPICS | May | William Mason Park Irvine, Calif. | Worth Blaney 5670 Wilshire Blvd. No. 360, Los Angeles, Calif. 90036 | Out and back, hilly; certified | 196 (1978) | 2:31:58 2:58:31 | Todd Ferguson Sue Petersen |
| 190 | SILVER LAKE | Mar. | Newton, Mass. | Fred Brown 157 Walsh St. Medford, Mass. 02155 | Point to point | 493 (1978) | 2:18:26 | Dave Severence |
| 191 | SILVER STATE | Sep. | Davis Creek Park Reno, Nev. | Martha Dow c/o Athlete's Foot 580 N. McCarran Blvd., Sparks, Nev. 89431 | Loop, some hills; certified | 335 (1977) | 2:30:19 3:10:26 | Ron Zarate Joan Ullyot |
| 192 | SKYLON INTER-NATIONAL | Oct. | Buffalo, N.Y., to Niagara Falls, Ont. | Frank Neal 10 Beard Ave. Buffalo, N.Y. 14214 | Point to point, flat, possibly a headwind | 1,624 (1977) | 2:20:31 2:58:16 | Richard Hughson Ellen Turkel |
| 193 | SMOKY MOUNTAIN | Feb. | Civic Center Building Oak Ridge, Tenn. | Harold Canfield 502 Alandale Rd. Knoxville, Tenn. 37920 | One large loop on straight rural roads, flat; certified | 57 (1978) | 2:29:55 3:07:56 | Marshall Adams Mary Lindahl |

U.S. marathons (*cont.*)

| | Race | Mo. | Place | Contact | Conditions | Finished | Records | |
|---|------|-----|-------|---------|-----------|----------|---------|---|
| 194 | SONOMA STATE | Oct. | Sonoma State College Rohnert Park, Calif. | Bob Lynde Physical Education Dept., Sonoma State College, Rohnert Park, Calif. 94928 | Out and back twice on different rolling loops | 263 (1977) | 2:26:10 3:02:00 | Jan Sershen Penny DeMoss |
| 195 | SOUTH PARK | Jun. | Moline, Ill. | Mike Reroat Cornbelt Running Club 3538 9th Ave. Ct. Moline, Ill. 61265 | One loop | 43 (1978) | 2:31:46 3:53:53 | Dan Cooper Eloise Caldwell |
| 196 | SPACE COAST | Nov. | Wickham Park Melbourne, Fla. | Bob Lawton Space Coast Runners Box 94 Cocoa Beach, Fla. 32931 | One flat loop | 144 (1977) | 2:20:37 3:09:46 | Dean Foster Sue Ellen Trapp |
| 197 | SPOKANE HEART | Sep. | Spokane, Wash. | Edward Rockwell American Heart Association of Washington S. 11 Washington Spokane, Wash. 99204 | Point to point; certified | 101 (1977) | 2:31:51 | Jim Birnbaum |
| 198 | STEAMBOAT DAYS USA | Jul. | Winona, Minn. | Winona YMCA Winona, Minn. 55987 | Four loops | | 2:31:07 | Kerry Mayer |
| 199 | ST. PETER DAIRY DAYS | Jun. | St. Peter, Minn. | Vicki Huff 508 St. Julien St. Peter, Minn. 56082 | Out and back on rolling hills | | | [New race in 1978.] |

| # | Race | Month | Location | Contact | Course | Runners (Year) | Times | Winners |
|---|------|-------|----------|---------|--------|----------------|-------|---------|
| 200 | SUGAR RIVER TRAIL | Oct. | New Glarus, Wis. | Sugar River Trail Headquarters Box 781 New Glarus, Wis. 53574 | Point to point, no hills; certified | 308 (1977) | 2:31:11 3:06:53 | Bill McBride Mary Czarapata |
| 201 | SUMMIT COUNTY | Aug. | Lake Dillon Dillon, Colo. | Summit Visitors Service Box 669 Dillon, Colo. 80435 | Out and back, some hills; certified | 62 (1977) | 2:37:02 4:09:13 | Jon Sinclair Cherri Meyer |
| 202 | SUN BEAR MID-NIGHT RUN | Jun. | Eielson AFB, Alaska | Wayne Grieme 5179B No. St. Eielson AFB, Alaska 99702 | Out and back, flat | 30 (1977) | 2:41:05 3:02:41 | Ben Beach Marian May |
| 203 | SUNDOWN SALUTE | Jul. | Milford Dam Junction City, Kan. | Jerry Mathis 732 Crestview Junction City, Kan. 66441 | Point to point, flat | 68 (1978) | 2:50:56 6:54:57 | Stephen Brumit Patricia Holderman, Nikki Wheaton |
| 204 | TEXAS RELAYS | Apr. | Zilker Park Austin, Texas | Roy Pool c/o Austin YMCA 1100 W. First Austin, Texas 78703 | | 96 (1978) | 2:27:04 3:08:42 | George Mason Dorothy Doolittle |
| 205 | THIRD OLYMPIAD MEMORIAL | Feb. | Washington University St. Louis, Mo. | Jerry Kokesh c/o Marathon Sports 13453 Chesterfield Plaza, Chesterfield, Mo. 63017 | Point to point; certified | 386 (1978) | 2:16:35 2:53:16 | Ron Tabb Terri Anderson |
| 206 | THREE RIVERS FESTIVAL | Jul. | Memorial Coliseum Fort Wayne, Ind. | Cal Mahlock WKJG-TV 33 2633 W. State Blvd. Fort Wayne, Ind. 46808 | Out and back; certified | [750 started in 1978.] | 2:25:22 2:41:47 | Thomas Blumer Celia Peterson |
| 207 | TRAIL'S END | Feb. | Seasider Hotel Seaside, Ore. | Seaside Chamber of Commerce, Box 7 Seaside, Ore. 97138 | Out and back, fairly flat; certified | 1,357 (1978) | 2:14:43 2:47:02 | Brian Maxwell Irene Griffith |

219

# U.S. marathons (*cont.*)

| | Race | Mo. | Place | Contact | Conditions | Finished | Records | |
|---|---|---|---|---|---|---|---|---|
| 208 | TRI-STATE | Oct. | White Cloud, Kan. to Folk City, Neb. | Louis Fritz RR1, Box 21 Verdon, Neb. 68457 | Point to point, some hills | 92 (1977) | 2:21:36 3:54:34 | Bob Busby Sylvia Wiegand |
| 209 | UNITED BANK MILE-HI | May | United Bank 17th and Broadway Denver, Colo. | United Bank of Denver P.O. Box 17382 Denver, Colo. 80217 | Point to point, flat, 5,200 feet; certified | 700+ (1978) | 2:30:53 3:11:51 | Skip Houk Pam Olson |
| 210 | UNIVERSITY OF NORTHERN IOWA | Apr. | UNI Track Cedar Falls, Iowa | Lynn King Track Coach University of Northern Iowa Cedar Falls, Iowa 50613 | Point to point, flat | 44 (1978) | 2:27:33 3:08:40 | Dave Elger Stacy Roberts |
| 211 | USTFF | May | Cessna Stadium Wichita, Kan. | Coach Herm Wilson Wichita State University, Campus P.O. Box 18 Wichita, Kan. 67208 | Mostly flat, out and back; certified | 56 (1978) | 2:24:44 3:11:25 | Mark Stevenson Amy Johns |
| 212 | VALENTINE RUNNING FESTIVAL | Feb. | Eglin Air Force Base, Fla. | Buford Potter Playground Area YMCA, Box 1361 Ft. Walton Beach, Fla. 32548 | One loop | 54 (1978) | 2:19:34 3:14:45 | Jeff Galloway Becky Sears |
| 213 | VALLEY OF THE FLOWERS | Jun. | Huyck Stadium Lompoc, Calif. | Joe Sciame 1305 N. Orchard St. Lompoc, Calif. 93436 | One loop with some hills; certified | 147 (1977) | 2:34:31 2:50:34 | Michael Sayward Kathy Jewell |
| 214 | VFW POST 662 | Mar. | VFW Post Plain Street Lowell, Mass. | Daniel Coakley VFW Post 662 190 Plain St. Lowell, Mass. 01852 | One loop of rural asphalt | 449 (1978) | 2:18:26 3:14:47 | David Severance Jennifer Rice |

| # | Name | Month | Location | Race Director | Course | Entries (Year) | Times | Winners |
|---|------|-------|----------|---------------|--------|----------------|-------|---------|
| 215 | WALLA WALLA VALLEY INTERSTATE | Apr. | Walla Walla College, Wash. | Gerald Smith, CABL Walla Walla College College Place, Wash. 99324 | Out and back | 65 (1978) | 2:41:19 | Vic Gilliland |
| 216 | WASHINGTON'S BIRTHDAY | Feb. | Agricultural Research Center Beltsville, Md. | Bob Rothenberg DC Roadrunners 6N Hillside Rd. Greenbelt, Md. 20770 | Three laps; certified | 307 (1978) | 2:22:14 3:04:32 | Bob Doyle Marilyn Bevans |
| 217 | WAYNESBORO | Oct. | City Building Waynesboro, Va. | Marathon Association, Box 426 Waynesboro, Va. 22980 | Point to point, no hills; certified | 93 (1977) | 2:25:10 3:26:57 | Bill Rodgers Katherine Thomas |
| 218 | WEST BLOOMFIELD | Mar. | High School West Bloomfield Township, Mich. | Maurice D. Freed Race Director 7200 Brookridge West Bloomfield, Mich. 48033 | Three loops of rolling hills, variable surfaces | 114 (1977.) | 2:24:55 3:13:37 | Robert Hunt Alexa Kraft |
| 219 | WEST LAFAYETTE | Jul. | West Lafayette, Ind. | Steve Kearney 205 W. Porter Ave. Chesterton, Ind. 46304 | | 36 (1977) | | |
| 220 | WEST VALLEY | Feb. | High School San Mateo, Calif. | West Valley TC Box 1551 San Mateo, Calif. 94401 | Five flat laps; certified | 293 (1978) | 2:15:48 2:53:49 | Doug Schmenk Judy Gumbs-Leydig |
| 221 | WESTERN HEMISPHERE | Dec. | Overland Ave. and Culver Blvd. Culver City, Calif. | Carl Porter 4117 Overland Ave. Culver City, Calif. 90230 | Two laps, flat; certified | 85 (1977) | 2:15:21 2:43:55 | Bill Scobey Jacqueline Hansen |
| 222 | WHITEWATER COLLEGE | Apr. | Whitewater, Wis. | Rex Foster Track Coach UW-Whitewater Whitewater, Wis. 53190 | | 2 (1976) | | |

U.S. marathons (*cont.*)

| | Race | Mo. | Place | Contact | Conditions | Finished | Records | |
|---|---|---|---|---|---|---|---|---|
| 223 | WINDY | Mar. | Carmel Clay Junior High Carmel, Ind. | Jack Beasley 11040 Winding Brook Lane Indianapolis, Ind. 46280 | Two loops of flat to rolling asphalt; certified | 77 (1978) | 2:26:06 3:11:09 | Bill Gavaghan Lora Cartwright |
| 224 | WISCONSIN MAYFAIR | May | Mayfair Shopping Mall Milwaukee, Wis. | G. Roger Bodart Wisconsin Mayfair Marathon Mayfair Association Mayfair Shopping Mall 2500 N. Mayfair Milwaukee, Wis. 53226 | Two hilly loops through parks | 288 (1978) | 2:23:41 3:03:05 | Tony Rodiez Cindy Therriault |
| 225 | WHITE ROCK | Dec. | White Rock Lake Dallas, Texas | Sue Rhiddlehoover c/o Aerobics Activity Center 12100 Preston Rd. Dallas, Texas 75230 | Three flat laps; certified | 250 (1977) | 2:15:11 2:53:43 | Jeff Wells Dorothy Doolittle |
| 226 | WORLD MASTERS | Jan. | Chapman College Orange, Calif. | Bill Selvin 2125 N. Tustin, No. 3, Orange, Calif. 92665 | One loop, without hills; certified | 394 (1977) | 2:17:44 2:58:28 | Dave White Judy Milkie |
| 227 | YONKERS | May | Yonkers, N.Y. | New York RRC Box 881 FDR Station New York, N.Y. 10022 | Four laps, certified | 548 (1978) | 2:18:52 2:58:50 | Ron Wayne Nina Kuscsik |

| No. | Race | Month | Location | Organizer/Address | Course | Entrants (Year) | Time | Winner |
|---|---|---|---|---|---|---|---|---|
| 228 | BAYFEST* | Sep. | Corpus Christi, Texas | Corpus Christi Roadrunners Box 3012 Corpus Christi, Texas 78404 | | 25 (1977) | 2:42:29 4:23:44 | Clent Mericle Cissy Grill |
| 229 | PITTSBURGH MAGAZINE | Oct. | North Park Pittsburgh, Pa. | Marathon Organizer Pittsburgh Magazine 4802 Fifth Ave. Pittsburgh, Pa. 15213 | Six flat loops around the lake; certified | | | [New race in 1978.] |
| 230 | CASCO BAY | Sep. | Portland Exposition Building Portland, Maine | Casco Bay Marathon Box 3172 Portland, Maine 04104 | One loop coastal and rural roads; certified | | | [New race in 1978.] |
| 231 | ATLANTIC CITY | Oct. | Albany Ave. and Boardwalk Atlantic City, N.J. | Ed. League Box 732 Atlantic City, N.J. 08404 | Three out-and-backs, flat; certified | 65 (1977) | 2:28:44 | Herb Lorenz |
| 232 | CLARENCE DEMAR | Aug. | Keene, N.H. | Fred Brown 157 Walsh St. Medford, Mass. 02155 | | | | |
| 233 | DIXVILLE NOTCH | Sep. | Errol, N.H., to Colebrook, N.H. | Walter H. Childs Box 1484 Springfield, Mass. 01101 | Point to point asphalt; certified | 16 (1977) | | |
| 234 | DURHAM FIRST | Oct. | Wallace Wade Stadium Durham, N.C. | Chamber of Commerce, Box 610 Durham, N.C. 27702 | Two out-and-back loops, rolling; certified | | | [New race in 1978.] |
| 235 | HISTORIC GETTYSBURG | Sep. | High School Gettysburg, Pa. | Chamber of Commerce 11 York St. Gettysburg, Pa. 17325 | Rolling out-and-back course | | | [New race in 1978.] |

* Nos. 228–248 are late entrants and therefore not in alphabetical order.

U.S. marathons (*cont.*)

| | Race | Mo. | Place | Contact | Conditions | Finished | Records | |
|---|------|-----|-------|---------|------------|----------|---------|---|
| 236 | MARQUETTE | Sep. | Negaunee, Mich. | Chamber of Commerce 501 S. Front Marquette, Mich. 49855 | Point to point on asphalt descending 570 feet | 49 (1977) | 2:35:14 3:39:45 | Scott Lachniet Denise Green |
| 237 | POTOMAC VALLEY | Sep. | Lakeforest Mall Gaithersburg, Md. | Potomac Valley Marathon Festival Lakeforest Mall 701 Russell Ave. Gaithersburg, Md. 20760 | Two laps out and back on sidewalks; certified | | | [New race in 1978.] |
| 238 | YMCA GRAND VALLEY | Nov. | Grand Valley College Field House Grand Rapids, Mich. | Dan Ahearn Central YMCA 33 Library St. Grand Rapids, Mich. 49503 | Out and back, rolling | 127 (1977) | 2:26:42 3:37:31 | Barney Hance, James Carter Karen Holappa |
| 239 | LEATHERNECK | Jun. | El Toro Marine Corps Air Station Irvine, Calif. | Marathon Organizer El Toro Marine Corps Air Station Irvine, Calif. | | 311+ (1978) | 2:28:47 3:30:35 | Jean Ellis Janet C. Ledder |
| 240 | COLUMBUS | May | Columbus, Ohio | | | 45 (1978) | 2:41:22 4:09:30 | Ernie Watts Lorna Richey |
| 241 | SANTA MONICA | Aug. | Santa Monica City College Santa Monica, Calif. | Mary Esposito Santa Monica Rec. Dept. 1685 Main St. Santa Monica, Calif. 90401 | | | | |

| No. | Race | Month | Location | Contact | Notes | Finishers (Year) | Time | Winners |
|-----|------|-------|----------|---------|-------|------------------|------|---------|
| 242 | STORM LAKE | Sep. | Storm Lake, Iowa | Tom Huseman
510 Lake Ave.
Storm Lake, Iowa
50588 | | | | [New race in 1978.] |
| 243 | MIDNIGHT SUN | May | Fairbanks, Alaska | | | 32 (1978) | 2:43:56
3:32:02 | George Morse
Maureen Casamayou |
| 244 | SAN DIEGO | Oct. | Coronado Island
San Diego, Calif. | Bill Casper
San Diego County
Heart Association
3640 5th Ave.
Box 3625
San Diego, Calif.
92103 | Point to point,
some hills | | | [New race in 1978.] |
| 245 | HOMESTEAD–
ROSEBURG
TRACK CLUB | Jun. | Roseburg, Ore. | | | 63 (1978) | 2:36:43
3:24:50 | James Rocha
Judith Kidd |
| 246 | SAMMAMISH
VALLEY | Jun. | Issaquah, Wash. | | | 67 (1978) | 2:36:28
3:00:01 | Richard Holloway
Gail Volk |
| 247 | OKTOBERFEST | Sep. | La Crosse, Wis. | LaCrosse Festival
Inc., Box 1716
La Crosse, Wis.
54601 | | | | |
| 248 | HIBERNIAN | Sep. | Ligonier, Pa. | Dan Deasy
114 Greenside Ave.
Pittsburgh, Pa.
15220 | Out and back,
severe hills | [35 started in
1978.] | 2:30:20 | Skip Brown,
Mark Studnicki |

**Photo 21 (ABOVE)**
Individual attention bestowed on a winner at the 1978 Atlanta
Marathon. (*Photo by Cindy Brown*)

**Photo 22 (OPPOSITE)**
The torrent of runners breaks at the start of the Marine Corps
Reserve Marathon. The eventual winner, Kevin McDonald (No.
3164), is already among the early leaders. Winning time: 2:19:36.
(*Photo by Phil Yunger*)

Canadian marathons

| | Race | Mo. | Place | Contact | Conditions | Finished | Records | |
|---|---|---|---|---|---|---|---|---|
| 1 | ALBERTA | May | Bowness Park Calgary, Alta. | Bill Wyllie 2932 13th Ave. N.W. Calgary, Alta., Can. T2N 1M2 | Two laps | 82 (1977) | 2:28:32 3:35:47 | Peter Moore Debra Lane |
| 2 | GOLDEN MILE | May | Kildonan Park Winnipeg, Man. | Randy Longmuir 136 Seven Oaks Ave. Winnipeg, Man., Can. K2V OK5 | Laps | 24 (1977) | 2:45:45 3:39:26 | Jim Wadler Kim Longmuir |
| 3 | ILE D'ORLEANS | Oct. | St. Pierre I.O. to St. Jean I.O., Que. | Jean-Guy Cote 26 Rue Goudreault St. Brigitte de Laval Que., Can. GAO 3KO | Point to point | 65+ (1977) | 2:36:43 3:22:00 | Marc Corcoran Elionor Thomas |
| 4 | MARATHON DE MONTREAL | Mar. | Perras Blvd. and 49th Ave. Montreal, Que. | Michel Roase 12 232 Armand Bombardier Montreal, Que. Can. H1E 1W7 | Four laps | 89 (1978) | 2:23:10 3:08:08 | Jerome Drayton Maria Brzenska |
| 5 | MOLSON | Sep. | Douglas Park Regina, Sask. | Molson Saskatchewan Brewery Ltd. 1300 Dewdney Ave. Regina, Sask. Can. S4R 1GR | Laps | 37 (1977) | 2:31:55 | Phil Davis |
| 6 | NATIONAL CAPITAL | May | Carleton University Ottawa, Ont. | National Capital Marathon Dept. of Community Development Recreation Branch 111 Sussex Dr. Ottawa, Ont., Can. | Out and back on asphalt parkways | 1,750 (1978) | 2:16:02 2:47:37 | Brian Maxwell Chris Lavalee |

228

| # | Race | Month | Location | Organizer | Course | Participants (year) | Time | Winner |
|---|------|-------|----------|-----------|--------|---------------------|------|--------|
| 7 | NEWFOUNDLAND | Jul. | St. John's, Nfld. | Joe Ryan Newfoundland Track and Field Assn. St. John's, Nfld., Can. | | 5 (1977) | 2:44:16 | Mike Green |
| 8 | NORTHERN LIGHTS | Jun. | Espanola Arena Espanola, Ont. | Norman Patenaude Site 20, Box 25 RR No. 2 Sudbury, Ont., Can. P3E 4M9 | Six flat laps; certified | 24 (1977) | 2:40:06 | David Welch |
| 9 | SKYLON | Oct. | Buffalo, N.Y., to Niagara Falls, Ont. | Frank Neal 10 Beard Ave. Buffalo, N.Y. 14214 | Point to point, flat, possible headwind | 1,624 (1977) | 2:20:31 2:58:16 | Richard Hughson Ellen Turkel |
| 10 | TORONTO POLICE | Aug. | Exhibition Stadium Toronto, Ont. | D. R. Deke McBrien 590 Jarvis St. Toronto, Ont., Can. M4Y 2J5 | Out and back, perfectly flat | 207 (1977) | 2:18:42 3:06:09 | Brian Armstrong Susan Kahler |
| 11 | VANCOUVER LION'S GATE INTERNATIONAL | May | Stanley Park Vancouver, B.C. | Dan Basham 2032 Deep Cave Cres., Vancouver, B.C., Can. V7G 172 | Five flat laps | [600 started in 1978.] | 2:20:50 2:48:55 | John Hill Beverly Blanchard |
| 12 | BELLEVILLE | Sep. | Belleville, Ont. | Wolf Tausendfreund 202 Front St. Belleville, Ont., Can. | | | | |
| 13 | ELWYN DAVIES | Sep. | Chinguacousy Park Brampton, Ont. | Elwyn Davies 7 Kirkland Rd. Brampton, Ont., Can. L6V 2W5 | Two laps, asphalt, flat | 47 (1977) | 2:33:— | Max Barr |
| 14 | GRAND PRIX | Oct. | Toronto, Ont. | Ontario Track and Field Assn. Box 612, Station F Toronto, Ont., Can. M4Y 2J5 | | | | |

# British marathons

| | Race | Mo. | Place | Contact |
|---|---|---|---|---|
| 1 | AAA | May | Sandbach, Cheshire | AAA |
| 2 | BARNSLEY ROAD RUNNERS | Dec. | Barnsley, Yorkshire | Barnsley Road Runners Club Barnsley, Yorkshire |
| 3 | BORDER HARRIERS | Jun. | Silloth to Carlisle, Cumbria | P. A. Nash 87 Petteril St. Carlisle, Cumbria |
| 4 | GOLDENLAY POLYTECHNIC | Jun. | Windsor Castle Windsor, Middlesex | J. E. Micklewright 75 Sutton Rd. Heston, Hounslow, Middlesex |
| 5 | HUDDERSFIELD | Mar. | Huddersfield Yorkshire | |
| 6 | WELSH AAA | Aug. | Newport, Gwent | D. J. Jones 3 Maesgwyn Maesteg, Mid-Glamorgan |

## Photo 23
Bill Rodgers and Garry Bjorklund lead the way in the 1977 New York City Marathon. Rodgers was the eventual winner (2:11:29) with Bjorklund fifth in 2:15:17. (*Photo by Phil Yunger*)

| | Race | Mo. | Place | Contact |
|---|---|---|---|---|
| 7 | ROAD RUNNERS CLUB CHAMPIONSHIP | Jul. | Milton Keynes, Bedford | Y. Gutteridge 40 Kelvin Close Bellfield, High Wycombe, Buckinghamshire |
| 8 | ROTHERHAM | Sep. | Rotherham, Yorkshire | Rotherham Harriers and Athletic Club Rotherham, Yorkshire |
| 9 | RUGBY | Sep. | Rugby, Yorkshire | Stuart Holdsworth 102 Frobisher Rd. Bilton, Rugby, Yorkshire |
| 10 | RYDE | May | Ryde, Isle of Wight | Marathon Secretary Ryde H.A.C. 31 Oakfield High St. Ryde, Isle of Wight |
| 11 | UNIGATE | Oct. | Harlow, Essex | Harlow Athletic Club Harlow, Essex |

## West German marathons

| | Race | Mo. |
|---|---|---|
| 1 | ACHERN | Apr. |
| 2 | BERLIN–MASTERS | May |
| 3 | BERLIN | Sep. |
| 4 | COLOGNE | Apr. |
| 5 | DAVERDEN | Jun. |
| 6 | DILLINGEN | Aug. |
| 7 | DONAUESCHINGEN | Oct. |
| 8 | DORTMUND | Oct. |
| 9 | DULMEN | May |
| 10 | ESSEN | Oct. |
| 11 | HAMBURG | Oct. |
| 12 | HERXHEIM | Aug. |
| 13 | HUSEM | Sep. |
| 14 | JULICH | Oct. |
| 15 | OSTERODE | May |
| 16 | RODENBACH | Apr. |
| 17 | RODENBACH | Sep. |
| 18 | ULM–SOFLINGEN | Oct. |

# Appendix III
# Marathon Reading

Concurrent with the boom in running and in marathoning there has been an explosion in published material for road-running enthusiasts. Much is duplicated, and much is quickly outdated, so it is important to discriminate when selecting books and regular journals. The following appendix offers our ideas on the journals available to you in the pursuit of the marathon; it is up to you to select those which will entertain and instruct you.

## Magazines

*Running Times*  12808 Occoquan Rd., Woodbridge, Va. 22192

This journal initially focused on the eastern half of the United States, but it is currently expanding to cover the country. It includes articles, succinct reporting, and comprehensive listing of coming events. Starting in a brown heavy-paper format, it has expanded to color photographs, which complement the magazine's already excellent photographic coverage. The magazine has a responsible editorial policy directed to the benefit of its readers. It enjoys an excellent reception among serious runners, perhaps because the nucleus of its staff are all experienced marathoners.

*Runner's Gazette*  102 W. Water St., Lansford, Pa. 18232

The *Gazette*, published as a newspaper tabloid six times a year, caters to Eastern runners. It is not widely advertised and yet it is reasonably well known, a tribute to its readability. It emphasizes both the winners and middle-of-the-pack runners in a comprehensive coverage of major races. Generally a race is written about rather than limited to a list of results, so the reader gains a feeling for the course and the day as well as the statistics. The newspaper format makes the journal difficult to store, reread, and refer to. Photographs are good but the layout tends to ramble. It is a friendly magazine, something which cannot be said about all others in this list.

*Runner's World*  1400 Stierlin, Mountain View, Calif. 94042

To some extent this journal must have some of the credit for developing running in the United States. For many years it was the only available journal and it was read avidly by leading and beginning runners. It has offered invaluable advice in training for marathoning and has helped to advance the sport. Unfortunately it has been caught up in the boom phenomenon and is now a glossy bookstall journal directed mainly toward the novice. Color is used extensively and attractive ladies are used to enhance the large amount of advertising that it carries. The reader is now treated to any and all running information with the exception of significant race results or reports.

*Running Review* 654 So. Prince St., Lancaster, Pa. 17603

Another Eastern journal geared very locally to the Washington–Pittsburgh–New York area, emphasizing complete race results. Sometimes these make little sense except as a record, since few race descriptions appear among the articles. While it does have articles on various aspects, it does not cater especially to the marathon runner.

*Running* P.O. Box 350, Salem, Ore. 97308

This is a "Magazine for the Thinking Runner" according to the editors and it aims for a national circulation. Its contents are divided into two categories. There are some technical articles on such topics as training, diet, and injuries which may be of some use to marathoners. It also contains articles on philosophical and psychological aspects of running which are of dubious value unless you're into that sort of thing. It does not cover races, nor does it specifically cater to marathoners' interests.

*Track and Field News* Box 296, Los Altos, Calif. 94022

Probably one of the oldest running publications, although its primary interests are track and field events. It is especially attractive to fans of the sport and statistics buffs. Until recently marathons and long-distance running received scant coverage, but this has changed with the recent boom in the sport. Now a marathon may even enjoy the distinction of being a lead article. Photographs are excellent. It is totally devoted to the competitive field, and numerical results are of great importance in its articles. There are very few offerings on aspects of training, preparation, or recovery except as they occur in interviews. The variety of sports dealt with make it attractive.

*On the Run* World Publications, Inc., P.O. Box 366, Mountain View, Calif. 94042

This is a new tabloid, to be published twice monthly according to the initial editorial. Its format is a direct copy of *Runner's Gazette* and its content much the same as is carried in *Runner's World*. There seems little additional reason for its existence except that it may be sold at other newsstand outlets that would otherwise not carry running journals. However, despite its lack of objective, the initial issue did contain one article of interest to marathoners by Amby Burfoot. It may contain others too so it is probably worth looking out for an occasional issue.

Then there are a number of local magazines which cover only runners and running in a specific area. They can still make for very interesting reading and the cross-fertilization of ideas in races and race planning can be valuable. Problems encountered in staging races in one area can find solutions through those applied elsewhere. Moreover, the practicing marathoner can often find articles of interest among those directed at 26-milers in other areas.

Here are a few of the major regional magazines which go beyond the normal club magazine in interest and application:

*Nor-Cal Running Review*   Box 1551, San Mateo, Calif. 94401
   Aimed at the northern California region, all around the bay.
*San Diego Track Club News Letter*   5994 Broadmoor Dr., La Mesa, Calif. 92041
   Serving the far south of California, the land of sun.
*Rocky Mountain News*   c/o 1525 S. Lansing St., Aurora, Colo. 80012
   Covering the Colorado and Wyoming areas in which races generally appear to be vertical or at least high.
*Stride On!*   P.O. Box 372, Michigan City, Ind. 46360
   Principally aimed at the Midwest with flat and rolling courses.
*Yankee Runner*   19 Grove St., Merrimac, Mass. 01860
   Covering competitive events in the New England area and the 7.6-mile and 8.2-mile events which seem to abound there.
*The Hoosier Runner*   2116 W. Euclid Ave., Muncie, Ind. 47304
   Covering Indiana and northern Illinois.
*RRC N.Y. Association Newsletter*   N.Y. RRC, 226 East 53rd St., New York, N.Y. 10022
   Devoted to racing in the New York City area, much of which is limited to Central Park.

In addition to these national and regional magazines, each local club may have its own journal. This may be little more than a results sheet or schedule of events, but in some cases, even with only volunteer help and small financial backing, these journals have become good reading. It is worth trying to subscribe to the one nearest to you.

Recently another national magazine has been announced which appears to be financially and editorially well based.

*The Runner*   One Park Ave., New York, N.Y. 10016
   This journal has at the time of writing only produced a sample brochure with sample articles. In format it follows a median between the bookstall *Runner's World* and the racing devotee's *Running Times*. It is too early to guess at its success.

Finally a journal which at least in name caters to the practicing marathoner:

*Marathoner*   Box 366, Mountain View, Calif. 94042
   This quarterly journal, recently published by World Publications, the parent organization for *Runner's World*, appears to be destined to take over the functions of the marathoning issue of that magazine. The first issue was devoted to a listing of nearly every marathoner's best time in the previous year if he or she had run in under 3 hours on one occasion. That seemed to guarantee the same number of sales! Other articles were devoted to ultra-marathoning results as well as to personal experiences of marathoners themselves. At the present time it *is* of interest to the marathoner, both practicing and intending. It has an expensive format in heavy paper. The first issue

indicates that the journal could be good reference material. Photographs are excellent.

The most supportive of organizations for marathoners and long-distance runners in general is the Road Runners Clubs of America. It is a national confederation of over 140 local chapters and 33,000 members (as of early 1978) devoted to assisting runners. The local chapters stage the majority of everyday races and fun runs in the country, and they, together with the U.S. Track and Field Federation, sponsor major marathons. They do so without imposing financial burdens on marathon organizers or runners. Their journal is:

*Footnotes*  Road Runners Club of America, 11155 Saffold Way, Reston, Va. 22090
This quarterly journal is intended to inform members about other clubs' doings and about national activities as well as to provide background material. It is in a newspaper tabloid form, again making it difficult to store and reference. Cartoons and good photographs as well as well-chosen articles are included.

The Amateur Athletic Union sponsors some running as part of an overall program encompassing karate to weightlifting. Its attention to running is passing except for the revenue which it can potentially obtain. It is administered by local associations across the country, which often exist only to issue membership cards. The races staged are minimal. They vary widely across the country. The association does attempt to sanction marathons, a process which enables all runners and the race organizers to pay more to support other sports. In return for a sanction, the local AAU

**Photo 24**
A sampling of running literature. (*Photo by John Graham*)

chapter often provides nothing to the race, so it is fortunate that the USTFF will also freely provide sanctions without imposing restrictions on the runners. The AAU does not provide a journal or newsletters, even to members, although one aimed at runners over 40 (masters) has been privately started.

## Books

Then there are books worth reading, some for inspiration and some for instruction. For a long time, World Publications was the only publishing company specializing in books for runners, so they have published a large number of the best. From its list, those books which have been of most value to us as marathoners include the following:

*The Complete Diet Guide for Runners,* edited by Hal Higdon (1978)
*The Running Body,* by E. C. Frederick (1973)
*Practical Running Psychology,* edited by Joe Henderson (1972)
*Running with Style,* by the editors of *Runner's World* (1975)
*Athlete's Feet,* by the editors of *Runner's World* (1974)
*Food for Fitness,* by the editors of *Bike World* (1975)
*Encyclopedia of Athletic Medicine,* compiled by G. Sheehan (1972)
*The Boston Marathon,* by the editors of *Runner's World* (1974)
*Tale of the Ancient Marathoner,* by Jack Foster (1974)
*The Self-Made Olympian,* by Ron Daws (1977)
*The Foot Book,* by Harry F. Hlavac (1977)
*Thoughts on the Run,* by Joe Henderson (1970)
*The Long Run Solution,* by Joe Henderson (1976)
*The Complete Runner,* by the editors of *Runner's World* (1974)
*Fitness after Forty,* by Hal Higdon (1977)
*Women's Running,* by Joan Ullyot (1976)

Excellent books by other publishers include:

*On the Run from Dogs and People,* by Hal Higdon (Chicago: Henry Regnery, 1971)
*The Boston Marathon,* by Joe Falls (New York: Macmillan, 1977)
*Corbitt,* by John Chodes (Los Altos, Calif.: TafNews Press, 1974)
*My Run Across the United States,* by Dan Shepherd (Los Altos, Calif.: TafNews Press, 1970)
*The Conditioning of Distance Runners,* by Thomas J. Osler (A Long Distance Log publication, 1967)

Recently a popular book for all types of runners, although only minimally for marathoners, is:

*The Complete Book of Running,* by James F. Fixx (New York: Random House, 1977).

Many of the articles from the World Publications books already mentioned, together with some from *Runner's World* and some original material, have been loosely gathered together into

*The Complete Marathoner*, edited by Joe Henderson (Mountain View, Calif.: World Publications, 1978).

Other books about to be published which appear to have something to offer include

*Serious Runner's Handbook*, by Tom Osler (Mountain View, Calif.: World Publications, 1978).

Several books on training long-distance runners exist. Whether or not they have use to you depends on what sort of person you are and what type of body you have. Our experience shows that for marathon training these books, all from World Publications, have something to offer, but none is universally beyond question. Judge for yourself.

*Van Aaken Method*, by Ernst van Aaken, translated by. G. Beinhorn (1976)
*Training with Cerutty*, by Larry Myers (1977)
*Training the Lydiard Way*, by Arthur Lydiard and Garth Gilmour (1978)

Then there is an excellent German book which is currently being serialized in *Marathoner* magazine. It appears to be well worth obtaining as a complete volume. It is:

*Marathoning*, by Manfred Steffny.

Other books have been and are being published which include "running" or "runner" in the title but are of only peripheral interest to the marathoner, being concerned with philosophy, religion, health and diet in general, or other forms of racing (such as cross-country). They can provide an entertaining alternative to the main literature listed above.

This list has meant to be selective—it is not complete—but if you delve into some of these books and journals you will be lead to others that suit your particular tastes. We have omitted mention of many books on our own shelves because, in retrospect, they contributed nothing significant or which was not better said elsewhere.

Good reading!

# Further Reading

Chapter 1
**The Target**
Aiming at the Marathon

ANDERSON, BOB, and HENDERSON, JOE, eds. *Guide to Distance Running*. Mountain View, Calif.: World Publications, 1974.

COOPER, KENNETH H. *The New Aerobics*. New York: Bantam, 1972.

Editors of *Runner's World. The Boston Marathon*. Mountain View, Calif.: World Publications, revised January 1974.

——. *1976 Olympic Games*. Mountain View, Calif.: World Publications, 1977.

FALLS, JOE. *The Boston Marathon*. New York: Macmillan, 1977.

FIXX, JAMES F. *The Complete Runner*. New York: Random House, 1977.

HIGDON, HAL. *Fitness After Forty*. Mountain View, Calif.: World Publications, 1977.

NELSON, BERT, ed. *Olympic Track and Field*. Los Altos, Calif.: TafNews Press, 1975.

PLATT, RICK, ed. "1978 Marathon Guide." *Running Times*, No. 13 (January 1978).

"Year of the Marathon, The." *Runner's World*, Vol. 13, No. 2 (February 1978), p. 68.

Chapter 2
**Put Your Best Foot Forward**
Training Methods

ANDERSON, BOB. "Stretching." *Running*, Vol. 3, No. 1 (Dec. '77-Jan. '78), p. 17.

ANDERSON, ROBERT. "The Perfect Pre-Run Stretching Routine." *Runner's World*, Vol. 13, No. 5 (May 1978), p. 56.

BOWERMAN, BILL, and BROWN, GWILYM S. "The Secrets of Speed." *Sports Illustrated*, Vol. 41 (August 2, 1971), p. 22.

CLARK, TOM. "As You Race, So Must You Train." *Runner's World*, Vol. 12, No. 6 (June 1977), p. 32.

DAWS, RON. *The Self-Made Olympian*. Mountain View, Calif.: World Publications, 1977.

Editors of *Runner's World. The Boston Marathon*, Mountain View, Calif.: World Publications, revised January 1974.

――――. *Exercises for Runners*. Mountain View, Calif.: World Publications, 1973.

――――. "Featuring Marathoning," *1975 Marathon Handbook*. Mountain View, Calif.: World Publications, February 1975.

――――. *Runner's Training Guide*. Mountain View, Calif.: World Publications, June 1975.

――――. *Running with Style*. Mountain View, Calif.: World Publications, 1975.

"Fartlek—What It Is and Isn't." *Track and Field News*, Vol. 28, No. 3 (April 1975), p. 46.

FOSTER, CARL, and DANIELS, JACK. "Running by the Numbers." *Runner's World*, Vol. 10, No. 7 (July 1975), p. 14.

FREDERICK, E. C. "So You Want to Run a Marathon?" *Running*, Vol. 3, No. 2 (Spring 1978), p. 6.

GRAHAM, JOHN. "Marathon Test Times." *Runner's World*, Vol. 11, No. 3 (March 1976), p. 50.

HENDERSON, JOE. "1977 National Running Week." *Runner's World*, Vol. 13, No. 3 (March 1978), p. 40.

HITTLEMAN, RICHARD. *Introduction to Yoga*. New York: Bantam, 1974.

"Ian Thompson—from Nowhere to No. 1." *Track and Field News*, Vol. 28, No. 1 (February 1975), p. 43.

MAXWELL, BRIAN. "Training to Race Marathons." *Runner's World*, Vol. 13, No. 2 (February 1978), p. 80.

MEYERS, LARRY. *Training with Cerutty*. Mountain View, Calif.: World Publications, 1977.

MOORE, KENNY. "Watching Their Footsteps." *Sports Illustrated*, Vol. 46 (May 3, 1976), p. 81.

"1977 Marathon Calendar." *Runner's World*, Vol. 12, No. 2 (February 1977), p. 58.

"A Positive Interval Addiction to Speed." *Runner's World*, Vol. 13, No. 6 (June 1978), p. 70.

PROKOP, DAVE. "Clayton, Drayton, and Hill," in *Guide to Distance Running*, Bob Anderson and Joe Henderson, eds. Mountain View, Calif.: World Publications, 1971.

"RACER'S Recordbook, 1977 Boston Marathon Official Computer Results." Published by the Boston Athletic Association, 1977.

RENNIE, DOUG. "Less Is More." *Runner's World*, Vol. 12, No. 11 (November 1977), p. 50.

SLOVIC, PAUL. "What Makes a Marathoner." *Runner's World*, Vol. 8, No. 10 (October 1973).

UHRIG, H. T. "Physiology of Distance Running," in *Guide to Distance Running*, Bob Anderson and Joe Henderson, eds. Mountain View, Calif.: World Publications, 1971.

VAN AAKEN, ERNST. *Van Aaken Method*. Mountain View, Calif.: World Publications, 1976.

"Viren's Four Phases." *Track and Field News*, Vol. 30, No. 1 (February 1977), p. 40.

WARDE, ROBERT. "Coming on Strong After 50." *Runner's World*, Vol. 12, No. 11 (November 1977), p. 43.

WILT, FRED, ed. *How They Train, Vol. II: Long Distances.* Track and Field News, 1973.

YOUNG, KEN. "The Theory of Collapse." *Runner's World*, Vol. 8, No. 9 (September 1973).

Chapter 3
### You Are What You Eat
Diet

BURFOOT, AMBY. "The Meatless Runner." *Runner's World*, Vol. 13, No. 2 (February 1978), p. 48.

CLARK, LINDA. *Go, Caution, Stop, Carbohydrate Counter.* New Canaan, Conn.: Pivot Health Special, Keats Publishing Inc., 1973.

*Count Your Calories*, Dell Purse Book 1532. New York: Dell, 1968.

HIGDON, HAL, ed. *The Complete Diet Guide for Runners and Other Athletes.* Mountain View, Calif.: World Publications, 1978.

HOYT, CRAIG. *The Athlete's Diet, "Food for Fitness."* Mountain View, Calif.: World Publications, January 1975.

KAUFMAN, DAVID A. "Fructose Facilitation: A Way to Delay the Onset of Fatigue." *Running Times*, No. 9 (September 1977), p. 22.

MEYERS, LARRY. *Training with Cerutty.* Mountain View, Calif.: World Publications, 1977.

MOORE, KENNY. "A Gentle Radical Running Scared." *Sports Illustrated*, Vol. 47 (October 17, 1977), p. 32.

VOLLMER, MARION W. *Food—Health and Efficiency.* Nashville: Southern Publishing Association, 1964.

VON HANDEL, PETER. "Carbohydrate Packing" in *The Complete Runner*. Mountain View, Calif.: World Publications, 1974.

"Waldemar Cierpinski," *Runner's World*, Vol. 13, No. 3 (March 1978), p. 68.

Chapter 4
### Putting It to Yourself
The Effect of Stress on the Body

COSTILL, D. L., and WINROW, M. A. "Maximal Oxygen Intake Among Marathon Runners." *Archives of Physical Medicine and Rehabilitation*, June 1970, p. 317.

COSTILL, D. L. "Physiology of Marathon Running." *Journal of the American Medical Association*, Vol. 221, No. 9 (August 28, 1972), p. 1024.

Editors of *Runner's World. The Boston Marathon.* Mountain View, Calif.: World Publications, revised January 1974.

FREDERICK, E. C. *The Running Body.* Mountain View, Calif.: World Publications, September 1973.

GRAHAM, JOHN. "What a Difference the Day Makes." *Runner's World*, Vol. 11, No. 6 (June 1976), p. 49.

**Photo 25**
Winter marathoning in the Northeast. (*Photo by Jim O'Brien*)

HIGDON, HAL. *Fitness After Forty*. Mountain View, Calif.: World Publications, 1977.

MOORE, KENNY. "Watching Their Steps." *Sports Illustrated*, Vol. 46 (May 3, 1976), p. 81.

"U.S. Age Groups Records." *Runner's World*, Vol. 13, No. 2 (February 1978), p. 102.

Chapter 6
**Trials and Tribulations**
Problems During Training

GRAHAM, JOHN. "It May Not Be Old Age." *Runner's World*, Vol. 13, No. 3 (March 1978), p. 10.

HLAVAC, HARRY F. *The Foot Book*. Mountain View, Calif.: World Publications, 1977.

MIRKIN, GABE. "The Proper Care of Running Injuries." *Sports Medicine Consultant*, February 1975, p. 104.

OSLER, THOMAS J. The Conditioning of Distance Runners. A Long Distance Log Publication, August 1967.

SHEEHAN, GEORGE, compiler. *Encyclopedia of Athletic Medicine*, booklet of the month #12. Mountain View, Calif.: *Runner's World*, 1972.

SUBOTNIK, STEVEN I. *The Running Foot Doctor*. Mountain View, Calif.: World Publications, 1977.

ULLYOT, JOAN. *Women's Running*. Mountain View, Calif.: World Publications, 1976.

241

Chapter 8
## The Finish Line and More
Success and the Future

HENDERSON, JOE. *Jog, Run, Race*. Mountain View, Calif.: World Publications, 1977.

MARSHALL, NICK. "1977 Ultramarathoning." *The Marathoner*, Vol. 1, No. 1 (Spring 1978), p. 38.

MAXWELL, BRIAN. "Training to Race Marathons." *Runner's World*, Vol. 13, No. 2 (February 1978), p. 80.

OSLER, TOM. "Ultramarathoning Secrets." *Runner's World*, Vol. 13, No. 5 (May 1978), p. 52.

Appendix I
## Marathon Performances

Editors of *Runner's World*. *The Boston Marathon*. Mountain View, Calif.: World Publications, revised January 1974.

————. *1976 Olympic Games*. Mountain View, Calif.: World Publications, 1977.

FALLS, JOE. *The Boston Marathon*. New York: Macmillan, 1977.

KUSCIK, NINA. "The History of Women's Participation in the Marathon." *Road Runners Club, New York Association Newsletter*, No. 72 (Summer 1977).

"Marathon Times." *Runner's World*, Vol. 13, No. 2 (February 1978), p. 98.

NELSON, BERT, ed. *Olympic Track and Field*. Los Altos, Calif.: TafNews Press, 1975.

# Index